Illusions
of
Equality

Illusions
of
Equality

Deaf Americans in School and Factory

1850–1950

Robert M. Buchanan

Gallaudet University Press
Washington, D.C.

Gallaudet University Press
Washington, DC 20002

Library of Congress Cataloging-in-Publication Data

Buchanan, Robert (Robert M.)
    Illusions of equality : deaf Americans in school and factory,
1850–1950 / Robert Buchanan.
      p. cm.
    Includes bibliographical references and index.
    ISBN 1-56368-084-X (hardcover : alk. paper)
    1. Deaf—Education—United States—History.   2. Deaf—
Employment—United States—History.   I. Title.
HV2530.B83   1999
305.9′0813—dc21   99-40421
                                             CIP

All photographs courtesy of the Gallaudet University Archives.

For my mother and father

Contents

Abbreviations

ADA	Americans with Disabilities Act
AFPH	American Federation of the Physically Handicapped
ASL	American Sign Language
CAID	Convention of American Instructors of the Deaf
CCC	Civilian Conservation Corps
CEASD	Conference of Executives and Administrators of Schools for the Deaf
CIO	Congress of Industrial Organizations
DMJ	*Deaf Mute's Journal*
ESA	Empire State Association of the Deaf
FEPC	Fair Employment Practices Committee
GCAA	Gallaudet College Alumni Association
GPO	Government Printing Office
GYAC	Goodyear Aircraft Corporation
MCAD	Metropolitan Civic Association of the Deaf
NAD	National Association of the Deaf
NFB	National Federation of the Blind
NFSD	National Fraternal Society of the Deaf
NID	National Institute for the Deaf
NRA	National Recovery Administration
OVR	Office of Vocational Rehabilitation
PCEH	President's Council on Employment of the Handicapped
PSAD	Pennsylvania Society for the Advancement of the Deaf
SWJD	Society for the Welfare of the Jewish Deaf
TSC	Temporary State Commission
USES	United States Employment Service
WMC	War Manpower Commission
WPA	Works Progress Administration

Acknowledgments

This study would not have been possible without the generous support and assistance of deaf and hearing individuals from around the United States. Above all, I am indebted to Laura Mumford, whose careful reading and criticism were an extraordinary act of friendship. At the University of Wisconsin my greatest obligation is to Tom McCormick, whose constant support and brilliant mind were of immeasurable assistance. Special thanks go to Linda Gordon, Stan Schultz, and Harold Scheub for their roles as mentors and readers. I am truly grateful to friends such as Caryn Goldberg, Tricia Egan, Nancy MacLean, Kathy Brown, Ted Pearson, Megan Ballard, Kim Santiago, Jenny Jones, Bambi Riehl, Earl Mulderink, Paul Taillon, and the Bassett and Follet families.

The staff at numerous institutions provided immeasurable assistance. I am particularly indebted to colleagues at Gallaudet University, including Ulf Hedberg, Michael Olson, Marguerite Glass-Englehart, Ivey Pittle Wallace, and John Van Cleve, who provided much needed help and support. In addition, I want to thank editor Christina Findlay, whose professional and thoughtful efforts were especially welcomed. Thanks also go to colleagues at the University of Wisconsin and the Wisconsin Historical Society: Jon Peters, Lorraine Adkins, Ellen Burke, and the late Judy Cochran.

Institutions in the deaf community that graciously allowed me to review their records include the New York Society for the Deaf; the Fanwood School in White Plains, New York; the Marie Katzenbach School in Trenton, New Jersey; the Wisconsin School for the Deaf in Delavan; the National Fraternal Society of the Deaf; and the National Association of the Deaf. I am especially grateful for the aid of deaf and hearing leaders such as Jean and Bobbi Cordano, and the late Waldo Cordano; Ben Schowe Jr.; Robert Lankenau; Alvin and Minnie Hawks; Lois Hume; Henry Buzzard; Alan B. Crammatte; Pat Dierson; and Eve Dicker. I trust I have honored their confidence.

Finally, my deepest thanks go to my cousins, aunts, and uncles, whose accomplishments epitomized the highest traditions of the deaf community, and to my family—including Suzanne and Adin—whose unwavering support and assistance made this study possible.

Introduction

This historical study considers the working lives of deaf men and women in the United States from the mid-nineteenth century to the establishment of an industrial-based working class during World War II. It examines the strategies deaf adults used to prepare for, enter, and advance through the nation's mainstream workforce. In doing this, deaf workers are portrayed, to the extent possible, as they saw themselves. In the working world, they typically sought to de-emphasize their identity as sign language-using deaf persons and to be integrated into the mainstream work force. In their schools, however, they usually favored a bilingual approach, celebrating the centrality of American Sign Language and recognizing the value of English. In fact, as early as the latter half of the nineteenth century, deaf people defined themselves socially as members of a distinct community with shared formative experiences and language as well as full members of hearing society.[1] Outside the workplace, deaf adults have long defined themselves as bicultural, bilingual Americans.[2]

This study also demonstrates that the accomplishments and failures of deaf workers are inextricably linked to the language, identity, schooling, and general status of deaf adults. In addition, the position of deaf workers has been constrained by the changing relationship between the dominant able-bodied hearing culture and other minority communities and marginalized groups in this country.

Consequently, this book attempts to explain the varied factors within the deaf community and U.S. society at large that have alternately restrained and advanced the fortunes of deaf workers. I argue first that sign language-based educational methods have been of particular importance in shaping the identity, intellectual growth, and vocational success of this nation's deaf citizens. Indeed, the nineteenth century's greatest advance was the development of an incomplete but extended national system of sign language-based vocational and academic instruction for deaf students. Through the efforts of hearing and deaf leaders, education thus was recast from the privilege of the few to a right of the majority, and deaf people in the United States were brought into close association.

Second, I claim that the most intractable obstacles restraining deaf workers were centered not in the workplace as, one might expect, but in the classroom. By the late nineteenth century, a powerful constituency of hearing educators, parents, and professionals—oralists—opposed the creation of a signing deaf community and sought to assimilate deaf children and adults into mainstream society. Oralists gained control of the nation's schools where they forced deaf adults from the classroom and administrative positions, undermined vocational instruction, and replaced instruction in sign language with marginally useful oral-based approaches dependent upon speech and speechreading to convey information. My research indicates that the reduction or suppression of sign language restrained the academic, vocational, and intellectual progress of many, if not most, deaf students.

These developments, in conjunction with the limited years of schooling available to most students, left them ill-prepared to assume anything more than marginal positions in agriculture, industry, and commerce. In particular, my research strongly suggests that the ascendancy of oral-based methods was a hollow, even illusory victory. Even as they were dispersed across the nation, deaf adults vigorously and passionately advocated for sign language and opposed any efforts to ban their beloved language or impose methods that relied exclusively on oral-based approaches. This record of sustained resistance through shared linguistic and cultural identification is remarkable, if not unique, in American history.

Furthermore, I argue that compromise on these pedagogical differences was never reached, as these debates were linked to a broader intractable struggle over the very existence of the developing deaf community. Throughout the period of this study, the pervasive racist, ethnocentric, and assimilationist practices and values of the dominant culture restricted the rights and standing of all minority communities—including, of course, deaf adults.

Although distinguished by its American Sign Language-based communication system and its own cultural identity, the deaf community nonetheless internalized the dominant gender, racial, and class prejudices of hearing society. Consequently, racial, class, and gender divisions influenced the choices made by white, male, middle-class deaf leaders regarding appropriate strategies to enter and advance through the economy, and they weakened leaders' commitment to aiding employment rights for all deaf people.

The formative institutions in the deaf community re-created these divisions. School administrators, whether deaf or hearing, established vocational programs that favored male students while slighting women. The majority of African American students attended inferior, segregated schools and were excluded from deaf organizations. Sharp economic divisions resulted from widely disparate educational and vocational opportunities. Although most deaf students never advanced beyond primary-level instruction, a small but influential elite completed secondary programs, graduated from Gallaudet College, found well-paying jobs, and assumed prominent positions in the deaf community.

In contrast to their pathbreaking efforts to define and defend their right to use sign language, deaf leaders and adults were typically cautious, even deferential, regarding their status and rights as workers. By the latter half of the nineteenth century, male deaf leaders had promulgated an influential gender-based code that influenced employment strategies used by deaf workers through the close of World War II. These leaders insisted that states provide academic and vocational instruction, especially to male deaf students, who in turn were expected to become successful workers and respected representatives of their community. This code failed to address the communication difficulties and widespread discrimination most deaf people confronted when they entered the mainstream economy.

Deaf leaders and workers debated and proposed additional employment strategies, but these strategies augmented rather than overturned this conservative precept. Most leaders sought to educate employers about the capabilities of deaf workers, believing that they lacked the power to directly challenge entrenched habits. The first four decades of the twentieth century brought only intermittent advances to the nation's deaf workers, and no development did more to hinder them than the continued dominance of oralist educational practices. The influence of federal and state agencies on deaf employment was mixed. In some situations, deaf workers were assisted by government efforts; in others they were discouraged or excluded from programs.

It was only during World Wars I and II that deaf adults were offered considerable short-term success as industrial employees, especially when employers encouraged the use of writing and sign language in the workplace.

Near the close of World War II, deaf leaders debated the issues that had influenced deaf employment for the previous fifty years. They rejected proposals to require government and private employers to hire deaf employees because they believed such legislation violated their long-standing code of individual responsibility and was appropriate only for "handicapped" individuals, from whom they sought to disassociate themselves. With the majority of adults employed in mid-level factory positions at the close of World War II, however, deaf working men and women faced a troubling future.

Chapter 1 examines academic and vocational instruction before oralist thought and practices became preeminent. Chapter 2 interprets the educational, vocational, and ideological conflicts between oralists and deaf and hearing opponents during the late nineteenth and early twentieth centuries. Chapter 3 traces the successful efforts of deaf and hearing activists to reverse a turn-of-the-century ruling by federal administrators to block deaf workers from government employment. Chapter 4 examines the influential but incomplete efforts of deaf activists to harness the power of the state government to oversee the status of deaf students and workers in Minnesota. Chapter 5 traces the influx of deaf women and men into the industrial workforce during the early decades of the twentieth century. Chapter 6 considers the efforts of deaf activists to reverse oralist rule at selected residential schools as well as the efforts of workers to enter New Deal work programs during the Depression. Chapter 7 centers on the movement of deaf workers into industry during World War II and their efforts to prepare for employment after the conflict. A brief epilogue sketches the status of deaf workers and the deaf community from the close of World War II to the contemporary era.

Although the geographic boundary of this book ranges across the United States, it is not a comprehensive national study, nor does it fully consider the experiences of all deaf workers in the diverse deaf community. Based primarily upon the records of organized state and national associations, this study focuses on the most highly educated and professionally successful white males, who dominated leadership positions in most deaf associations. Although I attempt to show the ways that economic-, race-, and gender-biased assumptions influenced these leaders, this study is not centered upon deaf women, deaf individuals of color, or marginally schooled and employed deaf adults. I look forward to additional studies that will more fully illuminate their important but neglected history.[3]

1

"For the Deaf of the Land"
Building Independence

The history of most deaf Americans prior to 1800 is undocumented.[1] By 1900, however, forty thousand deaf citizens had constructed a unique national community with its own visual language, schools, organizations, and businesses. Most deaf adults during the nineteenth century were laborers and artisans; many tilled the land; a small number were entrepreneurs, educators, and professionals. This chapter centers on the debates and strategies employed by deaf people to prepare for, enter, and advance through the nineteenth-century work force.

The most significant developments advancing the position of deaf workers occurred outside the workplace. Deaf men and women led efforts to provide general education and vocational instruction for themselves and for children like themselves. These efforts spurred them to build social and civic organizations in which they debated the status and responsibilities of deaf workers.

The deaf community in the nineteenth-century United States was culturally unique and economically vulnerable. Many adults favored sign language communication in their private lives and developed a social and linguistic identity distinct from their hearing neighbors. Yet, as workers, most sought their fortunes in the mainstream economy among hearing peers who did not sign and in the mainstream economy at positions that did not accommodate their unique auditory and linguistic attributes. Deaf leaders were concerned about these occupational constraints, but they nonetheless opposed the creation of special group rights for deaf workers. Rather, they promoted a de facto code that obligated the state to provide schooling and demanded that

1

educated deaf adults become independent—even model—wage earners and citizens.

Overall, the nineteenth century brought epochal advances in the working lives and general standing of many deaf people. Yet class, race, and gender biases within the developing deaf community itself constrained opportunities for many deaf adults and children,[2] thus paralleling mainstream, hearing society.

Efforts to establish schools were the nineteenth century's most influential development for the deaf community. In 1800, organized public vocational or academic instruction was generally unavailable: of the nation's several thousand deaf children, only a tiny minority from affluent families had private tutors or attended schools in Europe. Over the next century, however, a small number of educated deaf people created a national network of schools, sometimes working individually, occasionally in unison with other deaf people, and most often in conjunction with hearing leaders. By 1900, most deaf citizens regarded education as a right.[3]

The nation's first permanent public school for deaf students, popularly known as the American School for the Deaf, opened its doors in 1817 in Hartford, Connecticut. Thomas Hopkins Gallaudet, an evangelical Congregational minister, originally led the institution, assisted by Laurent Clerc, a graduate of and former teacher at the National Institute for the Deaf in Paris.[4] Gallaudet had visited Europe to learn more about efforts to educate deaf students and found in Clerc an accomplished teacher whose skills complemented Gallaudet's inexperience. In deciding to leave his home and travel to the United States, Clerc demonstrated a commitment to service characteristic of other deaf educational forerunners. He explained that his emigration sprang from a curiosity about travel and a commitment to see that his "unfortunate fellow-beings on the other side of the Atlantic" might possess the same educational benefits he had known.[5] By the end of its first year, almost forty pupils from ten states had studied at the American School.[6]

Religious assumptions influenced the character of the school Clerc and Gallaudet founded. Like other reformers of the Second Great

Awakening, Gallaudet believed his overarching duty was to bring his students closer to God and the Gospel. As he would later write, uneducated deaf children and adults knew nothing of morality or salvation, so they stood outside the reach of God.[7] If deafness had severed the ties between deaf people and God, sign language, he reasoned, would bring these souls into communion with their Creator.[8]

Consistent with the preindustrial artisan economy of the early nineteenth-century United States, Gallaudet designed the curriculum to prepare his students to become independent wage earners. Students followed a three-year program of general and vocational instruction, centered on written language, reading, and arithmetic, supplemented by study in revenue-earning workshops, taught by local artisans, in cabinet making, shoe making, and tailoring.[9]

The American School's influence was enormous. By virtue of its pathbreaking position and Gallaudet's and Clerc's expertise, the school served for decades as an unofficial training center for deaf and hearing teachers and for administrators. As personnel from other states typically adopted the methods and practices developed at Hartford, the school also became an informal center for learning and promoting sign language, the favored method of communication in class instruction and daily interaction.[10]

These advances in Connecticut encouraged aspiring deaf leaders, including American School graduates, who demonstrated their commitment to advancing the standing of deaf students by founding residential and day schools across the country.[11] In the first half of the nineteenth century, deaf people assisted in the establishment of two schools; between 1850 and 1875, they founded seven; between 1875 and 1900, they established an additional thirteen. By century's end, deaf leaders had been instrumental in helping to establish some thirty schools.[12]

Although dispersed in their efforts, most deaf school founders shared educational values and goals derived from the practices of the American School. The three most favored practices were: first, that sign language be the primary medium of instruction and communication; second, that both deaf and hearing adults be teachers and administrators; and third, that students receive sustained vocational and academic instruction.

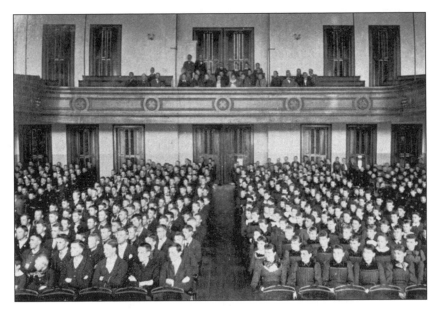

Deaf and hearing school leaders believed they were responsible for the spiritual as well as academic and vocational guidance of residential school students. Here students are shown in the chapel of the Illinois Institute.

Educational advances demonstrated that deaf men and women could be learned students and graduates as well as effective workers, teachers, and administrators. By the 1850s, some 250 of the 550 teachers and administrators in the burgeoning national network of schools were themselves deaf. By century's end, more than 2,500 children and adults had received instruction at the American School alone. Nationally, perhaps half of all eligible deaf students had received some elementary instruction.[13]

Establishing schools was only the first phase of a process that unfolded throughout the century. Through several decades, deaf activists and hearing educators worked at the local and state levels to strengthen programs at schools scattered across the nation. They advocated substantive measures including lowering the age limits for entering students, ending tuition charges, and enacting legislation to codify education as a right for deaf students and to mandate attendance. These reforms were typically noncontroversial, but advocates had to work steadily, often over a period of years, to secure them.[14]

Deaf and hearing educators labored with only modest success to improve vocational instruction during the second half of the nineteenth century. In state and national conventions of teachers and administrators, as well as in meetings of various state, regional, and national associations of deaf adults, members critiqued existing programs and called for more advanced and varied instruction for students.[15] No critic was more vigorous than John Carlin, a deaf artist and writer who had attended residential school in Pennsylvania. In 1853, at the third national Convention of American Instructors of the Deaf (CAID), a professional organization established in 1850, Carlin charged that eastern cities were flooded with poorly trained graduates of schools for the deaf, who were locked into undesirable trades with limited opportunities. "Shoe-makers and tailors are always expected to toil incessantly from dawn to midnight," Carlin charged, "with their backs and necks bent almost to the level with their works." These problems would grow, he warned, as long as schools provided students with neither adequate training nor sufficient trades.[16]

Carlin proffered an ambitious proposal for reform. He called upon administrators to broaden the range of trades taught in their schools, to pay students for their work, and to lengthen the period of instruction so that students could acquire sufficient training to become apprentices. Moreover, he argued that because many employers were unaware of the students' skills, school officials were obliged to act as brokers on behalf of their graduates—a claim numerous deaf activists would repeat in later decades.[17]

In the 1880s, Edward Hodgson, a vocational instructor at the Fanwood School in New York, became the deaf community's most persuasive proponent of advanced vocational instruction and most forceful critic of inadequate training. In 1880, at the founding convention of the National Association of the Deaf (NAD) in Ohio, Hodgson argued that because few students could acquire a position on the basis of academic training, industrial instruction was the most important aspect of schooling. School officials, Hodgson charged, seemed more interested in reducing costs than in providing systematic training. Students therefore left school with insufficient skills to compete for jobs.[18]

Hodgson used his position as editor of the school's nationally renowned newspaper, the *Deaf Mute's Journal* (*DMJ*), to build public pressure for change. In one representative editorial, he warned that without a trade, deaf adults were likely to be "sans friends, sans trade, sans food, sans everything."[19]

Educators like Hodgson and community-based leaders like Carlin decried existing conditions and called for systemic reforms,[20] but nineteenth-century deaf leaders were stymied by substantive economic and cultural constraints. Even by the outset of the twentieth century, few deaf people had any formal role in either determining or influencing school financial affairs. School administrators had secured widespread support for the concept of schooling, but obtaining funds to match their educational visions was far more difficult.[21]

The focus of most deaf leaders' reform efforts in the nineteenth century was on the work status of white males, not that of women or minorities. Vocational education for women, for instance, was periph-

As editor of the *Deaf Mute's Journal*, Edward Hodgson encouraged deaf advocates and average citizens across the country to use the newspaper as a forum for their views. The newspaper also became a platform for informing hearing leaders involved in educating and employing deaf people. Reprinted from *The Silent Worker*, November, 1894.

eral to other issues within the deaf community, despite the increasing participation of women in the industrializing economy and debates within hearing society about women's employment. Like their counterparts in public schools, most educators of deaf students assumed that women graduates would get married and likely not enter the paid workforce.[22] Vocational programs for women students consequently were narrow in range and poorly funded.[23] For example, schools often provided instruction that trained women for domestic service—generally as servants or cooks—or for sewing trades. Only infrequent exchanges regarding the vocational condition of women punctuated the conventions of teachers and administrators during the latter half of the century.[24]

Few such discussions questioned the character of programs for women; instead, most participants differed only in their degree of enthusiasm for particular domestic pursuits, although occasionally a few teachers and administrators would criticize instruction.[25] One teacher at a national conference in 1880 argued, for example, that few of her peers challenged the "popular notion that if girls learn to sew and sweep the house that is about all we can expect of them."[26] And as part of a broader critique of vocational instruction in 1893, Francis D. Clarke, superintendent of the School for the Deaf in Michigan, argued that "there is not a school for the deaf that is doing what it should to train its girls."[27] These kinds of remarks, though, were the exception.

In addition, racially-biased practices often neglected or excluded deaf African American children, just as gender-biased assumptions narrowed deaf women's educational opportunities. At national conventions held in the latter half of the century, few teachers and administrators, whether deaf or hearing, even mentioned African American students, although a handful of white community-based leaders intermittently advocated improving their schools.[28] In most southern states, deaf African Americans attended inferior segregated facilities—if schooling was available to them at all.[29]

Although frustrated in their campaigns to advance broad-based vocational instruction, educational leaders nevertheless successfully secured support for a national college for deaf students in the nineteenth century. Following calls from Carlin and others for the provision of postsecondary education in the early 1850s, influential hearing people—including Edward Miner Gallaudet, the son of Thomas H. Gallaudet—enlisted in the effort. The younger Gallaudet eventually secured private and congressional support for a college in Washington, D.C., and in the fall of 1864, thirteen students began classes at the National Deaf Mute College—later renamed Gallaudet College to honor the founder of the American School.[30]

Gallaudet College quickly became the most influential deaf educational institution in the nation, and its students became leading national figures. In ten years, more than one hundred students had attended classes; by the early 1890s, another three hundred had studied in Washington, D.C. In keeping with the original practices of the American School, students communicated in sign language and often studied with deaf professors. Former Gallaudet students assumed prominent stations in education, business, agriculture, and the ministry, as well as leadership positions in state and national associations in the deaf community.[31]

College administrators did not at first welcome women at the new institution. Like their peers in hearing society, few male leaders within the deaf community believed that women should attend college. For some two decades, school officials, including Edward Gallaudet, its first president, discouraged or shunned women applicants.[32]

A small number of deaf women protested their exclusion, however.[33] From the mid 1870s through the 1880s, these women labored to gain the attention of educational leaders with the deaf and hearing communities.[34] Activists such as Laura Sheridan, Angie Fuller, and Georgia Elliot wrote letters and appeared before educational conventions, combining argument with public pressure to advance their claim for higher education. Finally, in 1887, President Gallaudet agreed to admit women.

The efforts of these women are noteworthy not only for their success, but also for their scope and boldness. Male deaf leaders had typically avoided public debate outside the deaf community. The success of Elliot and others in persuading college leaders to admit women demonstrated that debate and confrontation could be effective.[35]

This advance for women did not, however, translate into advances for deaf African Americans, who were not welcomed into the college. Like white women, African American deaf students of both sexes faced systemic economic and social obstacles in any attempt to prepare for and enter college. Moreover, as segregationist Jim Crow policies took hold across the nation in the latter part of the nineteenth century, Gallaudet officials typically directed aspiring African Americans to petition for admission to nearby Howard University, a federally supported school for African Americans that had no formal program to accommodate those who were deaf.[36] It was not until after World War II that deaf activists helped desegregate Gallaudet College.

Leaders who built and strengthened schools were also committed to improving deaf adults' opportunities to obtain positions consistent with their abilities. In the latter half of the nineteenth century, deaf activists used meetings, correspondence, newspapers, and formal presentations to debate ways to improve deaf adults' livelihoods and to advance their standing as a group.

Out of this extended, collective self-examination, most participants came to agree that hearing people, rather than deafness per se, presented the most powerful obstacle to employment success. In their communications with hearing coworkers and employers, deaf workers typically relied on writing and did not aspire to positions that relied upon hearing or spoken communication (although individuals who were deafened after they became verbally proficient could and often did use spoken language). Nonetheless, most believed they should be considered for any positions they could perform, particularly where they could work independently or at least where rapid communication with nonsigning coworkers would not be expected. Most also agreed that hearing individuals often underestimated their abilities. Carlin's invective was illustrative. He railed against "benevolent men of business" who "blindly believe" that the inability to hear or speak prevents deaf individuals from performing many types of work.[37]

Deaf adults understood that hearing employers held great sway over their individual and collective advance; they disagreed, however, about how to handle or improve this vital relationship. A few argued that hearing employers would never equitably hire and promote deaf workers, so they sought to establish independent economic positions or enclaves. Others argued that deaf workers deserved specific rights, including priority for selected jobs. Most deaf leaders, however, thought resistant employers could be enlightened through persuasion and example. They also sought to strengthen state and national associations and to establish a code of personal responsibility within individual workers.

Whatever their disagreements regarding employers' attitudes, most leaders and commentators presumed that deaf workers were equal in ability—and often superior in diligence—to their hearing peers and that full membership in the deaf community was predicated upon the willingness to work. Transgressors risked censure or expulsion. Itinerant deaf people unable to secure steady work were criticized; solicitors of charity risked outright ostracism.[38]

Educators and leaders of state and national associations publicly denounced deaf itinerants or individuals who apparently chose not to work.[39] James L. Smith, president of the Minnesota Association of the Deaf and a teacher at the state residential school in 1885, explained his views in a speech before the state association. "If a deaf stranger from another place comes among you, meet him as a brother, offer to help him get work," he advised. But, "if he does not work, if he prefers to depend upon charity—then regard him as your enemy, and treat him as such."[40]

Deaf writers and leaders argued occasionally that censure of marginal workers was excessive or inappropriate.[41] In a brief debate at the 1883 NAD convention, for example, several members, including the respected Thomas Brown, founder of the New England Gallaudet Association, argued that the plight of migrant deaf workers was due to inadequate vocational training. Until such instruction was improved, more men would be forced to peddle or beg in order to survive. One person sided with Brown, requesting that organizations assist unemployed workers, but another participant demanded swift punishment of deaf tramps and peddlers. The brief exchange spurred no formal response: even the respected Brown could not sway his unyielding peers to consider including these unfortunate adults in their community.[42]

Many deaf adults understood that their opportunities as workers were linked, in large part, to their general standing in hearing society. This position greatly worried some, and a small number of deaf individuals doubted they would ever be treated fairly in hearing society. They worked to establish autonomous communities comprised primarily of deaf citizens. During the 1850s, the most publicized of these proposals circulated in the *American Annals of the Deaf*, a professional journal. Georgia resident John J. Flournoy in 1855 called upon deaf citizens to build an autonomous Deaf Commonwealth in the western territories. As long as deaf individuals remained in hearing society, he argued, they would be constrained by "rejections and consignments to inferior places."[43]

Most observers criticized Flournoy's proposal. William Turner, a hearing teacher at the American School, shared Flournoy's belief that deaf citizens could manage their own colony, but he rejected the scheme as impractical.[44] Laurent Clerc, too, dismissed the plan as unrealistic. Edmund Booth, an American School graduate and teacher, opposed the premise that deaf citizens needed refuge outside mainstream society.[45] Whatever their differences, however, most critics of the idea likely agreed with one correspondent who explained, "I am for a place, where all my deaf-mute brethren could live and be happy."[46]

Despite these criticisms, a small number of deaf citizens continued to promote the creation of enclaves for deaf adults. At the first NAD convention in 1880, one participant urged deaf workers to establish a settlement where deaf people and hearing friends could live and work free from prejudice.[47] The following year, Henry Rider asserted that hearing employers invariably mistreated deaf workers. He decried bosses who "willingly and easily shuffle us from employment to idleness and destitution."[48]

These arguments and initiatives ultimately enjoyed more notoriety than support. While deaf adults in rural and urban areas often lived and worked together in informal but close association, the financial and logistical burdens of formal colonies spelled their failure. Besides, most deaf workers sought their fortunes in society at large rather than in rural separatist communities.

Many nineteenth-century deaf leaders argued that agriculture was the best pursuit for the average deaf person, because it offered autonomy and opportunities unattainable in other occupations. Proponents emphasized that agriculturists were not subject to the biases of hearing employers; instead, success depended upon the skills of the individual. A typical letter to the *DMJ* extolled farming and warned of the pitfalls of other trades: farmers, one correspondent boasted in 1882, "meet with less opposition from the ruling class, and enjoy more liberty and independence, more rights and privileges, than the same class does in any other country in the world."[49]

A small number of advocates also questioned the sweeping prerogative of employers to hire or exclude deaf workers. In his 1882 directive to the *DMJ*, "Gatesby" argued that administrators of schools for deaf students were morally obliged to hire deaf employees and to train students for future vacancies. If school principals disagreed, activists should petition state legislatures. "This is right and just," he concluded. "We should not fold our arms behind and see such things remain undone."[50]

Others sought to broaden and renew state and national associations as a means to elevate the status of deaf workers. In the mid-1880s, Henry White urged NAD leaders to lobby on behalf of workers. A former Gallaudet College student, White believed that recent victories of women suffragists would result in an increased willingness on the part of hearing politicians to consider the views of deaf organizations and people.[51] Thomas Francis Fox, a widely respected teacher and NAD president, went further in 1889, proposing an international federation to protect the rights of deaf workers and citizens.[52]

Despite a readiness to propose these ideas, visionary leaders and enthusiastic convention members could not sustain a program of action consistent with their aspirations. They had worked for years to obtain nominal advances in schooling; but any undertaking to define and secure work-based advances would demand far greater efforts. Moreover, few women or men had the time or financial resources to attend conventions, much less to fight for innovative initiatives.

Plus, most deaf leaders embraced individual enterprise, rather than collective action, as the preferred strategy to assist workers. Organization officials and leaders favored an individualistic strategy that relied upon training, personal initiative, and responsibility, a strategy consistent with the entrepreneurial ethos typically associated in the African American community with Booker T. Washington. The government was expected to provide general instruction and vocational training to willing students, who were then obligated as educated deaf adults to become self-supporting workers. Advocates of this strategy understood the obstacles facing deaf workers; many had worked to strengthen schooling and had been underemployed themselves. Still, at least in their public pronouncements, they maintained that sustained personal diligence and determination alone would bring success.

Thomas Fox was one of the first leaders to argue publicly that educated deaf adults were obligated to become independent wage earners and citizens. In a presentation before the NAD in 1883, he argued that after receiving an education from the state, students were morally bound to earn their way by "honest industry" and to refrain from "idle, roving, and dissolute" activity. In fact, he held that graduates had won over employers by following these tenets.[53]

Henry Rider argued that each deaf person represented all his or her deaf peers. A gifted graduate of the New York School, he became a teacher, school administrator, and long-standing president of the Empire State Association of the Deaf (ESA). In a speech before the association in 1875, he argued that the example of one would aid all. "Live so that you will command the respect and approbation of your employers," he explained, "and you will have won a great triumph not for yourself alone, but also for the deaf of the land."[54]

Hodgson edited the *DMJ* for quite a few years, from the late 1870s through the 1930s. He never advised readers to lower their aspirations when confronted by resistance, but he cautioned that success demanded years of effort, often in the face of indifferent employers.[55] In a representative editorial in 1882, he advised young workers to be prepared "to start at the bottom, and with a stout heart, clear head, and willing arm, climb upward by hard work and faithful attention to duty."[56]

Hypatia Boyd, one of the few leaders to address women workers, agreed with the theme of self-control and self-reliance articulated by her male peers.[57] Between 1899 and 1901, she penned a series of essays in the *Silent Worker,* a New Jersey-based periodical written and published by deaf people, in which she surveyed professional positions suitable for deaf women. She argued that success at any position depended upon patience and industry. In one typical article she praised a friend whose success as a bookkeeper served as a "silent and modest example" for fellow workers, reminding her readers that discipline and selflessness were expected of women as well as men.[58]

This code of personal responsibility, although never formally proclaimed, ultimately served as an exacting expectation for both deaf students and aspiring workers.[59] Troubled by the uncontested authority of employers, proponents of the code nevertheless did not challenge this prerogative. Instead, they placed the onus on individual workers to establish themselves in the face of persistent adversities. Deaf leaders thus acted as disciplinarians and exemplars to steel students and workers against discrimination and disappointment. Much as Thomas Hopkins Gallaudet had pursued the reformation of society through individual salvation, these leaders predicated the advance of their community upon the success of each worker. Contrasting illustrations from New York, however, reveal the positive reach as well as the cautionary limits of this approach.

At St. Ann's Episcopal Church for the Deaf in Manhattan, the precepts of personal responsibility and persuasion brought workers modest successes.[60] Established by the Reverend Thomas Gallaudet, the eldest son of Thomas Hopkins Gallaudet, and his deaf wife Sophia Fowler Gallaudet, St. Ann's was the first church in the nation intended to bring deaf and hearing parishioners together. A graduate of Trinity College and an instructor at the New York School since the early 1840s, Gallaudet received his ordination in the Episcopal Church in 1851 and established St. Ann's in 1852. His decision to found St. Ann's reflected the convergence between his own spiritual beliefs and a long-standing secular commitment to deaf people.[61] In fact, the church was also open to blind parishioners and others with disabilities, regardless of race and color.

As Amos Draper, a deaf professor at Gallaudet College, explained later, Gallaudet meant St. Ann's to be a "working church" in which he "aimed not to simply preach the word, but to live the word."[62] At the same time, the church's development coincided with the growth of the area's deaf community as, by midcentury, deaf students from across the region in search of employment had migrated to New York City.[63]

Gallaudet sometimes met with wary employers to enlist their support in hiring deaf workers. Because he believed that apprehensions about communication underlay most employers' reluctance to hire deaf people, he discussed ways to convey information to deaf employees, such as writing, fingerspelling, and sign language.[64] Although he favored private, informal means to assist workers, he also employed public appeals to request aid from the city's hearing residents.[65]

Perhaps more important, Gallaudet strongly encouraged deaf and hearing parishioners to assist unemployed individuals. Deaf parishioners invited community members to various gatherings where they exchanged information regarding prospective employers and occupations.[66] Hearing members of the St. Ann's congregation were encouraged to learn manual spelling and sign language in order to communicate with deaf parishioners and prospective coworkers.

These activities at St. Ann's are noteworthy. Their successes demonstrated to the deaf community itself that deaf workers were especially qualified to counsel and assist their peers. They also illustrated that deaf and hearing parties could find ways to communicate effectively. Finally, they indicated that the urban economy provided a range of positions at which deaf workers could excel—provided cooperative employers could be found.[67]

Whatever the successes of St. Ann's Church, however, deaf people in general faced systemic, even insurmountable, challenges in the nineteenth-century workplace. In fact, the limits of the self-help ethos were revealed in a series of disputes regarding federal hiring policies from the late 1880s through the 1890s. During the latter half of the century, a small number of deaf men worked in the state and federal Civil Service, often at clerical positions that emphasized written communication.[68] Despite these inroads, deaf leaders were alarmed in 1885 at reports that government officials had prevented deaf candidates from applying for employment. Worried that any instances of exclusion might encourage more systemic restrictions, leaders of New York's ESA worked with Edward A. Fay, the hearing editor of the *American Annals of the Deaf* and a vice president at Gallaudet College, to organize an investigation.[69]

The investigation quickly reinforced the deep concerns of these leaders. On the positive side, initial correspondence between Fay and the secretary of the U.S. Civil Service Commission, R. D. Graham, revealed that no formal rules or practices forbade the employment of deaf candidates.[70] Nonetheless, deaf observers, including Edward Hodgson, worried that Graham's assurances would not protect deaf applicants from antagonistic local officials and thus called for ongoing monitoring of the government.[71] The issue faded from public discussion until 1888, when a second observer argued for concerted action against the government. "Are we mutes always to be imposed upon, suffer wrongs and simply, because we cannot hear, must we endure them without complaint?" asked Brooklyn resident George Reynolds in the *DMJ*. Reynolds argued that deaf citizens were duty bound to invigorate their local, state, and national organizations—to "combine and demand our rights"—or else they would be powerless to challenge future restrictions. "[I]n union alone there is strength," Reynolds warned.[72]

Reynolds's fears were prescient.[73] In 1893, following reports that two deaf candidates were denied permission to take examinations for positions as clerks in the U.S. Railway Service, national and state leaders quickly launched a second investigation.[74] This time, correspondence with John T. Doyle, secretary of the Civil Service, revealed that deaf applicants had been prevented from taking an employment exam with the Railway Mail Service.[75] The general superintendent of the service had decided that railway employment presented too many risks for deaf workers.[76] Current deaf employees would not be affected, but all future deaf applicants would be turned away. This decision, Doyle concluded, was neither discriminatory nor improper.

In fact, the exclusionary directive was consistent with overall policy. Civil Service officials shaped the work force by controlling examination and placement procedures that determined which, if any, positions would be open for examination by candidates "defective" in speech or hearing. In addition, local appointing officers could reject even those "physically incapacitated" candidates qualified by examination.[77] Activists countered that the exclusionary rule was unwarranted because deaf workers were employed at the time of the new ruling. Still, according to Civil Service policy and federal law, their claims, although outwardly reasonable, had no standing.

In the end, Smith and the leadership of the organized deaf community chose not to challenge the Railway Mail Service directive. Occasional newspaper articles in the following years described the accomplishments of remaining deaf Railway Mail Service workers or warned of obstacles to applicants in other departments of the Civil Service. Otherwise, this issue faded from public debate or discussion.[78] Deaf workers were excluded because law and custom had converged to limit sharply their already narrow workplace rights.

Most deaf workers enjoyed greater educational and vocational opportunities after the opening of the American School in 1817. A network of private and public schools strengthened their intellectual and vocational standing, and secondary and collegiate studies brought success to a small number of artisans, educators, and professionals. Advances in education were not equally available to all deaf Americans, however. Racial and gender divisions narrowed the boundaries of membership in the deaf community and contributed to the educational and economic segmentation of deaf women and men.

Racial exclusion was at once the most limiting and the most accepted demarcation. Like their peers in the hearing world, white deaf leaders sanctioned segregation and blocked deaf African Americans from their national organizations. In civic life, they left unchallenged a system that denied most southern African American deaf children an education and ensured their economic marginalization as deaf adults. For example, one reviewer of the 1890 census estimated that only 20 percent of African American deaf males and 13 percent of deaf African American females even attended school.[79] Available anecdotal evidence further indicates that African American deaf women and men were largely excluded from skilled trades and the professions. Most men were laborers or farmers; most women toiled as laborers, servants, or laundresses.[80] Thus, two parallel communities developed with little interaction between them: the first, comprised primarily of whites, has been described by hearing society—as well as by most deaf citizens—as "the deaf community"; the second, for the most part unrecognized even today, was comprised of deaf African American women, men, and children.[81]

Traditional gender-biased precepts and practices also limited the cultural, educational, and occupational opportunities of deaf white women. Few deaf men paid attention to women's educational and occupational concerns, despite the women's activism in state and national organizations. Deaf women won a substantive victory when they were finally admitted to Gallaudet College, but a restricted system of vocational training still left most who were in search of paid employment with nothing other than marginal positions in sewing trades, factories, and domestic service.[82] In contrast, a college degree enabled a small number of women to secure professional positions, often in education and the fine arts. Evidence from residential schools, deaf organizations, and government records suggests that white deaf women enjoyed greater occupational mobility than deaf African Americans of either sex, but significantly less than their white male counterparts.

Gender-biased values rooted in hearing society also constrained the employment strategies of male deaf leaders, who rejected rights-based demands for work opportunity in favor of codes that emphasized personal responsibility and economic independence as the sine qua non of deaf manhood and worth. Within this ideology of masculinity, most deaf leaders believed that they were obligated, as men, to overcome economic obstacles, but such a code obscured the presence of racial, educational, and class privileges that segmented the deaf community. Moreover, in coming decades, this ethos would undermine efforts to align with other groups of citizens with disabilities even as it greatly narrowed efforts to establish workplace rights.

White men enjoyed the greatest occupational opportunities among deaf adults because of their access to the broadest array of educational, vocational, and community resources. Surveys by residential schools, deaf organizations, and the government at midcentury indicated that the majority of deaf men were employed in agriculture and in semiskilled and skilled craft positions.[83] A small number of men—likely those with the strongest academic and vocational training—secured well-paid positions in such fields as the applied arts, woodworking, printing, teaching, and business.[84]

As these divisions stratified the deaf community in the nineteenth century, the beliefs and practices of hearing educators and employers defined the community's educational and vocational opportunities.[85] Indeed, by the latter decades of the nineteenth century, growing numbers of hearing professionals and parents, drawn by alluring promises that deaf children could be "restored" to society by being taught to speak and understand oral vocabulary, called for the dismantling of the emergent community, the closure of residential schools, the elimination of sign language, and regulation of the reproduction of deaf adults. United by their common language and shared sense of identity, as well as by the belief that they had a right to influence the terms of their education and employment, deaf women and men mobilized to oppose these changes. In the latter half of the nineteenth century, deaf adults were thrust into the most turbulent period in their history.

2

"Our Claims to Justice"
Challenging Oralism

In November 1883, Alexander Graham Bell appeared before the National Academy of Sciences to deliver the results of his research. Deaf graduates of residential schools, he claimed, socialized in associations, used sign language, intermarried, and had deaf children far more often than did deaf individuals in society at large. If left unchecked, the continued reproduction of deaf adults would establish a "defective variety" of the human race. In order to avert this "great calamity," Bell called for the closing of residential schools and the replacement of deaf teachers and sign language with day schools led by hearing instructors who would train deaf children to speak and read spoken English.[1]

Bell was part of a broader group of hearing individuals—including parents of deaf children, government officials, and educators—who fervently opposed the development of an autonomous community of deaf citizens and sign language-based schools and instead sought to anchor the education of deaf children to oral methods. Instruction in lipreading and articulation, advocates contended, would enable students not only to speak but also to comprehend spoken conversation. In short, these methods would "restore" deaf citizens to their "full humanity" and enable them to pursue a wide range of jobs throughout society.[2]

Many deaf men and women fiercely countered these proposals. Robert McGregor, National Association of the Deaf (NAD) president, warned that "no greater calamity can befall future generations of the deaf" than replacement of sign language with Bell's pure oral methods.[3] The usually temperate Edward Hodgson charged that advocates of sign language prohibition were guilty of "intellectual murder," and that a "day of reckoning" awaited anyone who thus harmed deaf students.[4]

These debates were part of a struggle over the identity and future of the nation's forty thousand deaf citizens that was waged from the 1860s through much of the twentieth century. This chapter traces the responses of deaf adults to these oralist proposals, especially as they influenced deaf employment. Deaf leaders argued that oral instruction undercut the status of deaf workers by stealing time and funding from much needed academic and vocational instruction, despite the fact that few students would be able to use their rudimentary oral skills in the working world. Above all, leaders sought to preserve the system of education they had helped create, so that soon the majority of deaf leaders came to call for a *combined system* of instruction that included *both* oral methods and sign language.

Many hearing educators were ambivalent about the development of a national deaf community, and this ambivalence erupted into open opposition in the early 1870s. They began to criticize deaf adults for establishing state, regional, and national associations. Surprisingly, these initial critiques came not from proponents of the pure oral method (although they did indeed oppose such organizations), but from hearing teachers and administrators, including Edward Gallaudet, who supported sign language yet charged that deaf associations impeded the intellectual and social growth of their members. Critics urged deaf individuals to strengthen their relationships with hearing coworkers and friends and to lessen those with other deaf women and men.[5]

Such critiques were rooted in a long-standing paternal ethos that underlay the efforts of most hearing adults to assist those who were deaf. In the late nineteenth century, deaf adults were full citizens under the law; few hearing citizens, however, saw them as their peers.[6] Since 1817, hearing professionals—many influenced by their evangelical training—had devoted their lives to the advancement of deaf children and adults. Yet, in speaking out against deaf social organizations, they revealed that they did not see deaf people—even those adults who were educated and self-sufficient—as fully independent and capable of judging their own best interests.[7]

In the 1870s, Edward Gallaudet's counsels against purely deaf associations reverberated throughout the deaf community, where leaders overwhelmingly opposed his position.[8] Henry Winter Syle, a graduate of the American School and of Yale and Trinity Colleges, an Episcopal minister, and a founder of the Pennsylvania Society for the Advancement of the Deaf (PSAD), flatly dismissed Gallaudet's criticisms. "A society of deaf-mutes for mutual enjoyment, improvement, and pecuniary aid," he concluded, "has at least as much *raison d'être* as any of the innumerable similar societies of hearing people."[9] In any case, deaf citizens themselves paid little heed to critiques like Gallaudet's. Between the 1870s and 1890s, the number and size of local, state, and national organizations swelled as deaf adults continued to build community associations.[10]

Deaf people effectively protected their beloved organizations, but they did not have the power to successfully defend the schools and sign language that had first brought them together as a community. During the first half of the nineteenth century, a few oral-based schools had come and gone, but they were not part of an effective national movement to establish an oral system.[11] Debate over the value of oral instruction erupted in the 1840s, especially after officials and educators traveled to Europe to appraise oral instruction and returned with sharply conflicting conclusions regarding the quality of oral instruction.[12]

Through the 1850s, however, sign language enjoyed steady support among most educators. At the national Convention of American Instructors of the Deaf (CAID) meetings, participants debated the preferred mix among sign language, fingerspelling, writing, and oral instruction, and whether to use "natural" sign language or a system of signs that represented English, but they did not challenge the central role of sign language in deaf education.[13]

Following the Civil War, however, determined oralists (as oral advocates were called) invigorated their efforts to establish an oral-based system in the United States. They established independent schools so that the schools could not be influenced by sign advocates, whose strength was in the state-supported residential institutions. By 1870,

The 12th Convention of American Instructors of the Deaf (CAID) was held in New York on August 23–27, 1890, and was also the first international CAID convention held in the United States.

oralists controlled three schools in New York and Massachusetts.[14] In a comment that reflected the motivation of many oralists, Caroline Yale, principal at the Clarke Institution for Deaf Mutes in Northampton, Massachusetts, explained that oral methods had "saved" her students from the "deaf-mute world." With a moral fervor that paralleled the drive of Thomas Hopkins Gallaudet to rescue the lost souls of uneducated deaf children, oralists sought to lead deaf children into the full grace of hearing and speaking society.[15] Between 1860 and 1930, oral advocates across the nation sought nothing less than to transform schooling from sign-based to oral-centered instruction.[16]

Oral proponents quickly gained decisive victories in their efforts to champion oral instruction and challenge manual methods. In 1868, in an attempt to resolve the growing methodological controversy, Edward Gallaudet invited administrators from twelve schools to Gallaudet College. He successfully pushed through an unwieldy compromise. Although critical of exclusively oral methods, he offered his support for instruction in lipreading and speech for students who could profit by these efforts.

This attempt to establish a balanced *combined* system of instruction changed little.[17] On the one hand, as an astute participant at the conference noted, the efforts of the Clarke Institution's staff to teach children to talk would not stop "for all the resolutions that the Conference passes." On the other side, Job Turner, a deaf teacher trained at the American School, argued that deaf adults had as much right to ask that hearing people learn fingerspelling as hearing people had to require that deaf individuals receive speech instruction. The conference failed to alter these differences or reach any compromise.[18] In fact, oralists had only begun to advance their methods and were not about to agree to a self-imposed limit on their instruction.

Some sign language advocates wavered under the pressure as oralists increased their national presence and stature. In 1870, a conflicted Edward Gallaudet effectively denigrated sign language, claiming that it was incapable of conveying the range of thought expressed in written language. Although he believed any effort to prohibit signing would be foolhardy and destructive, he advised hearing teachers against unduly defending an inadequate language system in order to support deaf students.[19]

A few deaf leaders also faltered in their absolute defense of sign-based instruction. Henry Syle, a staunch defender of deaf associations, backed away from sign language at CAID's 1876 national convention, arguing that it did not properly prepare students for communication with the hearing world. "[O]ur object," he explained, "is to fit our pupils to go out into the world among men who know English, but know no signs."[20]

Aided by scientist, teacher, and émigré Bell, oralists solidified their influence among education specialists and the U.S. population at large.[21] They advanced their arguments directly within the institutions of hearing society, rather than at residential schools or the associations of deaf adults. Deaf advocates and their allies were a tiny minority, scarcely known and generally misunderstood by the public, who typically viewed deaf adults through negative stereotypes. The public's general ignorance of deaf people greatly hastened their acceptance of

In 1870, Edward Gallaudet faltered in his support of sign language and claimed it fell short
of written communication.

claims by oralists—many of whom, like Bell, were the educational,
medical, and scientific elite of the United States.

Oralists in the United States enjoyed the benefits of a victory engineered by European oralists in 1880. At an international convention
of educators of deaf students in Milan, Italy, participants agreed to a
resolution that declared that speech instruction promised the greatest
advances to deaf students. Oral advocates, who had organized the
meetings, maintained that the resolution represented an international
agreement to promote speech methods and prohibit sign language.[22]
Out of more than 150 participants, however, only one was deaf, and
only five, including Thomas and Edward Gallaudet, were from the
United States. As one oralist later asserted, after Milan the word went
out across the world: "You shall speak."[23]

Still, even in the face of these developments, deaf adults and sym-
pathetic hearing people worked to challenge oralists' arguments and
practices and to defend sign language. In 1872, Benjamin Pettingill, a
hearing teacher at the Pennsylvania Institution for the Deaf, published
a simple but powerful critique that punctured the basic rationale of
oralists. The inability to speak or follow spoken communication, Pettingill explained, was an inconvenience that could be redressed by

writing and was therefore not the grave malady claimed by oralists. The difficulties deaf people confronted in learning English were not due to their use of signing—a natural language and medium for communication—but to the fact that spoken English was an artificial language for visually-oriented deaf children. In order to build English vocabulary, he called for teachers to strengthen instruction in writing, reading, and fingerspelling. In fact, Pettingill unknowingly anticipated late twentieth-century sociolinguistic studies by arguing that immersion in a signing environment stimulated the intellectual growth and linguistic aptitude of children. From the perspective of activists like Pettingill, oralists had it backwards: uninhibited use of sign language, not its banishment, would best promote the intellectual development and expressive abilities of deaf children.[24]

Deaf activists also sought to deflate oralists' alluring claims about the ease with which deaf children could develop readily usable speaking skills. In 1879, Alphonso Johnson appeared before New York's Empire State Association (ESA) to predict that hearing parents would be singularly attracted to oralists' promises that they could restore speech to their deaf children. As a teacher, Johnson understood that oralists' could fulfill their pledges only at great cost. In devoting enormous time and energy to learning how to articulate such common phrases in the oralist lexicon as "Pa and Ma," or "I love you," most children were forced to limit, if not forfeit, their general education. This exchange, Johnson claimed, was unacceptable.[25]

While teachers advanced an experience-based critique of oral methods, deaf activists published and circulated their opinions, convened meetings, and passed resolutions of censure in an effort to halt or slow the practices advocated by oralists.[26] If this debate had been dispassionate and pedagogical, advocates of a flexible combined system of instruction might have prevailed. Proponents of a pure oral system recast the issue, however, successfully turning it into a broader referendum over the very identity of deaf children.

By the 1870s, oralists had increasingly come to rely on the nascent field of evolutionary theory to advance their arguments. With the 1859 publication of Charles Darwin's *The Origin of Species,* they found new arguments to critique sign language, advance spoken English, and question the very standing of deaf individuals.[27] Oralists argued that over the course of human history superior languages had replaced inferior languages. In this process—described by one historian as "linguistic Darwinism"—spoken language had properly supplanted sign language.[28]

Oralists claimed that spoken language was the truest measure of human advance, distinguishing humans from their primitive predecessors.[29] Just as manualists had employed sign language to save the souls of uneducated children, oralists argued that spoken English was the key to earthly progress and necessary to full citizenship.[30] Having defined themselves as the progressive champions of deaf children, oralists rapidly strengthened their position among educational administrators, placing both manualists and proponents of a combined-system on the defensive. Through the last decade of the century, oralists established their own professional organizations, surpassed the number of manualists and advocates of a combined system, and prepared to increase the use of oral methods in the nation's classrooms.[31]

In addition to battling for ideological dominance, oralists in the late nineteenth century worked to wrest control of education from advocates of sign language or a combined system by implementing the measures proposed by Bell at the National Academy of Sciences in 1883: the establishment of local day schools, elimination of sign instruction from residential schools, and replacement of deaf teachers with hearing instructors. Oral day schools were most often self-contained elementary classes for deaf children within a public school. Deaf students were supposed to attend academic and speech classes together, in either a distinct class or building, but were to join in common social activities with hearing children. After completing elementary studies, deaf students were expected to attend hearing high schools. This process, oralists argued, best prepared students for integration into mainstream society and at a lower cost than residential schools.[32]

Most deaf leaders and teachers opposed *oral* day schools, not day schools per se.[33] Edward Hodgson pointed out that pure oralists sacrificed vocational instruction for promises they could not guarantee: "What matters it if the [deaf student's] general education suffer and industrial education be neglected, as long as the gaping public is mystified by 'speech given to the dumb.'"[34] He urged readers to judge day schools by their usefulness in preparing students for independent lives. "The place to look for genuine 'results' is not at schools," he explained, "but in the great big busy world which men and women live in."[35]

Deaf leaders joined with like-minded administrators of combined systems in various efforts to block the expansion of oral day schools across the United States. In Portland, Maine, national leaders from the oral and manual blocs clashed from afar, as each sought to influence local officials who were considering whether to renew a local school. In 1894, Portland's newspapers carried a series of exchanges that pitted American School officials and deaf activists against Bell and Yale.[36] After city officials decided to continue the day school under the combined method, one deaf activist celebrated the decision but argued that the determination should not have been made without the direct participation of Maine's deaf residents. Henry White, a gifted rhetorician, graduate of the American School and Gallaudet College, and founder of the Utah School for the Deaf, faulted school administrators for their failure to consult directly with deaf adults. "What of the deaf themselves?" he asked. "Have they no say in a matter which means intellectual life and death to them?"[37]

At a national level, oral day schools never became the influential laboratories envisioned by their architects. Teachers were unable to provide the range of classes and services foreseen by their original sponsors. With limited funding and few or no vocational services, these schools were no match for the diversified, although poorly funded, programs available at most residential schools. By 1901, sixty-five day schools, scattered in fourteen states, educated less than 1 percent of the national pool of deaf students; by 1913, the percentage had increased, but only to less than 15 percent; and as late as 1930, fewer than 20 percent of the nation's deaf students attended day schools.[38] If oral activists were truly to transform instruction in the country, they would have to try some other way of achieving their goals.

Beginning in the 1880s, oralists set out to eliminate or reduce sign language in the nation's residential schools.[39] The Pennsylvania School for the Deaf provides a case study of this trend. Established in 1820 and briefly led by Laurent Clerc, who established a signing tradition, the Pennsylvania School began to provide speech instruction in 1870,

mirroring national patterns. In 1884, Albert Crouter assumed responsibilities for the school and, despite his own proficiency in sign, began
to reduce and then to restrict sign language usage in the school.[40]

Crouter initially stated that the conversion to oralism was an experiment. As the first step, he directed that all students be initially
instructed in an exclusively oral environment. Those who showed
minimal progress there would be transferred to manual classes and
their academic progress assessed again. By 1889 Pennsylvania administrators declared the oral program a resounding success, with 90 percent of all students studying under oral instruction. Nearly all of the
10 percent deemed "oral failures" also failed in the school's remedial
manual program as well, according to this assessment. A historic turning point in education had arrived: apparently, oral-centered education had proven successful at the nation's largest and, by the late nineteenth century, most influential residential school.[41]

Attempting to foster an environment that would support oral instruction, Crouter presided over a new campus established in 1892
outside Philadelphia, in suburban Mt. Airy. The school was physically
divided into two distinct departments: the first for the majority of
students to be taught in a pure oral environment; the second for "oral
failures" to be instructed in sign language. If signs could not be eliminated from the campus, at least they could be remanded to a confined
section, away from the sight of the promising students. Sign language,
Crouter declared, was an unwanted reminder of a decadent past.[42]

Incredulous deaf leaders doubted Crouter's successes. Oral instruction had been tried intermittently at residential schools since
1840 and used exclusively at the Clarke Institution since 1867, but
deaf leaders had never budged from their argument that these methods could not work for most students. Articulation was extraordi-
narily time consuming, and lipreading, they argued, was more an art
than a science that could be readily taught to everyone. Some students
acquired a modicum of proficiency; most struggled; all but a few students found their skills unequal to the rapid spoken communication
outside the classroom or in the workplace.

Without the power to investigate Pennsylvania's experiment directly, skeptical deaf leaders studied reports and anecdotal accounts
from students and teachers. They eventually wove together discrete

pieces of information, statistics, and observations into a provisional critique of the school. Hodgson claimed that the failure rate for manual students was likely due to overcrowding. In the oral program, each teacher had ten students, including those who had become deaf after learning to speak or who were hard of hearing. In the manual department, teachers had nearly seventeen students per class.[43] Minnesota's James L. Smith later pointed out that sign language was actually prohibited in the manual department. All students were forced to communicate by fingerspelling, a rapid but impractical and tiring approach mainly used by deaf adults as an adjunct to signed communication but never as the exclusive means of expression. Critics concluded that Crouter had created an untenable environment for the school's manual students. Adding insult to injury, he had then blamed students for their inability to prosper in this contrived situation.[44]

Despite criticism, by 1905 the majority of the nation's deaf students were instructed by writing and oral methods rather than by sign language.[45] Unlike the experience with the day schools, where oralist aspirations never found steady footing, the transformation of the Pennsylvania School was but the first of a slow and uneven pattern, as residential school administrators increased oral instruction and restricted sign language.

These administrators also sought to reduce the number and influence of deaf teachers. Before the 1870s, most debates over deaf instructors centered on pay issues rather than the suitability of deaf people as teachers.[46] By the 1880s, however, deaf teachers—especially those who used sign language in academic rather than vocational areas—feared for their future.[47] Their apprehensions were well founded, as superintendents across the country promoted oral instruction, often by hiring hearing instructors with training in articulation and lipreading.[48]

Deaf teachers had little individual or collective power to reverse this broad trend, but deaf leaders, students, and hearing supporters joined them to resist oral-centered instruction and to contest the removal of deaf teachers from the academic classroom. Many turned to their newspapers and conventions to voice their opposition to these changes, to ask for help, and even to envision an end to oralist advances.

Students were often the most steadfast supporters of deaf teachers and incisive critics of hearing teachers, especially those unfamiliar with sign language or inexperienced with deaf pupils. Deaf teachers served as informal but influential role models for deaf children, typically raised in families without deaf adults present and in towns where other deaf people were not to be found. By contrast, new hearing teachers were often poorly prepared to become instructors, much less role models for their students. Writing to Hodgson's *Deaf Mute's Journal (DMJ)* in 1881, "Michigan Girl" lamented that some of her teachers had no experience with deaf students. She explained that she and her fellow students had taught their instructor sign language. She asked of these poorly trained instructors: "Should they not be called new pupils instead of teachers?"[49]

Some deaf critics viewed oralist school administrators as dangerous intruders. "Enos," a regular contributor to the *DMJ,* claimed that deaf workers faced fewer obstacles than were imposed upon deaf teachers by hearing school bureaucrats. He wrote that oralist administrators were parasites feeding on their students. "These aristocrats, after being warmed, fed, and grown sleek at our institutions, turn upon us and sting us all they can."[50]

Many deaf leaders worried that the removal of deaf teachers would ultimately prove disastrous to the education and development of deaf students. Robert McGregor, an instructor at Ohio's residential school, expressed his fears at the 1893 NAD national convention: "It will be a sad day for the deaf of America and the world at large when the deaf teacher is entirely eliminated. . . . Let us most earnestly pray God that this consummation may be forever deferred."[51]

Foreshadowing arguments advanced by student protesters at Gallaudet University nearly one hundred years later, several correspondents even argued that deaf teachers had a moral claim to positions at schools for deaf students. From New York, *DMJ* columnist "Infante" lashed out at Gallaudet College administrators, who had established a teaching program open exclusively to hearing instructors. Teaching jobs, "Infante" claimed, rightfully belonged to deaf graduates of Gallaudet College and this new program was an affront to deaf citizens.[52]

Henry White was one of the most far-sighted deaf activists of this period. He believed that deaf instructors had a moral claim to teaching positions, but he understood that such assertions were nothing if they were not based in law and protected by vigilant deaf adults. In 1885, he urged his peers to define, organize, and defend a new set of rights. "One thing must be made plain," White maintained, "if we wish to combat this lingering prejudice and secure justice . . . we must assert our claims to justice or we will never receive it."[53]

Deaf activists were unable to mount the type of national campaign White envisioned. Dispersed across the nation, lacking formal rights or protections, many deaf teachers were removed from the profession over a span of thirty years. Scattered protests occurred in deaf publications, as in Ohio in the late 1880s when nine deaf teachers were replaced by nine hearing teachers.[54] Such protests were insufficient to reverse or even slow this forced exodus, however. The number of deaf instructors peaked in the early 1870s: approximately 250 of 550 teachers and administrators, roughly 40 percent of the instructional force. By 1895, however, they represented little more than 20 percent of the instructional staff, and by 1917 hearing administrators reduced this figure to less than 15 percent.[55]

Oralists claimed that oral skills strengthened the employability of deaf adults. They reasoned that few employers would take the time to communicate with deaf employees via writing and even fewer would learn sign language. Speech and lipreading skills would place deaf employees on an equal footing with their hearing counterparts.[56]

Anecdotal evidence from school officials, however, undermined the claim that orally trained students used speech communication in the workplace. In an appearance before his fellow school administrators at their 1884 convention, Pennsylvania's Crouter conceded that oral methods were often too uncertain for vital communication, and writing alone could suffice.[57] Similarly, Yale of the Clarke Institution admitted that some students were simply unable to learn speaking skills in a reasonable period of time.[58] Infrequently, Crouter's and Yale's peers affirmed these positions. At the 1911 CAID convention, several superintendents expressed their support for oral skills, but at the same time acknowledged that they had little practical value outside the classroom, except when used among friends or family.[59]

Skeptics of the oral method also argued that deaf workers relied upon writing skills rather than oral communication in the workplace. Thomas Gallaudet, pastor of St. Ann's Church for the Deaf in New York City, claimed that among the hundreds of deaf adults he had known, most relied upon sign language or writing in their business relations.[60] Deaf Chicago publisher James Gallaher argued that the surest way to evaluate the value of oral skills would be to survey deaf adults in the working world. An investigation, he believed, would reveal that adults did not use their oral skills in either their social lives or their business affairs.[61]

Gallaher's contention had merit, and the claims of oral proponents were further weakened by an informal survey of deaf leaders conducted by administrators at the New York School in 1912.[62] E. Henry Currier, principal and former speech teacher at the school, asked more than three dozen prominent deaf men and women their views on sign language, pure oral methods, and the usefulness of both oral skills and sign language in business. All respondents condemned efforts to ban sign language and claimed that oral communication, especially lipreading, was ineffective in the business world. George Quackenbush, a teacher and interpreter, argued that orally trained students had more persistent employment problems, including lower wages, than deaf employees who shunned oral methods.[63] Jay Cooke Howard of Minnesota, a graduate of Gallaudet College and eventual NAD president, explained that in any business dispute, the lipreader would invariably be at risk because writing was the only reliable method of communication.[64]

Broader studies affirmed these contentions. Between 1899 and 1907, NAD leaders surveyed three groups: employers with deaf employees, deaf businessmen employed at roughly one dozen occupations, and deaf workers. The majority of employers preferred a combination of writing, sign language, and fingerspelling for communicating with their deaf workers; only one favored lipreading. Among deaf businessmen, the majority favored writing; lipreading was their least popular method. Finally, the majority of workers were unable to employ lipreading; in fact, they noted that some of their hearing coworkers had learned the manual alphabet.[65] A subsequent national survey reaffirmed the preliminary results of the NAD investigation. A poll of more than two thousand deaf adults, completed in 1913, revealed that *none* were willing to use lipreading and speech in their business affairs.[66]

A final, more in-depth survey, completed by Warren Robinson under the auspices of the CAID in 1914, further underlined the limited utility of oral skills in the workplace. A vocational instructor at the Wisconsin School for the Deaf and the head of the CAID's Industrial Section, Robinson conducted a survey of more than 350 deaf men and women from thirty-six states. Oral skills had some utility, but only to a minority of deaf adults: some 20 percent of the overall group used both writing and oral skills; less than 15 percent communicated orally. The largest number of respondents, more than 150 men and women or almost one-half of the sample, used writing to communicate with their hearing acquaintances.[67]

Respondents who rejected oral methods stated that such skills were impractical for everyday communication. As one New York resident explained, "I would like to see some of the pure oralists employ a deaf man in a position of importance in their own business where his accuracy of lipreading would have a few of their good dollars resting on it."[68]

A final canvass of more than 400 orally trained adults, completed in 1917, further undermined oralists' claims. Tellingly, almost 375 respondents—roughly 80 percent of the adults—did not use oral methods in their business affairs. And of the nearly 100 respondents who did use oral skills, all but a few had lost their hearing *after* they learned how to speak, suggesting that their previous hearing status, not oralist instruction, was the factor that made those skills usable.[69]

Despite such powerful and consistent findings, however, there is no evidence that these surveys diminished the enthusiasm of oral proponents or even influenced the ongoing communications debate. The findings did not circulate widely in either the deaf or hearing press. In fact, Robinson apparently never even compiled the results of his survey. Moreover, had this data been circulated, oralists would likely have contended that the studies simply indicated that the skills of deaf adults were poorly developed. Indeed, in the coming decades, as deaf critics' disapproval of oral programs grew and as mounting evidence pointed to the shortcomings of oral methods, proponents of those methods typically countered by arguing that more, not less, training was necessary before oral techniques would produce satisfactory results. In other words, oralism's failures merely reinforced the claim of its proponents that even greater efforts were necessary to bring about ultimate success.

By the early years of the twentieth century, oralist educators dominated the school culture and education of deaf students. Above all, their ascension derived from their broadly attractive claim that pure oral instruction could nearly eliminate the impact of deafness and enable deaf children to participate fully in hearing society. Pre-existing depictions of deafness as an affliction and the application of evolutionary theory to language itself further undercut the effort of deaf adults to critique these claims and to promote combined instruction.

Oralist practices soon governed the nation's classrooms. By the turn of the century, 40 percent of all students were taught without sign language. By 1920, oral advocates claimed that almost 80 percent of students were so instructed.[70] Advocates of sign language were also put on the defensive by the view that it would somehow impair the development of those who used it.[71] Oralist domination of school curriculum and administration heightened tensions between deaf administrators, students, and adults. As deaf opponents of oralism had predicted, oralists gained the reins of power only to preside over a system of instruction whose failings produced critics of the system rather than grateful beneficiaries.

The seeming victory of oralists was, in fact, fraught with contradictions. Outside the classroom, the life experiences of most students demonstrated daily the frailties of oralist claims. A small number of students were able to use their hard-earned skills to advantage. The majority of students and adults, however, relied on writing in the working world and on sign language within the deaf community.

Deaf adults uniformly resisted oralists' entreaties to abandon the community they had lovingly crafted. Students and adults continued to sign, socialize, and intermarry throughout the nineteenth century and into the twentieth. A small but influential contingent of students trained at Gallaudet College went on to lead state and national organizations.

Above all, deaf adults continued to defend their beloved language—the symbolic core of their community. In a speech before the NAD in 1896, Robert McGregor explained that deaf people "have a deep-rooted conviction that their happiness is bound up in signs, and they grapple them to their hearts with hooks of steel. . . . Like a stone wall they stand united, the whole world round, presenting a solid front to any interference in their use of signs." Oralists could try as they might, he contended, but in the end, sign language would "flourish to the end of time."[72]

In light of their conflicts with oral advocates, few deaf leaders thought it a propitious time to challenge openly any discriminatory or prejudiced employers. Furthermore, most of these leaders favored a code of self-reliance that emphasized individual initiative rather than collective action. Thus, they were not only deeply troubled but also unprepared to respond when, in 1906, the U.S. Civil Service Commission announced that deaf applicants would no longer be admitted into government service. Some feared that private employers would follow suit and close off their businesses to deaf employees, others worried this exclusion would encourage broader efforts to constrict their freedoms. Reluctantly, they undertook the first collective labor action in their history.

3

"Shoulder to Shoulder"

Protesting Civil Service Discrimination

In late October 1906, U.S. Civil Service commissioners General John Black of Illinois, Henry F. Greene of Minnesota, and James McIlhenney of Louisiana revised the guidelines for applicants to the Civil Service. They added *total deafness* and *loss of speech* to a list of more than ten conditions, including insanity and paralysis, that barred candidates from Civil Service examinations. In adding these conditions, commission members reversed the standing policy of some three decades that had granted the right of deaf candidates to apply for work in the government. This new ruling effectively barred deaf candidates from all positions in the Civil Service—including many occupations at which deaf individuals had labored since the late nineteenth century.

Stunned deaf leaders and hearing supporters condemned this ruling as discriminatory and groundless, and organized to overturn it. On December 1, 1908, after two years of open opposition and sustained lobbying by these activists, President Theodore Roosevelt reversed the commission's exclusionary ruling. Deaf applicants would be allowed to apply for all positions whose duties they were capable of performing, as determined by the commission.

This campaign marked a pivotal turning point in organizing ability and consciousness on the part of the developing national community of deaf citizens. First, it brought deaf individuals and their organizations together with hearing supporters from the education profession and from state and federal government, in the process achieving new levels of united activity among local, state, and national organizations of deaf citizens. Second, the campaign ironically aggravated relations and increased the distance between the organized deaf community and other people with physical disabilities. Third, and most important, it was the first national campaign of organized and public opposition against employers. Since the mid-nineteenth century, deaf leaders and workers had claimed the moral "right" to apply for positions for which they were qualified, but they had refrained from openly organizing against employers, generally out of concern that public conflicts might dissuade other employers from hiring deaf candidates. This effort demonstrated that open debate and confrontation could be a powerful tool against discriminatory employers.

The exclusion of deaf applicants from Civil Service positions contrasted with concurrent inclusionary trends that had begun to broaden the Civil Service workforce late in the nineteenth century and in the first decade of the twentieth century. Federal legislation and internal shifts in the Civil Service had provided new opportunities for previously excluded groups. In an attempt to regulate, if not eliminate, political patronage, the federal government had passed legislation to outlaw political and religious discrimination, and previously sealed Civil Service registers that ranked candidates were opened for public review.

Of particular importance for deaf candidates, these changes included standardized means of evaluating and placing workers, with an extensive and flexible system of administering examinations to applicants of varied ethnic and linguistic backgrounds. In 1906, more than 136,000 applicants took nearly 400 different examinations in territories and states across the continent. In Puerto Rico and the Philippine Islands, for example, exams were typically administered in Spanish and English.[1] Letter carriers in New York and Ohio were evaluated on their familiarity and fluency in Italian and Hungarian,[2] and elsewhere aspiring artisans completed examinations that evaluated their skills in their respective crafts but that required neither reading nor writing.[3]

These procedures provided a standard means of precisely identifying required skills for each position and evaluating potential applicants.[4] By the 1890s, they had already helped attract a small but increasing number of African Americans and women into the workforce[5] and seemed to suggest to deaf candidates that even if their verbal communication were limited, they would have ample opportunity to demonstrate their written communication skills and gain entrance into government service.

Yet government officials would not extend these inclusionary efforts to deaf workers. Instead, they moved against deaf applicants by adding the words *total deafness* and *loss of speech* to a preexisting list of "defects" that barred any applicant deemed physically or mentally unfit for examination. Along with insanity, blindness, paralysis, and nearly one dozen other conditions, deafness now disqualified citizens from entering the Civil Service.[6] Ironically, this exclusion came at a time when the Civil Service found it increasingly difficult to attract male candidates to positions that had been favored by deaf applicants, including typists, bookkeepers, and railway mail clerks.[7]

News of the Civil Service Commission's policy spread slowly through the national deaf community during the winter of 1906 and spring of 1907. Following brief notices in several school newspapers, deaf leaders first began to contest the policy in the spring of 1907. Reverend Oliver J. Whildin, a Gallaudet College graduate and an Episcopal missionary active with deaf congregations in the mid-Atlantic region, wrote to the Civil Service Commission on behalf of a deaf applicant blocked from taking an examination for the Government Printing Office (GPO).[8] The situation was ominous because printing, an especially popular trade pursued by the most talented students at many residential schools, had become the preeminent skilled trade open to deaf men and women.[9] The elimination of positions within the GPO would be a sharp blow to this growing corps of artisans.

Whildin received a succinct and disheartening explanation for the government's policies in early June 1907. Henry Greene, the acting president of the Civil Service, explained that the decision to bar deaf candidates resulted from previous difficulties in placing applicants who had passed entrance examinations. Although these aspirants had been certified by virtue of their exams, some appointing officers had refused to place them, arguing that their deafness prevented them from successfully fulfilling various responsibilities at particular positions. In light of this objection, commission members simply decided to exclude all deaf candidates. This prohibition, Greene assured Whildin, was neither intended to disparage the positive work record of current deaf workers, nor would it be used as a rationale to dismiss them.[10] In an open letter to the *Deaf Mute's Journal* (*DMJ*), Whildin challenged Greene's reasoning. Urging deaf people to organize vigorously against the directive, he argued that any annoyance hearing administrators might have at working with deaf workers was no basis for the exclusion of qualified candidates.[11]

Leaders of the deaf community quickly responded to Whildin's call to action and agreed to the outlines of a national drive to combat the ruling. Members of the Gallaudet College Alumni Association (GCAA)—including Whildin, E. Clayton Wyand from Massachusetts, and, most important, George Veditz, the brilliant and fiery NAD president—established a committee to direct efforts against the ruling. Unlike in 1893, when deaf leaders reasoned that the risks of a divisive and potentially unsuccessful public campaign against the Railway Mail Service outweighed the benefits of overturning the exclusionary policy, in 1907 they argued that the risks of inaction greatly outweighed those of a public battle. Deaf leadership in the United States thus joined the first concerted employment-based national protest campaign.[12]

Deaf committee members engineered a plan to reverse the policy. Wyand would direct an initial effort to discredit the rationale of the exclusionary policy. He set out to gather testimonials and endorsements from deaf workers and administrators within the government that would attest to the fitness and effectiveness of deaf workers. The replies he received that fall and winter were overwhelmingly supportive and confirmed the positive work records of deaf employees in various Civil Service offices. Leaders hoped that these testimonials would reveal the exclusionary directive to be capricious and without basis. One deaf writer noted the bitter irony in the government's actions, which supported some deaf workers yet classified others as unfit. It "would be laughable, if it were not so unjust," he reflected.[13]

While Wyand worked to undermine the directive's rationale, Veditz drew upon longstanding tenets within the deaf community to mobilize the nation's deaf adults and hearing supporters. Throughout much of the nineteenth century, deaf leaders had centered their employment strategies on the simple argument that properly educated deaf citizens were suited for a wide range of positions that did not emphasize oral communication. By barring deaf applicants from all

Civil Service examinations, the government's ruling implied that deaf workers were incapable of successfully working at *any* position.

Veditz enlisted the nation's deaf newspapers in his efforts to convince deaf adults that the ruling threatened all deaf workers, not merely aspirants to government employment. In the *Deaf American,* an independent newspaper published in Nebraska, Veditz argued that private managers would follow the lead of the government and close off employment, reasoning "if the deaf-mute is not good enough for Uncle Sam he is not good enough for me." Moreover, Veditz claimed, by associating deafness with conditions including paralysis and insanity, the Civil Service ruling would discourage hearing employers, who were often uninformed anyway, from even considering deaf employees. And with employment already limited, the result would be outright disaster. The nation's schools for deaf citizens, he argued, would have their "usefulness sapped at their very foundation," and unemployment, poverty, and crime would follow. "No action ever taken so far in the history of the American deaf," Veditz warned, "has been as inimical to their material welfare."[14]

Veditz also worked to undermine the legitimacy of the Civil Service ruling. In a series of seemingly simple articles written by an unassuming character, Veditz exposed the paternalism of the Civil Service directive and challenged its rationale. Somebody "who didn't know nothin' about the deaf but thought he knew it all," he surmised, must have "sprung the rule." He explained that deaf workers had already demonstrated their abilities and worth and thus needed no special justification to continue in government employment. In fact, they were less likely to socialize and were often more industrious and efficient than their hearing counterparts. The government's ruling, Veditz concluded, "is certainly a most uncivil service that has been done to the deaf." If such an unassuming person could challenge the government, Veditz reasoned, surely the nation's deaf citizens could contest these actions.[15]

The support and active participation of the deaf community's numerous local clubs and state associations would be crucial to a broad national campaign. In the summer of 1907, state conventions across the country denounced the ruling. From Seattle, Gallaudet College graduate Olof Hanson brought the resources of the recently established Puget Sound Association of the Deaf to the campaign; on the West Coast, businessman and activist Oscar Regensburg rallied forces in Los Angeles; and in Chicago, George T. Dougherty helped secure the support of the Pas-a-Pas Club, one of the nation's largest, oldest, and most respected clubs. As Veditz would later note, "Every deaf mute of any consequence or public spirit in the country was actively enlisted in the cause."[16]

As the national campaign developed during the winter of 1907 and spring of 1908, deaf activists reiterated their belief that classifying deafness as a "defect" undermined the status of all deaf people. In correspondence with congressional representatives, Dougherty described deaf individuals as independent citizens interested in public affairs. Being associated with "the insane, the crippled, and criminals" in Civil Service regulations was bound to negatively influence potential employers. In his presidential address at the NAD convention in Norfolk, Virginia, the following summer, the impassioned Veditz called upon the assembled members and supporters to challenge the ruling. "Once let the government brand deafness as a disability that renders us ineligible for its service," he warned, "and it will not be long before the prejudice will spread among the employers at large."[17]

Opposition to the Civil Service directive extended outside the immediate, culturally deaf community. Although torn by debates over sign language and oral communication, professional educational organizations also opposed it. J. Schuyler Long, a deaf teacher at the Iowa School for the Deaf, led the effort to secure the opposition of CAID to the exclusionary ruling. Arguing that the directive unjustly placed deaf citizens in the same class with others deemed physically and mentally incapable, the CAID resolution called for the restoration of the "rights of the deaf as educated and competent citizens of the United States."[18]

A small number of superintendents and administrators from schools for deaf students also joined the efforts to overturn the Civil Service restriction; indeed, several fulfilled indispensable roles in the campaign. Gallaudet College president Edward M. Gallaudet worked to persuade federal administrators of the errors of the directive.[19] From the Midwest, Richard O. Johnson and Philip Gillett, superintendents of the Indiana and Illinois schools, lobbied with congressional

J. Schuyler Long advocated for deaf workers' right to be employed by the federal government. Several years later he published one of the first printed manuals to record, preserve, and promote sign language.

J. SCHUYLER LONG, '89
President 1906—1908

officials. From Maryland, Charles Ely, superintendent of the state school at Frederick, joined in the effort.

Johnson's correspondence with Senator Albert Beveridge in February 1908 was representative of exchanges that took place during the campaign. The unjust and "reactionary" ruling, Johnson charged, was a "grievous reflection" upon all deaf adults that was rooted in a "discriminatory past" from which deaf citizens had labored to free themselves. Discounting any basis for the order, he claimed that there were hundreds of positions in the Civil Service at which deaf adults could be successful. Any problems with deaf employees, Johnson reasoned, could be resolved through consultation and proper placement of future candidates.[20]

In April 1908, with deaf leaders and hearing supporters continuing their campaign, the *Silent Worker* newspaper published selected correspondence between the Civil Service Commission and President Roosevelt that outlined the commission's rationale for barring deaf applicants. Commission members noted that "very few of these defective persons" applied and only a small number had passed their exams and gone on to be considered for employment even though they had been permitted to apply for Civil Service positions since 1883. Some of these few applicants were later rejected by appointing officers who determined that the applicants' hearing differences or loss of speech prevented them from fulfilling particular positions. Several candidates, Civil Service officials explained, had charged that they were unfairly disqualified and brought "constant complaint" against the agency. As a result of these conflicts, the commissioners concluded that open exams had improperly encouraged deaf candidates.[21]

After deciding that examinations were an inadequate means of matching deaf applicants with specific positions, the commissioners decided that the interest of all deaf petitioners was best served by barring their applications. This exclusion, however difficult, would relieve the Civil Service of any further "embarrassment" and the applicants of any additional disappointment. In fact, commissioners saw their ruling as an act of "kindness" that would spare applicants from "ultimate relentless rejection." Any other response, they assured the president, was a "fraud."[22]

Deaf leaders and supporters quickly condemned the commission's paternalism as well as its unwillingness to contemplate additional procedures to match workers with the varied positions within the Civil Service. In an accompanying article in the April *Silent Worker*, Johnson denounced the commission's rationale and repeated the demands being made by the deaf community. Johnson's correspondence is especially noteworthy for its espousal of long-standing core beliefs advanced by hearing educators and deaf leaders regarding job placement strategies for deaf workers. He dismissed as insupportable the rationale that only a small number of applicants were affected. Equity, not the number of candidates, was at issue: "the one deserves fair play and justice as well as the thousand," he countered. Deaf individuals had never requested "to be relieved by self-constituted official guardians" of their right to take examinations.[23]

In addition to dismissing the commissioners' actions, Johnson reviewed the demands of deaf activists and hearing supporters. Johnson called for the establishment of a comprehensive system of evaluation within the Civil Service that would examine the readiness of all candidates without "partiality or prejudice." Deaf workers, he pointed out, asked neither for assistance on account of their deafness nor for placement in positions where they could not fulfill all job requirements. Finally, he concurred that appointing officers retained the right to determine which positions were suitable for deaf candidates, but applicants held the privilege of requesting that any dismissals be reviewed. Deaf workers expected only that which was theirs as a "birth right": "the opportunity to aspire to public position through competitive examination."[24]

After eighteen months of lobbying by activists, however, the issue remained at a standstill, evident even in an assessment made by Edward Allen Fay, editor of the *American Annals of the Deaf.* Confident of ultimate success—the just demands of the deaf community would not be "forever disregarded"—Fay was less sure that victory would come in the foreseeable future. His reserve was appropriate: deaf Americans did not have the political clout to reach inside the Civil Service and force the commissioners to abandon their position.[25] Overall, activists could offer little evidence of progress.

Their direct exertions thus blunted, deaf leaders reinvigorated previous efforts to develop a broader network of public and private officials who would apply pressure to the recalcitrant commissioners. Edward Gallaudet asked past and present representatives involved in the oversight of Gallaudet University, as well as the school's board of directors, to petition Civil Service administrators. Gallaudet officials from Colorado, Kansas, New York, and South Dakota now joined superintendents Johnson, Ely, and Gillett. In turn, this broadened coalition of educators implored their congressional representatives to challenge the commissioners.[26]

As months passed, however, even this greater lobbying effort was unsuccessful. Veditz would later note that "[t]here seemed nothing left us but to furl our banners, reverse our arms and leave the field in dishonorable retreat." As a final effort, the disappointed leader wrote to President Roosevelt and requested a personal interview. He assured the president that if he would personally investigate the matter, he would find that unfounded prejudice against deaf workers, rather than problems of inefficiency or incompetence, underlay the commissioners' directive. In a final attempt to convince Roosevelt, Veditz argued that deaf workers, like the president, cherished traditional values of independence and self-reliance. They "revere you," he assured the president, "you represent the ideal living American."[27] In closing, he asked the president to consider a Biblical verse from Leviticus, which, he explained, laid claim for the rights of deaf individuals: "Thou shalt not curse the deaf, nor put a stumbling block before the blind, but shalt fear thy God: I *am* Lord."[28]

A week later Veditz received his reply. Civil Service Commissioner Black, rather than Theodore Roosevelt, responded to Veditz's correspondence with a candor that revealed the formidable obstacles facing deaf workers. The prohibition of deaf candidates, Black noted, was not a matter of prejudice but of basic policy. He opposed deaf candidates not because they were unreliable or inefficient but because they were deaf! There was simply no reason, he explained, for any department chief to favor the certification of a deaf candidate "to do work in any department or in any place, for which a man in possession of all his faculties might be certified." In addition, he dismissed Veditz's reference to Leviticus, which had warned against unfairly limiting deaf individuals. "The curse of which you speak," Black countered, "is not laid at the door of the men who are charged with the administration of the affairs of this government."

Despite his opposition to deaf workers in the civil service, Black also revealed that he would consider the request of any departmental directors predisposed to certify deaf applicants. Beyond this narrow and unexpected accommodation however, the campaign had apparently secured few, if any, advances.[29]

Disappointed but not deterred by Black's rebuff, Veditz and other leaders redoubled their efforts within and outside the deaf community through the summer of 1908 to enlarge the coalition of influential opponents. Within the deaf community, leaders sought anew to enlist the support of all deaf citizens, especially the membership of the varied state and professional associations. *DMJ*'s editor Hodgson drew upon the example of political activity among African American adults to urge deaf citizens to join and work within their state and national organizations. And ESA president Theodore Lounsbury even called upon the association's members to contemplate civil disobedience as a possible strategy to overturn the exclusionary policy. Excluded from government positions, deaf citizens were released from their obligation to pay taxes or otherwise assist the government, he wrote. "What is it to be deaf?" demanded the outraged leader. "Surely it is no crime."[30]

Leaders again reached outside the deaf community in their opposition to the Civil Service directive. Veditz asked Edward Gallaudet to contact James Rudolph Garfield Jr., secretary of the interior and former Civil Service Commissioner. His father, Garfield Sr., had been instrumental in supporting the development of Gallaudet College and Garfield Jr. had continued this tradition of involvement in the affairs of deaf people and the college. Perhaps President Gallaudet could persuade Garfield to request the Civil Service Commission to provide examinations for deaf candidates desirous of working in the Department of the Interior.[31]

As deaf people awaited the outcome of Gallaudet's efforts, they also looked to the upcoming presidential elections as a way to overturn the exclusionary ruling. Veditz contacted the presidential candidates asking each for his support. Democratic Party nominee William Jennings Bryan's response was ambivalent. Professing an inability to offer a definitive position on an issue not already included in his platform, he expressed his surprise that the ruling excluded deaf citizens from all positions.[32] Republican nominee William H. Taft, on the other hand, was direct: although he confessed his ignorance of the ruling, he agreed that deaf candidates should be allowed to compete for positions for which they were qualified.[33] Socialist Party candidate Eugene V. Debs offered the strongest endorsement. Opposed to any exclusion of deaf workers, he pledged to end all discrimination against deaf candidates and to consider the establishment of an evaluation system that would take into account the "disability" of "our deaf-mute brothers."[34] As the election approached, Veditz praised Debs's position but urged deaf citizens to vote for Taft as the most likely candidate to replace Roosevelt.[35]

After Taft's election, deaf leaders nonetheless persisted in their efforts to have President Roosevelt overturn the policy before Taft's inauguration. In late November, Olof Hanson of the Puget Sound Association of the Deaf forwarded a fervent letter to the president, asking him to imagine his feelings if his son were to become deaf and there-fore excluded from applying for positions for which he was capable. He urged Roosevelt against leaving office without first providing deaf citizens the "square deal" they expected from a leader with such a "high sense of justice."[36] In addition, Fay, Gallaudet, and Olof Han-son, among others, met with Secretary of the Interior Garfield in mid-November to enlist his support. Garfield subsequently met with the president and apparently again placed the demands of the deaf com-munity before him.[37]

In late November 1908, President Roosevelt repealed the exclu-sionary ruling. Twenty-five months after deaf people had been ex-cluded from government examinations, he reinstated their right to apply for selected Civil Service positions.[38] The two-year-old campaign had triumphed. One activist later exulted, "The mighty Civil Service fell, and great was its fall. As a result, the deaf will henceforth be regarded as a positive quantity of the first rank."[39]

Repeal of the exclusionary ruling brought tangible short-term ad-vances to deaf Americans. First, it lowered discriminatory barriers within the Civil Service and perhaps within the government. Further-more, leaders hoped that it would send an unequivocal message to any private employers who might have considered restrictive policies. Most importantly, it was a ringing moral victory for deaf leaders that strengthened the standing of deaf and hearing activists alike. The two-year campaign to achieve the repeal had brought them together in a common cause. With characteristic bombast, Veditz later explained that the effort had a powerful unifying impact: "The deaf themselves were a unit and fought shoulder to shoulder. The zeal was such that it accomplished the seemingly impossible feat of uniting them politi-cally."[40]

The campaign also signaled an intellectual and tactical break from the self-limiting and conservative approaches typically used against recalcitrant employers in the nineteenth century. In the past, deaf leaders, at least in public pronouncements, had argued that demon-strations of individual excellence rather than organized confrontation were the most appropriate responses against discriminatory bosses.

Given the predominance of deaf workers in small-scale agricultural and artisan-based fields, individual laborers could simply bypass discriminatory employers in favor of more amenable ones should efforts at persuasion fail. However, the increasing concentration of deaf workers in towns and cities and the rising power of industrial owners —whose hiring decisions could decide the status of vast numbers of workers—compelled laborers and leaders to consider more vigorous measures to secure and retain employment. The unwavering opposition of the Civil Service Commission to deaf workers demonstrated that some employers were not open to persuasion and that activists must use confrontation in addition to accommodation.

Although deaf and hearing activists broadened their tactical approaches, their ideological core ironically remained fixed in conservative exclusionary tenets largely unchanged since the preceding century. Throughout the Civil Service campaign, these activists never challenged the theoretical validity of the exclusionary classification system upon which the divisive directive rested, but instead argued that this association with "undesirable" groups unfairly denigrated capable deaf candidates. Citizens with physical differences, deaf or otherwise, thus remained divided—almost at odds with each other— while the sweeping power of employers, educators, and other professionals to define and thereby control these varied groups of citizens remained largely unchallenged. Although successful in mobilizing support against the Civil Service ruling, the activists' strategy distanced deaf workers from other disabled people and undermined any possibility that these groups might later join in shared effort to oppose common restrictions.[41]

This campaign also reemphasized the vast differences in power and position that separated deaf workers from their employers. Activists clearly understood that President Roosevelt's executive order had curtailed, but not eliminated, the discretionary power Civil Service personnel held over deaf candidates. Civil Service administrators never conceded that their policy was incorrect or excessive, and many deaf leaders expected that continuing obstacles would be placed in the way of deaf applicants. Veditz, for example, cautioned it would be "absurd" to believe that Roosevelt's action would end discrimination in government employment.[42]

There is no evidence that deaf leaders envisioned a broader set of rights regarding access to or mobility within government positions. Deaf and hearing activists neither challenged the right of Civil Service authorities to decide which positions would be open to deaf candidates nor asked for special consideration in the application process. Indeed, even the most strident leaders, such as Veditz, believed firmly that employers retained the power to determine qualifications for their respective workforces.

A more comprehensive strategy might have established a broader foundation for the employment of deaf workers, but at the cost of estranging government officials and private employers who sought exclusive authority regarding employment, dismissal, firing, and job classification. Instead, activists simply insisted that authorities had incorrectly barred deaf candidates from all positions. They struggled less to enlarge their rights than to recapture traditional claims usurped by the exclusionary ruling.

In the short term, however, these underlying concerns were eased by the actions of the incoming Taft administration. Through the winter and spring of 1909, deaf leaders consulted President Taft, members of his cabinet, and directors of various government agencies.[43] In fact, Taft issued an Executive Order that lessened the power of Civil Service managers to restrict deaf workers to certain jobs by mandating that all departments in the government furnish a list of positions open to deaf candidates. The administration later released a list of eighty-four positions open to deaf candidates.[44] In the following months, the secretaries of the Interior and Labor Departments declared they would favor deaf candidates.[45]

By the summer of 1910, deaf citizens had begun to benefit by the reversal of the exclusionary ruling and the progressive actions of the Taft administration. In June, Veditz thanked President Taft on behalf of the people who had been freed from "cruel injustice." In his presidential address at the August 1910 NAD convention, Veditz declared that the time had finally come for deaf citizens to savor their victories.[46]

Deaf leaders understood that celebration at this point did not lessen the long-term imperative to educate employers or to monitor their actions closely. Therefore, that year's NAD convention participants established a permanent committee to oversee the Civil Service Commission. Three years later, at the 1913 convention, committee members reported several cases of alleged discrimination against deaf candidates. "In every case," reported the NAD member investigating the cases, "the official hides behind the letter of the law, shrugs his shoulders, and asks why we find fault with him."[47] As they look ahead to the early decades of the twentieth century, deaf workers and leaders, though heartened by the repeal of the exclusionary directive, organized anew to defend their standing and rights.

While deaf leaders in the Civil Service campaign sought, in 1913, to protect the rights of government employees, others in Minnesota celebrated the establishment of the Division for the Deaf in the Department of Labor. Many believed the division would define new rights for the state's students and workers and strengthen the standing of sign language proponents at large. As word of the bureau spread across the nation, deaf leaders wondered if these progressive advances in Minnesota would become a model for the nation.

4

"For the Deaf by the Deaf"

Advocating Labor Bureaus

The pivotal conflicts in education and the workplace of the late nine-teenth and early twentieth centuries were not merely contests of ideas but clashes over power and influence. In the varied struggles chroni-cled in chapters 1 through 3—struggles over vocational instruction, sign language, oralism, and workplace discrimination—deaf activists advanced substantive, even persuasive arguments. Few in number and dispersed across the country, they typically lacked the power to imple-ment their ideas. No one understood this systemic shortcoming better than Minnesota's Anson Rudolph Spear, a visionary and versatile lob-byist, school superintendent, and former civil servant.

These ongoing conflicts erupted in Minnesota shortly after the turn of the century, as Spear and other deaf leaders charged that the apparent abandonment of sign language for speech and lipreading at the state residential school threatened deaf students and workers alike. Spear sought to establish an independent source of power to resist these changes, to provide students and workers greater control over their education and employment, and to elevate the standing of deaf adults in Minnesota. Spurred by him and national deaf leaders, the legislature established a labor bureau in 1913 that Spear hoped would establish vigorous new rights and powers for deaf people.[1] Although the bureau fell short of Spear's ambitious vision, it aided deaf workers in the state and also served as a model for activists across the nation, who worked to establish comparable bureaus designed to provide deaf adults greater power over their education and their working lives.

Anson Spear's efforts grew out of a long-standing consensus among deaf leaders that the hearing world needed to be educated systematically about deafness and the skills of deaf workers. Antebellum-era deaf leaders and hearing teachers had argued without success for school administrators to mediate with employers on behalf of their former students.[2] With the energies of most deaf leaders diverted to the ongoing struggle over oral- and manual-based approaches, however, the issue fell from sight until the close of the century, when worrisome reports of urban unemployment sparked new efforts.

In the 1890s, at local and national forums, deaf leaders again began to promote initiatives to aid deaf workers. At the National Association of the Deaf (NAD) conventions in 1896 and 1899, Gallaudet's Amos Draper and Minnesota's Olof Hanson urged workers to pool information regarding employers and pressed the NAD to distribute educational materials to managers.[3]

Outside the NAD conventions, Edward Hodgson used the editorial column of the *Deaf Mute's Journal* (*DMJ*) to remind readers of the ongoing need to educate the public and employers. "Argument and example alike," he explained, were necessary to impress upon employers and the public that deaf individuals were able laborers and citizens. "The enlightenment of one generation," he pointed out,

Through his advocacy of state-sponsored, independent labor bureaus led by deaf officials, Anson Spear sought to educate hearing employers about deaf workers. Spear hoped the bureaus would also oversee hearing school administrators who favored oral communication methods.

"does not descend like a legacy, to the generation that comes after it."[4]

Deaf leaders unfortunately had few resources to fund a national campaign to assist workers. The NAD was little more than a skeleton organization led by unpaid officers whose operating budget paled before the ambitious visions of its members. Although members supported entreaties made by Hodgson, Hanson, and others for further action, deaf leaders were forced to ask for assistance from outside their community.[5]

School administrators continued to thwart renewed efforts to broaden the responsibility of school officials to assist deaf adults in finding work. At the turn of the century, Warren Robinson, chairman of both the Convention of American Instructors of the Deaf (CAID) Industrial Department and the NAD Committee on Industrial Status, called upon his colleagues at the Conference of Executives and Administrators of Schools for the Deaf (CEASD) to establish labor bureaus at their schools.[6] The administrators rejected the proposal, however. Francis Clarke, superintendent of the Michigan School for the Deaf and a consistent proponent of advanced industrial training, conceded that deaf workers might not initially be accepted by hearing coworkers, but he also scoffed at the charge that employers habitually excluded deaf candidates. Ironically, drawing upon the arguments of deaf leaders from earlier decades, he argued that individual excellence was needed, not intervention by a school official.[7]

Demands for a labor bureau nevertheless grew among deaf leaders and hearing supporters during the first decade of the twentieth century.[8] In 1905 and again in 1908, Robinson—now joined by Elsie Steinke, an instructor at the Wisconsin School for the Deaf—argued that the organization should sponsor a national labor bureau.[9] The members rebuffed these requests: financial pressures, combined with the view that administrators had no responsibility to students once they left school, dashed any hopes for such a bureau.

The fortunes of deaf activists changed when they grounded their efforts in their own local communities, however. Spear led the efforts of Minnesota deaf activists to enlist the backing of deaf people in establishing an independent, state-sponsored bureau. Although he used his voice to communicate with hearing individuals (he acquired his

Warren Robinson pressed educators to establish labor bureaus at individual schools in
order to increase the employment rates of school graduates.

deafness after learning speech), he identified with the state's deaf community. He had graduated from the state residential school for the
deaf at Faribault, worked as a tailor, and briefly attended Gallaudet
College. After working in the Census Bureau in Washington, D.C., he
had returned to the Twin Cities in the early 1880s.[10]

In 1889, Spear moved west to launch a second career working on
behalf of deaf children in the newly-created state of North Dakota.
After lobbying the state legislature to establish a school, he was appointed the first superintendent in 1890. During his five-year tenure,
he established sign language as the primary medium of instruction,
built a department of vocational instruction centered around printing,
and was a steadfast proponent of hiring deaf women and men as academic teachers and vocational instructors. He constructed a solid
school program centered on these elements at the very time that oralist educators called for the elimination of sign language and deaf
teachers.[11]

Spear had long argued that deaf citizens had the ability and right
to control their education and employment. At the first reunion of
students from the Minnesota residential school in 1885, for example,
he charged that some of his peers were overly dependent on hearing

people. Self-reliance, pride in one's work, and sign language were all-important, he counseled.[12] His successes in North Dakota encouraged an even sharper appraisal of the status of deaf citizens in the state and throughout the region. While superintendent of the North Dakota school, Spear returned to Minnesota to argue that speech-based instruction undercut the intellectual development of students and weakened the position of all deaf citizens. "Myself able to speak and enjoy the society of those who hear," explained Spear in a speech before the Minnesota Association of the Deaf, "I would yet give up speech a thousand times than be deprived of the means of communication with those, who like myself, are deaf."[13]

Spear moved back to Minnesota in 1895 and quickly involved himself in local educational affairs.[14] Within months of his arrival, he met with members of the State Board of Control, who supervised the residential school.[15] He accused them of lax oversight of the school, although he praised the efforts of Jonathan Noyes, the school's newly-appointed hearing superintendent. Recounting his confrontation with the board in a letter published in the *Minneapolis Tribune*, he charged that incompetent foremen ensured that vocational instruction was a "pretense" and that general instruction was weakened by school supervisors who did not properly support deaf teachers. Indeed, he argued that board members were more interested in their own advancement than in that of the students and were not worthy of overseeing the school.[16]

In these arguments, Spear initiated a practice of passionate, open criticism of school administrators that would span two decades. He also introduced an unprecedented level of debate that opened to challenge all school administrator's actions and their worthiness to retain their positions. To Spear, hearing professionals did maintain the state's schools—but only at the behest of deaf adults. His views foreshadowed the arguments of activists a century later and exemplify an unending, if uneven, practice of self-advocacy among deaf people.

By the turn of the century, Spear was arguing that the state's deaf citizens needed to act boldly to protect their education and status as workers. He appeared before the Minnesota Association of the Deaf in 1901 to argue that legislation was needed to safeguard the rights of deaf citizens—apparently a reference to the national successes of oralists and the displacement of deaf teachers. In light of his earlier angry charges, his proposals at this time were surprisingly modest: he called for the state to build a second residential school and for all schools for deaf students to be classified as educational institutions on a par with other public schools. "[W]e should decide right now on some of the legislation we want," Spear concluded, "and then go after it and keep after it until we get it."[17]

An isolated Spear found few peers willing to support his recommendations. Although association leaders agreed to establish a committee to promote a second residential school, they were understandably wary of an open clash with school officials and refused to promote Spear's proposals. Most members likely shared his interest in establishing a second school, but they believed that sponsoring an independent legislative initiative could touch off an irreparable conflict with school officials. They clung to suggestion and negotiation, not open confrontation, as their only viable strategy. Spear feared for the state's students if the deaf community did not act decisively; but his peers feared that even these restrained initiatives brought unacceptable risk.[18]

Differences between Spear and other leaders were temporarily eclipsed when Superintendent James Tate moved to strengthen oral instruction and curtail sign language at the school. Between 1866 and 1896, Superintendent Noyes had enjoyed the support of the Minnesota Association of the Deaf. Trained at the American School in Hartford, Jonathan Noyes had supported deaf teachers and employed sign language as well as oral instruction. Indeed, even Spear praised his willingness to incorporate the views of deaf adults in formulating policy.[19] Tate initially enjoyed hospitable relations with the association when he succeeded Noyes in the mid-1890s. Between 1906 and 1912, however, he initiated a gradual but consistent effort to restrict sign language and expand oral instruction.[20]

Spear utilized mainstream newspapers and the deaf press to condemn oralist administrators in Minnesota and around the country. Superintendents, he argued were "humble servants of the people." Thus, they were well advised to "get down from their pedestals" and "learn from the experience of the deaf." He dismissed pure oral practices as a "rank fraud" and advised advocates of those practices to admit their failures. "Be honest for once," he admonished them, "and see if you do not sleep better."[21]

Spear believed that the abridgement of sign language and primary reliance upon pure oral methods especially endangered deaf workers. Speech and lipreading lessons at school, he argued, undercut the intellectual development of students and wasted time that would be better used in strengthening valuable vocational skills.[22] In light of the unilateral actions of school administrators, it was not surprising, he argued, that business leaders would discriminate against deaf candidates. In fact, he thought it a "matter of astonishment" that so many graduates had prospered as workers. Directing his anger at the Minnesota school superintendent, he warned of certain trouble. "If those misguided educators who chase the shadow and miss the substance, shall at last succeed in striking down the sign language in this country," he concluded, "well may we exclaim, '*God help the deaf.*' "[23] And so, in 1912, he set out to establish an independent labor bureau with the power to oversee the education of students and protect the status of workers.

Deaf workers and leaders from around the country, many of whom had fought against the exclusionary Civil Service directive, campaigned on behalf of the bureau. From Chicago, George Dougherty joined a letter-writing campaign as he offered the support of the city's long-standing community organization, the Pas-a-Pas Club.[24] From Iowa, J. Schuyler Long, a school administrator and intellect active in regional issues, cheered developments.[25] And from Wisconsin, Warren Robinson wrote to local newspapers to explain that deaf leaders had long promoted a bureau.[26]

Notable state politicians eased the proposed bureau through the legislative process. The bill was introduced by State Senator William W. Dunn of St. Paul, a visually-impaired representative known for his advocacy on behalf of deaf and blind citizens during his six terms, and ushered through to passage by State Representative William A. Campbell, also from St. Paul, who described himself as caring deeply about the initiative.[27]

Minnesota's tradition of progressive labor and social welfare legislation hastened the passage of the bureau legislation. Both the Bureau of Labor and the recently established Bureau for Women and Children involved state oversight of working conditions and workers.[28] Labor Commissioner William Houk was on board by the winter of 1912.[29] He may have had a special affinity for Spear's initiative because, like many deaf students, he began his working career as a printer and had been a member of the International Typographical Union.[30]

State support was further augmented by the advocacy of key members of the school's board of directors. Even as Spear unabashedly criticized school officials, he maintained positive relations with B. B. Sheffield, a member of the board for some fifteen years. Although Sheffield's views of Spear's criticisms are not known, he agreed with Spear that the bureau would effectively promote deaf students and workers.[31] In April 1913, Governor A. O. Eberhart signed the bill instituting the Division for the Deaf in the Department of Labor, the nation's first state-sponsored agency for deaf workers.[32]

But the new division paled in comparison to the more powerful agency Spear envisioned. In the original version of the bill, a deaf director was empowered to appraise vocational programs and communication methods in all state schools and to protect the "rights to employment" of deaf workers.[33] As codified, however, an administrator would simply promote the "general welfare" of deaf citizens by studying labor trends and assisting individual workers to find work.[34] Moreover, the division chief had neither the authority to evaluate communication methods and instructional programs nor any specified authority to oversee or regulate employers. The division had been stripped of its primary powers; at the very moment he had hoped to celebrate victory, Spear was divided.

Deaf leaders from around the country delighted in the legislation despite the fact that the division did not satisfy Spear's vision. James W. Cloud, principal of the Gallaudet School for the Deaf in St. Louis, exclaimed in the *Silent Worker* that the beneficial outcome of the agency "cannot be overestimated."[35] "[T]he finest piece of legislation yet accomplished for the deaf by the deaf," exulted George Veditz on the first page of the *DMJ*. "There is no other like it in existence, anywhere on earth," he continued, "and it will be to the everlasting glory of Minnesota to have led the way." He believed that even a weakened division would assist workers. In particular, he thought the division chief would be able to publicize the talents and independence of deaf workers, the majority of whom relied upon sign language. This coverage, he asserted, would weaken the "propaganda" of oralists and create new opportunities for workers. Even so, a reflective Veditz acknowledged the inadequacies of the division: "As it stands, the law is a fine thing for the deaf, as originally drafted by Mr. Spear it was finer still."[36]

Unlike his peers, Spear found little to celebrate. Although archival records do not indicate who scaled back the bureau, Superintendent James Tate certainly favored the revisions. At the CAID convention that summer, he openly supported a bureau, but only if organized as part of the state residential school and under his supervision. This support was enough for Spear to blame Tate for the diminution of the division.[37] In a presentation before the Minnesota Association that summer, he argued that Tate's alleged intercession was made possible because school policy was controlled "by one man alone, the superintendent. His word is law. There is no appeal." Given Tate's unilateral power, Spear maintained that additional measures were necessary to protect the education, industrial, and social position of Minnesota's deaf citizens. "It rests with this Association," he concluded, "to say whether or not we shall continue to allow this man to be the absolute dictator over the destinies of the deaf of this good State of Minnesota."[38]

Spear also renewed his charge that the leaders of the state association were unduly wary of fighting for greater power. In fact, he sought members' endorsement for a series of bold measures that would strengthen the influence of the Minnesota Association regarding oversight, administration, and instruction at the residential school. First, in addition to demanding Superintendent Tate's resignation, he proposed that all members of the board of directors be required to study sign language and that one position on the board be reserved for a school alumnus. Second, he demanded that teachers be given greater power in the administration of the school. Third, although supportive of oral and manual instruction, he insisted that sign language be allowed in all school activities. His proposals reflected a clear intent that deaf adults have a permanent, if subordinate, role in the school and that oral instruction not overwhelm sign language.[39]

Spear's fellow deaf leaders once again backed away from his call to action. Although the association's members shared his opposition to unchecked oralism, several of them, including Jay Cooke Howard, worried anew that his charges were counterproductive. So at the very time Spear sought support, he was isolated: he was not invited to discussions with the board of directors.[40]

Thus sidelined by his peers, an undeterred Spear looked ahead. He placed his efforts in a larger framework and took the debate to the NAD convention that summer, reminding his audience that deaf people had always sought to participate in decisions regarding their education and work. He argued that an independent labor bureau would be the greatest advance in fifty years, and he pledged to advance new legislation to strengthen Minnesota's bureau and to establish a national bureau in Washington, D.C. Greater action, not diminished expectations, was necessary.[41]

Spear's fears regarding the division in Minnesota were warranted. The agency had neither the resources nor the influence to overcome the social and economic hurdles confronting deaf students and workers. In fact, the agency began work two years late because the authorizing legislation had not included funding. Beginning in the summer of 1915, one individual with an annual budget of $1,000 was to travel the state and assist approximately 1,000 deaf adults and 350 deaf students.[42]

A deaf woman named Petra Fandrem was the first to lead the division. A graduate of the state residential school and Gallaudet College, Fandrem was selected from a pool of Civil Service candidates. Fluent in sign language and also able to communicate with her voice, she moved easily between the deaf and hearing communities.[43] Although neither Fandrem nor her successor left behind extended records describing their work, both completed brief biannual reports that sketched their activities and the problems faced by deaf students and adults.

In her brief tenure, Fandrem validated one of Spear's central arguments: employers regularly shunned qualified deaf applicants. Deaf adults had long claimed that many employers simply refused to consider them for employment, but no record of this practice existed in Minnesota, nor had deaf workers organized to challenge it. Fandrem, like Thomas Gallaudet before her, noted from discussions and meetings that resistant business people often claimed that writing out orders to deaf workers was too time-consuming. She labored to deflate this concern by explaining that the concentration and efficiency of deaf workers compensated for any communication impediments.[44]

Fandrem's successor, Luella Nyhus, encountered comparable problems in her meetings with employers. Nyhus was the hearing daughter of deaf parents, both of whom had graduated from the state residential school, and she too moved readily between both communities. She reported two seemingly contradictory findings after meeting with nearly seventy-five employers: first, she noted no "marked antagonism" toward deaf workers but second, an unidentified number of employers paid deaf workers less than hearing coworkers for the same work. Although she did not indicate the possible reasons for this pay differential, employers may have favored deaf workers because some would consent to work for less than prevailing wages. On a more promising note, she reported that local unions welcomed qualified deaf workers.[45]

Petra Fandrem was the Minnesota Labor Bureau's first leader. She left the bureau the following year, but continued to work for the state's association for the deaf.

Nyhus's work in the prewar era also affirmed arguments that inadequate training particularly limited deaf women. A survey revealed that male students had access to the broadest array of training programs. More than 200 men reported receiving instruction in areas that included carpentry and cabinet making, printing, tailoring, and barbering. In contrast, 96 percent of 250 women were trained in domestic science.[46]

This kind of gender-based inequity in job training was followed by gender-based job segregation. The 224 men surveyed were employed in more than 50 positions, the largest number as miscellaneous laborers, in printing, and as farmers. Of 98 women surveyed, however, all were employed in only eight distinct positions. More than 60 percent of these women labored as power machine operators.[47] Nyhus's efforts to assist unemployed women and men in finding work conformed to these patterns. Twenty of the 30 women with whom she worked in 1917 and 1918 were employed as either power machine operators or seamstresses. In contrast, she helped 62 men secure positions in nearly a dozen different fields, generally in artisan jobs that were often better paying and likely had more opportunities for advancement.[48]

With Nyhus guiding the division in Minnesota, Spear redirected his energies toward the establishment of a national bureau in the U.S. Department of Labor. His plan called for the national chief to be an experienced educator proficient in sign language and fingerspelling, a provision that was part of the original Minnesota proposal. Although Spear apparently expected the person in this position to be able to hear, his proposal cited a preference that all subordinates be deaf. The bureau director would evaluate the social and economic status of the nation's forty thousand deaf citizens, work with school officials to review communication methods and vocational training, educate the general public and employers regarding deaf laborers, and intervene against discriminatory employers to protect deaf workers' "rights to employment."[49]

Spear next secured congressional sponsors and the backing of deaf people. In March 1914, Minnesota's Senator Moses E. Clapp and Representative James Manahan forwarded proposed legislation to the House Committee on Labor. The following month, Representative

Clarence Miller and Representative John Edward Raker, a member of the board of directors of Gallaudet College, introduced comparable congressional legislation in the House Committee on Education.[50] Deaf leaders and citizens from around the country solicited Congress in an effort to promote the legislation. That spring, a smattering of individuals, alumni associations, clubs, and state as well as national organizations forwarded letters and petitions to Senator Clapp's office. NAD branches in Ohio and Chicago contributed petitions; alumni from the state residential school in Ohio lent their support; and from Chicago and Pittsburgh, members of state and local groups joined in. Despite this midwestern base of support, advocates were apparently unable to establish a viable national campaign and the future of the bureau was doubtful.[51]

The drive took an especially heavy blow when the Department of Labor refused to endorse the proposed bureau. In response to inquiries from the Committee on Education, where enabling legislation rested, Secretary of Labor James Wilson recommended that any decision regarding a bureau be postponed pending a national study of the status of deaf students and workers. In addition, officials in the Bureau of Labor Statistics offered reservations about a bureau largely staffed by deaf employees. There is no record that Spear contacted officials in the Department of Labor. If he did, it apparently had little impact; by the summer of 1914, government officials had stalled the legislation.[52]

The proposed bureau received two further blows that summer. First, a CAID subcommittee endorsed the bureau, but only after stripping it of the power to appraise communication methods at schools. With this stipulation, the subcommittee unanimously forwarded the proposal to the convention.[53] From Washington, D.C., a discouraged Senator Clapp reported that Congress was preoccupied with the war in Europe, and little immediate attention to the proposal could be expected. With some luck, Congress might convene a hearing during the following session.[54] Despite these setbacks, Spear urged deaf proponents of the bureau to reinvigorate their work.[55]

Meanwhile, deaf leaders continued to debate whether the division chief should review communication methods at schools, thus expressing the national deaf community's divisions over the effectiveness of directly challenging oralist school administrators. When the issue surfaced at the 1915 NAD convention, James Cloud argued that a "common ground" might be established with oralists—provided the bureau chief did not review communication methods. Alice Terry, a leader of the California Association of the Deaf, countered that bureau representatives would be especially well suited to educate hearing parents regarding sign language and oral approaches. In a unifying gesture, Cloud asked that Spear be honored for his work, and the assembled members agreed to continue their efforts to establish a national bureau mandated to review communication methods at schools.[56]

Between 1915 and 1918, deaf leaders and individuals worked without success to spur further congressional action. Then, coincidental with the country's entry into World War I in April 1917, members of the House and Senate reintroduced legislation. Deaf activists and organizations followed with a new round of petitions and suggestions.[57] From New York, the editor of a prominent metropolitan area newspaper for deaf readers argued that government intervention was necessary to spur reluctant employers to hire deaf workers.[58] NAD leaders, in an attempt to capitalize upon the war, pointed out that newly deafened soldiers would be able to turn to the bureau for assistance.[59] Finally, activists recruited teachers and administrators from schools across the country in an effort to broaden support for the bureau.[60] As Congress directed its attention to the widening European conflict, however, deaf activists had to grudgingly recognize that their national campaign had apparently failed.[61]

In February 1918, even as the war continued, visions of a national bureau were temporarily renewed as proponents secured a long-awaited hearing before the House Committee on Education. Shying away from commentary on school-based communication debates, deaf and hearing advocates testified that a bureau would reduce obstacles that blocked deaf workers from the trades and professions. William Souder, a NAD member active in the campaign to reverse the Civil Service exclusionary decree and an employee of the Census Bureau, explained that the aspirations of deaf workers were blunted by employers who unfairly judged all deaf candidates by the actions of one individual. Representative John Raker once again indicated his support, asserting that deaf men and women could succeed "in all walks of life" if given the opportunity to demonstrate their skills.[62]

The hearing was inconclusive, and it signaled an end to the campaign. Deaf activists had scarcely been able to attract the attention of Congress, and the bureau proposal languished and died in committee. Anson Spear never testified. Two months prior to the hearing, in December 1917, he had collapsed in Minneapolis and died.[63]

Anson Spear was a daring advocate for deaf students and workers, clearly ahead of his peers and his times in his willingness to risk conflict in pursuit of systemic change. In retrospect, however, his apparent belief that the deaf community could establish and sustain a truly autonomous state agency that would not be actively undermined by oralist educators seems naïve. Still, where else were deaf activists to turn? In seeking protection and redress from the state, they were following principles that had inspired countless progressive reformers in the hearing world. Spear's error, it seems, was to believe that hearing leaders in government, education, and business would be able to question and transcend prevailing norms and practices regarding the rights of employers and the alluring claims of oralists.

Had the U.S. Congress seriously considered a national bureau, it would likely have narrowed its mandate, much as Minnesota's legislature restricted its original Division for the Deaf. Neither school administrators nor oralist advocates would have stood by to allow the creation of an independent bureau sponsored by sign language proponents. Even if bureau proponents had been able to lessen the influence of school administrators, it is extremely improbable that Congress would have accorded deaf workers open-ended "rights to employment" not available to workers in mainstream society. Not surprisingly, an independent bureau intended to strengthen the rights of deaf workers was the vision of deaf activists and hearing supporters, not of Congress.

The work of the Minnesota division also underlined anew the broad disparities in power and understanding between deaf workers and their employers. Hearing managers continued to exclude deaf applicants for reasons deemed unfair by those applicants. Even if hired, deaf workers of both sexes were apt to have fewer job choices and be paid less than their hearing peers. In addition, deaf women faced gender-based restrictions common among their hearing peers. Confined to a narrow range of semiskilled positions, only a handful of deaf women had access to training that might enable them to pursue a broader range of positions.

The national campaign to create the Minnesota Division and the work it achieved thereafter were significant, however, even though deaf leaders in Minnesota were unable to overturn the structural obstacles hindering employment of deaf workers or to reverse communication policy in the schools. Although the division enjoyed neither the legislative mandate nor adequate staff to fulfill the ambitious vision Spear articulated, Fandrem and Nyhus increased the number of employers willing to hire deaf workers and enlightened the general public about deaf working men and women. Simultaneously, they helped adults find work when they might otherwise have been unemployed or underemployed.

Moreover, despite its limitations, Minnesota's division served as a model for and inspiration to deaf activists across the nation. Spear's vision of broader opportunities for working adults and of fuller participation by deaf adults in the education of deaf students had challenged and invigorated deaf workers and their leaders in the Midwest and in the nation. Within Minnesota, Spear's impassioned and occasionally intemperate advocacy had prodded the state's staid deaf community to a new level of activism. Between the opening of the Minnesota division and the end of World War II, deaf adults in more than a dozen states across the nation worked to establish comparable bureaus that aided thousands of workers.

At the final congressional hearing regarding the national bureau in February 1918, the president of Gallaudet College, Percival Hall, noted the migration of nearly one thousand deaf men and women from all parts of the country to Akron, Ohio, where they had been recruited by managers in the Goodyear Corporation.[64] Employed in the company's booming factories, these women and men also developed a rich and diverse social and cultural life. The growth of a "Silent Colony," as some deaf residents dubbed their rapidly growing community, suggested broad new possibilities for the standing of deaf workers. Some enthusiastic residents even claimed that the example of a thriving and fully employed community like the one in Akron would demonstrate to educators and employers alike the value of sign language and the abilities of deaf workers. Perhaps in Akron's crowded factories and busy streets, deaf working men and women would find the educational, economic, and social opportunities that they had long sought.

5

"For One's Daily Bread"

Entering Industry

In the spring of 1918, the nation's attention was drawn to Europe and U.S. involvement in World War I. The gaze of the country's forty thousand deaf citizens was directed, however, not to battlefields but to the factories of Akron, Ohio. There, managers had recruited nearly one thousand men and women to labor in the town's sprawling rubber factories. Eager deaf leaders hoped that the example of accomplishment set by these workers—tire builders, machinists, typists, chemists, and assemblers—would usher in an era of greater industrial and educational opportunities for all deaf men and women.

The national migration of hundreds of deaf adults to Akron was the culmination of nearly forty years of disparate and loosely organized responses by deaf people as the nation evolved from a rural, artisan-based economy to an urbanized, mass-based industrial setting. Amid these transformations, many deaf workers and leaders turned to their local, regional, and national organizations to debate how to best safeguard the standing of deaf workers. At the same time, leaders also consulted with school officials, prospective employers, and union and community organizations outside the national deaf community regarding the status of deaf students and employees. Significantly, several deaf activists championed proposals designed to secure new legal rights for deaf workers. Most deaf leaders, however, rejected these initiatives and sought instead to adapt traditional, more conservative educational campaigns to the nation's new industrial circumstances.

Many deaf workers and leaders, like their counterparts in mainstream society, were deeply troubled by industrialization. Doubtful that any reforms could make industrial work attractive to or even viable for deaf men and women, several deaf observers urged their peers to work in the agricultural sector.[1] In 1908, Robert Taylor, a teacher at the North Carolina School for the Deaf asserted that "[t]o enter the print shop or factory means for nearly all who do so, a life of slavery for one's daily bread." Agriculture, on the other hand, promised independence to deaf adults—even those who began as day laborers![2] Acting according to such critiques, a small number of deaf adults, including New York's Rider family, continued their efforts to establish self-sufficient cooperatives.[3]

Others drew upon the recent efforts of other minority groups to advocate for deaf farmers. William Cowles, a graduate of Minnesota's residential school who was forced to withdraw from the University of Minnesota for lack of funds, argued that the state should offer loans to aspiring deaf farmers. Just as emancipated African Americans had argued for governmental support during Reconstruction, Cowles reasoned that the state should provide deaf adults with access to capital in order to "work out their own salvation."[4] Like the entreaties of southern freedwomen and freedmen, however, Cowles's proposal was never realized. Moreover, few students were able to advance beyond rudimentary instruction: a survey completed in 1907 indicated that less than half of thirty-two schools provided sustained agricultural training.[5]

While the majority of deaf adults sought their fortunes within the industrial economy, deaf leaders were able to do little more than debate how to best utilize their scarce resources to achieve this objective. Wisconsin's Warren Robinson argued that schools were required to prepare students for the rigors of industrial competition. The credo of graduates, he explained, should be "[l]ife is a battle, not good cheer."[6] What would this preparation entail? Advocates of manual-training, including New York's Edward Hodgson, argued that schools should provide elementary mechanical instruction and trades training that would prepare graduates for entry-level positions in trades and industry.[7] Proponents of industrial instruction countered that only advanced training would enable students to be promoted beyond unskilled occupations.[8] A third group argued that industry-based apprenticeships were vital.[9] In the end, however, few schools had the resources to adequately pursue any such strategy.

Moreover, industrial changes that transformed production methods in the workplace left untouched the underlying gender-biased precepts that constrained schooling for women. Few educators and leaders saw any need to reshape vocational instruction for women, so most programs continued to emphasize domestic science and sewing in order to prepare female graduates to fulfill traditional roles as mothers and wives. Most deaf women therefore had few options in the paid workforce. A small fraction became teachers and professionals, and a small but increasing number obtained semiskilled positions in industry, typically as assemblers and power machine operators, despite school officials' representation of factory work as too grueling for women. The majority, though, labored as domestics and seamstresses. Most, including those who entered the paid workforce, went on to marry, confirming educators' prevailing belief that minimal vocational instruction was adequate for women.[10]

A few critics demanded broader female vocational instruction, faulted oral training, and decried the segregation of women in marginal industrial positions.[11] In an appearance before the National Association of the Deaf (NAD) in 1899, May Martin, an instructor at the Columbia Institution for the Deaf in Washington, D.C., charged that both prejudiced employers and oral instruction threatened women workers. Displaced from schools by hearing oral instructors and blocked by employers in many fields, they had few choices except garment work, for which most had some training.[12]

Yet women activists and educators lacked power either to transform instruction or to assist women workers. Moreover, only a handful of male educators and leaders, deaf and hearing, lent support to their arguments.[13] These women nonetheless exerted pressure on school administrators, educated their male counterparts, and persistently made demands that would eventually spur broader vocational opportunities.

As machine-based industrial production reduced the value of artisan-based vocational programs at schools, deaf proponents argued anew for training that would enable workers to keep up with economic changes.[14] A teacher at the South Carolina School for the Deaf explained that graduates needed access to advanced training facilities because most employers refused to hire deaf students for positions that demanded intellectual expertise.[15] Advocates, including Hodgson and Robinson, typically called for the establishment of an independent technical college or technical programs at Gallaudet College.[16] After President Edward Gallaudet agreed that the college could broaden teaching in the sciences, the National Conference of School Executives and Administrators announced their support for a technical department at the college.[17] The NAD and the newly organized Gallaudet College Alumni Association followed suit in 1893.[18]

Despite this support, Gallaudet College did not open a vocational department. President Gallaudet believed that a separate vocational branch was inconsistent with the college's mission as a liberal arts institution. Instead, in 1896 the administration provided several new technical courses, but they had little concrete effect. With Gallaudet College willing to admit only a small number of students each year, the vast majority of the nation's students still had no place to turn for advanced vocational instruction.[19]

Deaf leaders also continued efforts to inform employers and public officials of the accomplishments of deaf workers. No undertaking seemed more promising than the *American Industrial Journal,* a state-of-the-art magazine that profiled successful deaf workers and reported on topical labor issues. Four years after its promising start, however, fixed costs, limited financial backing, and a narrow subscription base forced editor Warren Robinson to shut down the presses. The journal, like scores of other short-lived newspapers, magazines, and publications promoted by ambitious deaf writers and leaders, was no more.[20]

Within their own community, deaf leaders, including those aligned with New York's Society for the Welfare of the Jewish Deaf (SWJD), established in 1912 by hearing and deaf leaders, continued a tradition of assisting needy individual deaf workers. In their efforts, SWJD employees, like their predecessors at St. Ann's Church, honored traditional precepts of the deaf community. Director Albert Amateau, likening his role to that of an interpreter, avoided charitable appeals as he sought to educate unknowing employers.[21] The society helped secure employment for some two hundred adults each year between its inception and the close of World War I. More than two-thirds were men who were employed as factory workers and artisans.[22]

Deaf leaders and activists were often union-trained printers and artisans, and they argued for deaf industrial workers to support unions.[23] Philip Morin, in a representative speech before the New England Gallaudet Association in 1906, maintained that individual deaf workers were apt to be overworked by employers; aligned with hearing workers in unions, they stood a better chance of being treated properly.[24]

As a labor activist, one deaf individual combined innovative legislative protections, comparable to those of the contemporary era, with traditional nineteenth-century standards of self-reliance. In 1900, George Sawyer demanded that deaf leaders promote legislation against prejudicial employers. "If there is a law against discrimination on account of color, race, or religion, and if any State legislature has made laws in the interest of working people," he appealed, "why cannot we get out a petition . . . to make laws against discrimination, on account of deafness?"[25] At the same time, he asked applicants to work without pay for a short time to demonstrate their reliability. This proposal elicited no response from either deaf or hearing observers. Moreover, had legislators become involved, they would likely have dismissed the idea as an infringement on the rights of employers.[26]

Thus, between the late nineteenth century and the first decades of the twentieth, deaf leaders and workers debated and employed a seemingly disparate range of individual and cooperative schemes and strategies to advance the rights of deaf workers. Their differences notwithstanding, most initiatives revolved around the longstanding goal of preparing for or securing access to the workforce. However, three examples—in Chicago, Detroit, and Akron—revealed that the industrial work situation, whatever its alluring possibilities, was, in fact, fraught with risk for most deaf workers.

Chicago's Automatic Electric Company was renowned as the first large industrial firm to actively recruit deaf workers in 1902, but it may also have been the first to fire deaf workers en masse. After two deaf employees who were hired on a trial basis in 1902 proved to be more productive than their hearing counterparts, management recruited more. Shortly, some 150 deaf women and men from Chicago and the Midwest labored in the brick plant, assembling telephones, among other things.[27] Their standing became precarious in April 1903, however, after machinists struck and appealed to fellow union members to join them on the picket line. Deaf workers, like their hearing counterparts, had joined the Telephone and Switchboard Workers' Union and soon marched outside the plant. The solidarity between deaf and hearing workers surprised managers, who had hoped that deaf workers would be so grateful for their positions that they would break the strike. A week later, the plant was reopened—after management acceded to a shorter workweek. Automatic Electric's deaf assemblers, in conjunction with their hearing coworkers, had won their first collective industrial contest in the new century.[28]

Ultimately, however, Automatic Electric's owners, not deaf assemblers, had the final word, for management fired large groups of deaf workers in retaliation for their role in the strike.[29] The company's deaf workers had proven themselves able employees and steady labor allies, and they had followed the canons championed within their community—only to face the streets. Their experiences revealed the vulnerability of minority employees in the face of the largely unconstrained and arbitrary power of employers. After all, self-interest, rather than any extraordinary commitment to diversifying the workforce, had initially spurred management to hire deaf people. Moreover, there is no available evidence that other employers followed Automatic Electric's lead. Chicago's first substantive gathering of deaf industrial workers came and went with little notice.

Several years later, deaf workers in Michigan sought employment at the rapidly expanding Ford Motor Company. Between 1908 and early 1914, following in Art Tremaine's footsteps, a few deaf applicants secured employment at Ford. According to lore within the deaf community, Tremaine and his peers demonstrated such extraordinary diligence and efficiency that they soon won over skeptical supervisors, who later informed Henry Ford of the success of these pioneers.[30]

This initially individualized and grudging acceptance was replaced by a policy of open admissions in January 1914, as deaf workers were swept up in one of the century's most momentous changes, Ford's institution of the assembly line. The start of the assembly line in the winter of 1913 had revolutionized production methods and gravely threatened labor relations, as management sought to reduce an automobile's assembly time from twelve hours to a little more than ninety minutes.[31] Working conditions in the new industrial system were so brutal that tens of thousands of hearing workers resisted its imposition. In 1913, fifty thousand workers left the plant and management discharged another eight thousand. Over the course of the year, the company had to hire one thousand workers to retain one hundred.[32]

Henry Ford acted decisively to stem this unacceptable level of turnover. On January 12, 1914, he doubled the daily pay for male workers and promptly attracted thousands of applicants from across Michigan and the Midwest.[33] Deaf people were especially interested in another announcement that accompanied the new wage policy: no applicants, company officials proclaimed, would be refused employment on account of their physical condition. In effect, the Ford Motor Company became the first major national firm to establish a policy of nondiscrimination regarding deaf workers or other applicants with physical differences.[34]

Why did Ford decide to hire workers with varying physical conditions? Although he needed to stabilize employee turnover, there is little evidence that deaf or other minority group applicants could be hired in sufficient numbers to halt such a turnover. Ford's biographer, William Greenleaf, observed that this policy instead reflected an engineer's "horror of waste and of inefficiently utilized human energy."[35] Ford agreed with most deaf leaders who believed that charity for persons with physical disabilities was unnecessary and demeaning. Self-sufficiency, he claimed, was within reach of all citizens. "We are too ready to assume without investigation," he explained, "that the full possession of faculties is a condition requisite to the best performance of all jobs."[36] Ford understood a simple yet vital axiom embraced by the majority of deaf and disabled workers: physical differences could be rendered insignificant by placing laborers in positions where they could demonstrate their particular abilities and skills. He also argued that the workforce of industries should mirror the diversity of the larger population.[37] Although his anti-Semitism, gender prejudices, and racism undermined this position, his interest in hiring disabled workers seemed genuine.

Ford instituted a methodical system to determine the placement of workers. Medical personnel and engineers identified the specific capabilities required for each position in the corporation.[38] Of the eight thousand jobs within the company, for example, more than four thousand were suitable for workers with physical differences, including almost seven hundred positions for legless workers, ten for blind individuals, and thirty-seven for deaf persons.[39]

Deaf workers publicly endorsed Ford's initiatives, but few sought employment. A small number of deaf men migrated to Michigan, but the overall number of deaf Ford employees never greatly increased from what it had been before these initiatives. By the summer of 1915, roughly two dozen deaf people worked at the company.[40] By January 1916, this number increased to around fifty workers, or just over one-half of 1 percent of the workforce.[41]

The apparent collective disinterest in working at Ford likely reflected the limited nature of most positions. The jobs identified as appropriate for deaf adults were primarily low-skilled, repetitive stations where workers labored in isolation with only slight opportunity for advancement. Less than eight hours of training were required to master the task in 40 percent of the positions considered suitable for deaf people.[42] Nevertheless, deaf leaders publicized Ford's initiatives in the hope of somehow promoting progressive hiring policies. "No particular consideration has to be given to deaf and dumb employees," Ford explained in a memoir. "They do their work one hundred per cent."[43] Although deaf publicists could not have asked for a more solid endorsement, praise from the nation's industrial giant did little to close the gap of ignorance and inexperience that separated deaf workers and hearing employers in most industries.[44]

The most promising large-scale recruitment and employment of deaf industrial workers, however, took place in the factories of the Goodyear and Firestone companies in Akron, Ohio, between 1915 and 1920.[45] Previously, a small number of deaf workers had gained entrance into Akron's rubber factories through individual demonstrations of ability and through the personal intervention of particular managers.[46] The experiences of Harry Ware, reportedly the first deaf man to obtain work in the factories, are representative of the barriers that faced others.[47] After working at odd jobs, Ware moved to Akron in 1910 and was repeatedly rebuffed in his initial efforts to find work at the Goodyear, Goodrich, and Diamond companies. It took a personal visit to the home of one supervisor before Ware began work at Diamond.[48] Between 1911 and 1913, a small number of deaf men, including Ware, were hired at Goodyear, although doubtful managers regularly rejected the entreaties of other deaf applicants. These early workers were outstanding employees, and by the spring of 1914, more than a dozen deaf men worked at Goodyear, Firestone, and Goodrich,[49] a tiny corps of deaf employees who had breached a small fissure in the wall of exclusion. War in Europe would tear down the wall.

World War I transformed Akron and the lives of its deaf residents. Between the outbreak of war in August 1914 and the country's entry into the conflict in April 1917, production in the city's rubber-based factories skyrocketed, as industrial leaders strained to meet war-driven orders.[50] Thirty thousand workers—including native-born men and women, immigrants, and a small number of African Americans—arrived in Akron between 1914 and 1917, drawn by company recruitment drives and the hope of landing steady work.[51] Akron bustled with activity as factories ran three shifts a day.[52] "Rubber City" may have been one of the fastest growing locales in the United States: between 1910 and 1920, the city's population increased some 200 percent.[53]

Amid these changes, industry leaders struggled to fill the expanding factories. The entrance of the United States into the European conflict and the conscription of almost three million men into service further strained industrial needs in Akron and elsewhere. With the nation's first large-scale conscription since the Civil War under way, an editorial in the *Akron Beacon Journal* voiced the concerns of industrial leaders: "Akron today needs all the good workmen it can get."[54] Against this backdrop, the top managers in the Goodyear Corporation decided in the fall of 1915 to actively recruit deaf men.[55]

Deaf workers flocked to Akron from around the country. Newspaper accounts from cities across the Midwest reported that deaf communities were depleted as residents left for Akron.[56] One journalist published travel information, including directions to the factory, and the names of managers who worked with deaf recruits.[57] By spring of

1917, two hundred deaf newcomers were working and Goodyear officials requested an additional one thousand men.[58]

Who were these newcomers? Although no precise records were maintained, the majority of Akron's deaf migrants—especially the early arrivals—seem to have been single white males in their twenties and thirties. Goodyear personnel directed their initial recruiting toward males, as they believed that only men could master the taxing piecework production system on which most jobs were based.[59] As the war progressed, the company recruited women, and many came to the city on their own. The educational and class level of these deaf migrants ranged widely, including not only many who had only attended secondary school, but also the nation's most accomplished deaf professionals and artisans.

The majority of deaf workers, like rubber company employees in general, labored on the production line at semiskilled piecework. Hundreds of men labored as tire builders, probably the most common of all positions.[60] One tire builder explained that the position demanded "machine gun speed and accuracy," but most began to master the challenges of this position within a week; after a month, nearly all were accomplished laborers.[61] The majority of deaf women likely worked on the production line as well.[62]

The willingness of Goodyear's managers to accommodate a varied range of communication methods was the cornerstone to the effective integration of deaf workers and probably the era's most significant advance. Deaf workers employed writing, sign language, fingerspelling, and, only infrequently, oral methods. In fact, company officials hired hearing men and women as interpreters in order to employ squads of deaf workers. Teams of deaf tire builders often worked on the same shift, supervised by hearing managers familiar with sign language.[63]

Consequently, deaf workers apparently held a broader range of positions at Goodyear than at any other single company in the nation. They were successfully integrated into skilled technical and professional positions—including management and office work, as well as work in the rubber, chemical research, and mechanical departments.[64] Initially excluded from the machine shop, more than fifty men later were trained as machinists, toolmakers, and lathe hands.[65] Another sixty deaf men joined the company's elite Flying Squadron, where they became familiar with a range of positions.[66] Other deaf men and women were employed as drafters, payroll auditors, and chemists. In addition to his responsibilities as a chemist, Kreigh Ayers helped supervise the "Silent Colony," as reporters dubbed the assembly of deaf workers.[67]

Employment at Goodyear was the primary, but not exclusive, attraction of Akron for deaf people. Many newcomers were drawn to the city's diverse social life. Between five hundred and one thousand deaf men and women lived within one square mile, most of them young and socially inclined. As one commentator explained, "You deaf who have no deaf friend within walking radius—much less one with your own likes and dislikes—think what that means."[68]

Goodyear officials promoted numerous social and recreational activities—company welfare initiatives—designed to build camaraderie and loyalty among their hearing and deaf workers. More than seventy-five deaf workers took advantage of college-preparatory classes in business English and mathematics offered at the Goodyear Institute in 1917. A. D. Martin, a tire finisher and graduate of Gallaudet College, obtained the backing of Goodyear and officials at Gallaudet to offer preparatory classes that would be recognized by the college. Students worked at Goodyear's first shift and studied in the evening. Many attended Gallaudet College during the year and worked at Goodyear during the summer. In return for their support, Goodyear acquired a highly educated, loyal deaf workforce.[69]

Organized sports between the deaf and hearing communities were common, and company-sponsored and independent teams competed in many venues. Basketball and bowling were both popular, but no team attracted more attention than the football team.[70] The Goodyear Silents football team was the pride of the deaf community between 1917 and 1922, as the team members established a regional reputation for their extraordinary prowess. Deaf residents poured out as a group for the games, often forming parades through the East Akron neighborhood as they made their way to the playing field. Folklore has it that few spectators actually watched the game, as they were distracted by the opportunity to sign with friends and make acquaintances in the crowded grandstands.[71]

The popularity of the Goodyear Silents sports teams highlights the importance of social outlets for deaf people who built a community in Akron, Ohio. Shown here is the men's basketball team.

Akron's deaf citizens built numerous organizations that offered a broad range of business, social, and philanthropic activities. These efforts centered on local, regional, and national concerns, as they also encompassed deaf and hearing worlds. Deaf Akronites organized and conducted their own worship services, produced and acted in dramas, danced at masquerade balls, viewed silent movies, held charity drives for needy elders, debated within local literary clubs, attended lectures, and reminisced at reunions. The Gallaudet College Alumni Association, the National Fraternal Society of the Deaf, and the NAD were represented in Akron by the largest and most active branches in the country.[72] Deaf residents also held drives to support the war effort, collecting funds and materials for soldiers and the Red Cross.[73] Is it any wonder that one individual, a deaf Native American from Okla-homa, moved to Akron just to join the city's community of citizens? Akron's deaf residents had built a rich, perhaps unparalleled, commu-nity life.[74]

As the international conflict that underlay the creation of Good-year's deaf workforce ended in November 1918, however, many work-ers wondered if the close of the war would bring an end to their jobs and community. For the next two years the status of the deaf work-force was uncertain as the city adjusted to a peacetime economy.[75] The deaf community was greatly heartened in early 1919 when the Fire-stone Corporation initiated a campaign to recruit deaf workers. Ben Schowe, an industrious recent graduate from Gallaudet College with experience as a machinist, was named to lead this effort.[76] Moreover, that winter, Goodyear officials announced their intention to establish a separate division for deaf workers.[77]

The summer of 1920 did not bring expansion, however, but the forced dissolution of the deaf community, as layoffs swept the city.[78] In July, Goodyear laid off 100 deaf workers and Firestone released 50. By September, less than a dozen men remained at Firestone and only 125 at Goodyear.[79] Amid these tumultuous changes, some residents clung to the hope that company officials would renew production.

But the layoffs were permanent. The expansion of Goodyear, Fire-stone, and Akron's factories had depended upon the unusual war-driven demand in the rubber products industry, and by 1920 this had collapsed.[80] Management at Goodyear and Firestone scaled back pro-duction and let go thousands of workers. Wages were cut and work hours increased for those who remained. When workers were rehired, company policies favored long-standing Akron residents. By the win-ter of 1921, the majority of Akron's deaf community had been forced to leave the city.[81] Even as the factories emptied, many deaf workers fought to retain the communal life that had drawn so many to the city. Several clusters of Akronites found work at other locations where they sought to recreate small colonies.[82] Some workers and families desperately tried to stay in Akron. Fifty employees volunteered to leave so other workers with families might be retained.[83] Despite these efforts, by the winter of 1921, the majority of Akron's deaf community had been forced to leave the city. The Silent Colony was no more.

Goodyear and Firestone attracted deaf workers with the promise of permanent work, solid wages, and a large deaf community.

The case of Thomas Blake, an NAD organizer and Goodyear employee, underscored the limits of the educational and occupational advances in Akron. Blake appeared before the 1920 NAD Convention, even as workers were being laid off at Goodyear, to argue that deaf adults were full participants in the national economy. In past economic hard times, deaf workers were typically advised by teachers and leaders to go "back to the farm." Those days, he concluded, were over.[84] But he spoke too soon. Following the layoffs, the editor of the *Ohio Chronicle* described the numerous requests he received from workers in search of employment. In an open letter to the readers of the newspaper, he advised unemployed deaf men to look for work as hired hands on small farms.[85]

Deaf citizens and hearing supporters in Akron and across the country optimistically argued that the industrial policies in the city would help create more jobs for deaf workers nationwide. Anecdotal reports from deaf leaders and commentators during the course of the war were favorable. Several reports identified large-scale firms whose managers wanted to hire deaf workers.[86] In the auto industry, deaf people were employed at plants across the Midwest and continued working at Ford.[87] In Connecticut, administrators in Bridgeport's Remington Arms Work announced in 1916 their interest in hiring an unlimited number of deaf employees.[88]

That a growing pool of employers hired deaf workers, however, did not mean that other employers had ceased to exclude deaf workers. Managers in Bridgeport's Winchester plant cited the fear of accidents and refused to hire deaf candidates. Indeed, in Akron itself, most reports confirmed the charges of local residents that the Goodrich Corporation never opened its doors to deaf workers.[89]

During the course of the war, several deaf commentators advanced proposals to limit the right of employers to bar deaf workers. J. Frederick Meagher, for example, demanded that the government require private firms to hire deaf employees as part of their federal contract, which was a proposal similar to that advanced by World War II-era African American labor leader A. Philip Randolph.[90] In 1917, another observer argued for the NAD to promote legislation to mandate the hiring of deaf workers at private companies.[91]

These commentators found no open expressions of support in the deaf community, however. Their proposals, like George Sawyer's innovative turn-of-the-century recommendation, appeared and disappeared, seemingly unnoticed. Although deaf leaders had never conceded the moral right of employers to prohibit deaf applicants from the workplace, they agreed, if only through inaction, that any public challenge to the legal rights of employers was ill conceived if not dangerous.[92]

Many deaf leaders and workers also hoped that the example of Akron's workers would also boost the number of sign language proponents. After all, management at Goodyear supported sign language by encouraging its use among employees and by hiring interpreters to facilitate communication between hearing and deaf personnel. Perhaps school officials would follow the lead of industry. As one observer from Alabama explained, "The deaf are indeed being 'restored to society' though not in the way some of our faddists expected. They are doing what all their educators with their multiplicity of methods could never do for them—working out their salvation industrially."[93] Certainly these results called into question any contention that oral skills assisted deaf workers in their daily lives. Nonetheless, there is no evidence that the example of Akron's Silent Colony influenced the ongoing educational conflict.

Sometime after Firestone and Goodyear had released their deaf employees, the editor of a midwestern newspaper for deaf readers cited the appearance of an advertisement recruiting deaf men and women for work in an industrial laundry. This announcement, the editor contended, was proof that deaf workers had succeeded in their longstanding efforts to enter industry.[94] After decades of debate and effort, though, this was not the industrial salvation that deaf adults in Akron or around the nation had desired. Unfortunately, even greater problems lay ahead for the country and for vulnerable deaf workers, as they soon became enmeshed in a national economic hardship of unparalleled severity and length.

6

"Conspiracy of Silence"

Contesting Exclusion and Oral Hegemony

The Great Depression brought widespread unemployment to forty thousand deaf adults and continued educational failure to fifteen thousand deaf students in the United States.[1] Economic downturn illuminated the inadequacies of vocational programs. Deaf people engaged in frustrating and often unsuccessful negotiations to secure work from either increasingly disinterested private employers or the recalcitrant state and federal officials who managed the era's governmental work programs. Deaf teachers and community leaders again sought to revamp technical instruction, and the continued determination of oralists to suppress sign language at public schools spurred broad and, in some instances, unprecedented opposition.

Efforts of deaf people to upgrade secondary-level vocational instruction were largely in vain in the 1930s.[2] Deaf teachers, although persistent, had little power now that their numbers had been reduced to less than 10 percent of the overall teaching force and less than half of all vocational instructors.[3] The frustrations of Iowa's J. Schuyler Long, one of the nation's few remaining deaf administrators, underscored this collective powerlessness. At the 1931 convention of school administrators, Long appealed to his hearing peers. "Do you know the world as the deaf man finds it?" he asked. "The place to test the success of an educational system is not in the schoolroom nor in the conversations over the social teacups," he explained, "but out where men toil and earn their daily bread."[4]

In addition to their efforts to upgrade vocational programs, deaf critics praised the few school administrators who successfully ex-

Some deaf activists used comics to illustrate the ironies and problems inherent in deaf education and deaf employment. Illustration by Byron Burnes for *Vocational Teachers* 2 (June 1931), p. 4.

panded instruction. For example, Edmund Boatner, superintendent of the American School for the Deaf, established courses in welding, mechanics, and typewriter repair beginning in 1938, despite severe budget constraints. In two years, school officials helped one hundred students, as well as nonmatriculating adults, find positions at area firms, including some that previously had been closed to deaf workers.[5]

The national economic downturn also undercut the efforts of deaf teachers to fulfill their long-standing goal of building an advanced institution for technical instruction.[6] Throughout the 1930s, scattered activists from across the nation put forward proposals for such a school.[7] The efforts of Peter Peterson, an instructor at Minnesota's residential school, revealed activists' limited influence. Rather than calling for a national effort as attempted by earlier activists, Peterson proposed that deaf leaders ask Henry Ford to underwrite establishment of a college. "All we need is a Moses to lead us through the wilderness," he claimed.[8]

Despite their continued inability to spur the establishment of accessible, advanced vocational instruction, deaf activists in several cities secured limited federal support for community-based programs where deaf adults studied basic vocational and general academic subjects. Between 1934 and 1937, for example, William Marra, a recent graduate of Gallaudet College, helped more than 2,500 of Kansas City's working adults strengthen their skills. One single mother enrolled after being fired from her factory position because of her poor writing skills, and was rehired after attending classes. These efforts, although limited in reach, underscored the unmet need for instruction for countless other deaf adults.[9]

Few deaf students of either gender received up-to-date instruction, but the situation of female deaf students was most troubling. Reiterating charges first put forward in the nineteenth century, deaf critics claimed that administrators continued to use female students to perform institutional tasks and reduce school expenses but did little to prepare them for employment.[10] Margaret McKellar, a Gallaudet College student, warned that without proper instruction most deaf women would be confined to "the vast army of unskilled laborers, doing household work, scrubbing floors, working in factories and laundries with small chances of ever advancing their standard of living."[11] These criticisms were confirmed in a 1933 survey of some 250 alumni from three dozen schools. Although the majority of respondents wanted to enter the paid workforce, they left school ill prepared because most never graduated.[12]

Deaf women found their employment restricted by formidable gender, economic, and racial barriers as well as by inadequate training.[13] Surveys consistently revealed that deaf women were usually segregated in marginal industrial positions. One study of former pupils of Indiana's residential school, for example, noted that most women were employed in menial positions at machine and laundry work.[14] Across the South, educational facilities for African American deaf students were poorly funded, if available at all. In Louisiana, for example, there was no school for deaf African Americans until 1938. The situation was even more perilous for African American women, whose status was scarcely acknowledged by educators. Given these constraints, most African American deaf women were consigned to work as domestic helpers or unskilled laborers.[15]

Ultimately, the status of vocational programs could not be separated from the ongoing conflict over communication methods. As the national economic downturn forced administrators to reduce their budgets, deaf leaders charged that oralist practices dangerously undercut vital vocational programs and the very standing of students. Warren Smaltz, the leader of the Pennsylvania Society for the Advancement of the Deaf, claimed that oralist administrators engaged in a "conspiracy of silence" regarding their failures.[16] Norman Scarvie, a vocational instructor at Iowa's residential school, was equally adamant. He charged that school officials neglected the "70 percent of our boys and girls who graduate out the back door."[17]

Irreconcilable differences continued to separate oralist administrators and deaf adults. Among the deaf community's activists, Roy Conkling, publisher of the independent newspaper *American Deaf Citizen,* may have been the decade's most persistent and prescient critic of oralist practices.[18] A graduate of the Ohio School for the Deaf and an alumnus of Gallaudet College, the undaunted Conkling wrote under the pen name Surdus Junius or "deaf warrior," to directly challenge the state's right to suppress sign language and mandate pure oral methods. The suppression of sign language, the ouster of deaf teachers, and the imposition of oral methods, he charged, had created "slave conditions" from which deaf adults would eventually liberate themselves.[19]

As in previous decades, deaf leaders challenged oralist practices and administrators at schools across the country. In Texas, Idaho, Virginia, Georgia, and Montana, the efforts of activists to defend sign language and combined methods or to halt the summary dismissal of deaf teachers met with limited success.[20] The Texas campaign merits examination for its successes as well as its failures. On the one hand, Lone Star activists gained widespread, perhaps unprecedented, support from both hearing and deaf adults in their politically sophisticated drive against the coercive superintendent of the state residential school. On the other hand, they were unable to muster broad support for their more compelling claim that the suppression of sign language undercut the intellectual development of children and often required coercive measures to be enforced.[21]

Deeply upset after meeting with students at the Texas School for the Deaf in the winter of 1937, leaders of the Texas Association of the Deaf initiated a campaign against Superintendent T. M. Scott. Scott was a political appointee who had presided over the Texas School for some fifteen years. Leo Lewis, president of the Texas Association, explained that he had visited with students in several classes and asked them if they understood the spoken communication of their teacher. "Not one knew. They are making mummies out of children, not educating them," he charged in an independent newspaper.[22]

Texas Association leaders knew that legislative support was vital if they were to oust Scott. After interviewing employees, former stu-

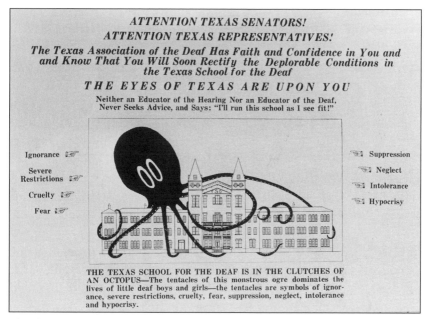

ATTENTION TEXAS SENATORS!
ATTENTION TEXAS REPRESENTATIVES!
The Texas Association of the Deaf Has Faith and Confidence in You and and Know That You Will Soon Rectify the Deplorable Conditions in the Texas School for the Deaf
THE EYES OF TEXAS ARE UPON YOU
Neither an Educator of the Hearing Nor an Educator of the Deaf, Never Seeks Advice, and Says: "I'll run this school as I see fit!"

Ignorance
Severe Restrictions
Cruelty
Fear

Suppression
Neglect
Intolerance
Hypocrisy

THE TEXAS SCHOOL FOR THE DEAF IS IN THE CLUTCHES OF AN OCTOPUS—The tentacles of this monstrous ogre dominates the lives of little deaf boys and girls—the tentacles are symbols of ignorance, severe restrictions, cruelty, fear, suppression, neglect, intolerance and hypocrisy.

The fight for the Texas School for the Deaf illustrates that the tradition of vigorous advocacy and action typically associated with contemporary deaf activists has longstanding routes in the deaf community. A variety of this announcement appeared in deaf journals across the country during 1939.

dents, and parents, activists forwarded charges to members of the Texas House Eleemosynary Committee who monitored the school. The charges accused Scott of dozens of violations, including refusing to meet with deaf parents, arbitrarily firing instructors, improperly expelling students, and allowing staff members to beat students.[23] "We are convinced our school is not fulfilling the purpose for which it is created," the Texas Association charged, "that instead it is confusing our heads, breaking our hearts, and tying our hands."[24]

State officials responded favorably. Alarmed by the breadth and severity of these accusations—especially the charges of physical punishment—members of the oversight committee began investigating Scott's efforts in 1938. State representatives interviewed Scott, Lewis, students, and parents, collecting hundreds of pages of testimony.[25] Brushing away the criticism, Scott assured state officials that 80 percent of his students could read lips.[26] "The sign language means nothing in the world to a deaf person, if they are taught the lipreading," he maintained.[27]

As Scott's fate hung in the balance, Texas Association leaders worked to strengthen their momentum. To this end, they held an emergency convention to enlist the support of former students, parents, and adults, and they circulated a petition calling for the removal of the superintendent.[28] Lewis also criticized school policies in the *Modern Silents*, the newspaper he published. Charging that widespread student resistance to oralism and the suppression of sign language forced supervisors to use physical force to maintain order, he asked pointedly: "Why the need for this doubled staff of nursemaids or whip wielders or whatever you choose to call them?" Texas Association leaders also presented the State Board of Control—the agency responsible for oversight of the school—with an extraordinary, even unprecedented document: a petition, with more than 7,500 names, demanding Scott's resignation. There was no doubt that the state's deaf citizens, joined by deaf and hearing supporters from outside the state, were united in their resolve to change the situation.[29]

This determined and well-documented drive had revealed Scott as an expendable embarrassment. In December 1938, the state's House Eleemosynary Committee held new hearings in which parents and students once again criticized school management.[30] Students at the

Texas School for the Deaf—in a demonstration suggestive of the protests that would shut down Gallaudet University half a century later—boycotted classes and marched to the state capitol to protest.[31] In early 1939, members of the State Board of Control agreed to appoint a new superintendent.

The deaf community's victory, although remarkable, was not complete. Scott's ouster greatly lessened the climate of coercion, and his successor invited members of the Texas Association and parents to the school for consultation.[32] Still, these substantive changes did not signal a rejection by state officials or hearing parents of oral-centered practices. Although Texas Association leaders supported the combined method and recommended that all teachers be fluent in sign language, they declined to press these positions, lest the focus be shifted away from Scott. Officials ended the physical and psychological abuses of the Scott administration, but there is no indication that hearing parents or officials agreed with deaf adults that pure oralist practices were themselves abusive.

In this period, along with their efforts to upgrade and transform education, deaf people continued to fight mightily to strengthen their individual and collective employment. Between 1928 and 1933, the nation's deaf working men and women had no effective national organization to help them. At the NAD, the administrations of Arthur Roberts (1923–30) and Franklin Smileau (1930–33) directed only cursory attention to employment issues for most deaf working men and women.[33] The cost of this inattention was registered in the winter of 1930–31 when the organization offered no response to the summary exclusion of deaf men from a public work project that employed twenty thousand men in New York City.[34] Amid these troubles, it was not surprising that some critics wondered if the venerable organization would survive the national economic downturn.[35] Unlike the weakened NAD, the National Fraternal Society of the Deaf (NFSD) had a broad membership base with more than seven thousand members in 1931. (The NFSD is described in detail in chapter 7.) Yet Arthur Roberts, president from 1931 through 1951, kept the powerful organization centered upon its traditional fiduciary responsibilities and turned away any proposals to expand its mission.[36] As the economy grew worse, anxious deaf workers turned to their local and state organizations.

Despite their limited means, deaf men and women organized through existing community institutions to help the neediest deaf adults and their families. Akron residents gave food and money through local social groups. Houston citizens channeled support through the NFSD branch and churches with deaf congregations. New Jersey NAD members gave food and coal to deaf residents.[37] Still, these efforts did little to stem the unemployment that stymied increasing numbers of deaf adults.[38] By 1932, for example, more than 40 percent of three hundred deaf people surveyed in Maryland were unemployed.[39] By the spring of 1933, deaf citizens, like their hearing peers, turned to the newly elected president for assistance.

After Franklin Roosevelt triumphed in the 1932 presidential election, deaf adults and NAD officers individually petitioned the federal government to encourage private employers to hire deaf workers. Frank Thompson, an unemployed printer, sent General Hugh Johnson, the chief of the newly established National Recovery Administration (NRA), a ten-page letter that recounted his failed efforts to find work. Thompson closed by conceding that he had recently been forced to become a street peddler.[40]

Deaf petitioners' requests for assistance raised substantive issues for the Roosevelt administration. Was the government prepared to regulate private employers? If the government acted on behalf of deaf workers, what would be the implications for other groups of workers? Not surprisingly, the administration backed away from the simple but potentially innovative requests of its deaf petitioners.[41] Rather than questioning the traditional prerogatives of private employers, the administration embarked upon an unparalleled campaign to provide federally sponsored work for millions of unemployed adults. Deaf adults then demanded a place in the varied work programs of the New Deal and before long, the acronyms CCC, for Civilian Conservation Corps, and WPA, for Works Progress Administration, were added to the fingerspelled lexicon of American Sign Language.

The admission of deaf applicants to the CCC seemed assured because thousands had already proven themselves at the demanding physical labor envisioned by the corps.[42] As more than two million adults and families traversed the United States in search of food and work in the spring of 1933, administrators from the Departments of Agriculture, Interior, War, and Labor hastily established CCC rural work camps throughout the country. Entrance requirements were straightforward: applicants needed to be free from physical conditions that would make it "impossible or inadvisable to attempt hard physical labor in the forests."[43] Although they clearly seemed eligible, deaf applicants were uniformly refused admission to the CCC. Between 1933 and 1942, more than two million American men labored in the nation's forests and parks, but not one tree was felled or one mile of trail cleared by a deaf man.[44]

Through the Depression, deaf applicants and hearing supporters from around the country organized to challenge CCC administrators.[45] William Allen sought entry and wrote to Robert Fechner, the head of the corps, to argue that the CCC's exclusion was yet another example of unfair treatment, because deaf men had often been the first to be let go from their jobs. The Oklahoma resident charged that many families had lost their homes and most men were "barely eking out a scanty living . . . roaming the country looking for work."[46] Ignatius Bjorlee, the superintendent of the Maryland School for the Deaf, was likely the most persistent CCC critic.[47] A hearing graduate of Gallaudet College who was raised with deaf brothers, the perceptive Bjorlee debated with CCC administrators and Congress between 1935 and 1940 in a dogged campaign to roll back the exclusionary policy. He thought the exclusion to be baseless. "[S]ociety was perfectly willing to absorb the deaf in practically all lines of activity when there was a shortage of labor," he explained, "but with this shortage removed we are given to understand that the deaf, because of their handicap, are incompetent to do those things which they were doing in a most satisfactory manner prior to the present labor crisis."[48]

Never successfully altered, the CCC's exclusionary policy provides a case study of the ways that hearing officials relied upon stereotype and self-interest to dismiss deaf demands for equal treatment. CCC administrators typically responded to critics by claiming that deaf men posed undue accident risks,[49] although they never provided data to support their contention.[50] In fact, program leaders flatly rejected proposals from officials in Minnesota and Mississippi that the CCC cosponsor trial camps to provide such data.[51] Some CCC administrators also stereotyped deaf adults as inadequate workers, suggesting that prejudice was at the heart of their reluctance to accept them in their programs. At one congressional hearing, CCC officials ridiculed the prospect of employing deaf men by countering that they were not running an "asylum."[52] Ultimately, though, bureaucratic self-interest rather than intractable prejudice was probably the greatest impediment to deaf applicants. In April 1935, Fechner conceded that deaf men could work at some positions but further explained that their admission would likely encourage other "handicapped" groups to demand inclusion. Expansion of the CCC workforce to include these *other* groups, he insisted, would be a "real menace" to safety.[53]

Deaf adults might have been included in the corps if Fechner and other administrators had not misrepresented them as afflicted and undesirable hazards but rather had accorded them the status of other minority groups. For example, CCC administrators established projects for almost one hundred thousand Native Americans and were pressured into including African Americans into camps.[54]

Fortunately, all New Deal administrators did not share the actions and attitudes of CCC personnel. The WPA admitted deaf workers, but the workers often had to negotiate with inexperienced and misinformed officials who doubted deaf workers' ability to be integrated successfully into the massive and diverse jobs program.[55] Founded in May 1935, the WPA employed roughly two million men, women, and students, including an undetermined number of deaf adults.[56] The scope of conflicts between deaf participants and WPA administrators first came to light in 1937 when Marcus Kenner, NAD president, was deluged by letters after he asked deaf adults to report instances of unfair treatment.[57]

In fact, deaf leaders around the nation often met with local, state, and district administrators to challenge cases of exclusion or to increase the number of the types of positions open to deaf workers.[58] In Akron, for example, deaf leaders Kreigh Ayers and Ben Schowe had to convince the local administrator that deaf workers were fit for even the most elementary work projects. After several meetings in which Schowe and Ayers cited the many positions successfully mastered by deaf men and women in the city's factories and businesses, the administrator conceded she had acted hastily and agreed to incorporate deaf workers.[59]

The contradictory administration of state and federal relief programs corroded relations between deaf leaders and state and federal officials. On the one hand, New Deal initiatives assisted hundreds, perhaps thousands, of deaf men and women by providing them with varied, if limited, employment opportunities. On the other hand, the pattern of individual discrimination and wholesale exclusion greatly troubled wary deaf leaders, some of whom concluded that arbitrary administrators turned away competent deaf adults almost as readily as they provided assistance.

Vulnerable deaf workers and leaders increasingly worried about the heightened influence of these governmental administrators as the nation's economy continued to tumble through the 1930s. That deaf workers had to enlighten hearing adults about their schooling, training, and abilities was not at all new. The growing number of work programs, however, seemed to greatly magnify the influence of often misinformed professionals. Deaf adults, worried Iowa's Tom Anderson, were now "at the mercy of the 'welfare worker,' the 'placement officer,' or anyone clothed with some fancy title and charged with finding jobs." The prospect of this dependence greatly troubled otherwise independent deaf adults, perhaps as much as their economic worries.[60]

Anderson's concerns about the dangers of relying on uninformed professionals were well founded—at least according to job seekers in New York City. In the fall of 1933, deaf adults had initially welcomed Margarette Hemle, who had been hired by area schools to assist deaf alumni in finding work.[61] Inexperienced with deaf adults and unable to sign, however, Hemle faced the formidable task of securing jobs for graduates as well as the stream of adults who turned to her for assistance.[62] Within a year, angry critics charged that she pressured deaf applicants into accepting subminimum wage positions.[63] Federal advocates had established this wage category—set at 75 percent of the standard minimum wage—as an inducement to employers to hire disabled workers.[64] Deaf leaders, who did not see deaf workers as disabled, initially paid little attention to the subminimum wage issue until complaints about Hemle's practices were exposed.[65] Deaf workers so resented their consignment to poorly paid positions that they dubbed their meager paychecks the "Hemle wage scale."[66] Although the exact number of poorly compensated workers is not known, Hemle met with more than 1,500 job seekers between 1933 and 1940.[67]

Damaging actions by federal and state administrators and a fear of dependence spurred most deaf leaders to oppose direct federal financial assistance to deaf adults, such as that available to visually-impaired citizens. The Social Security Act of 1935, for example, funded sheltered workshops and pensions for blind and visually-impaired citizens considered incapable of securing regular employment.[68] Deaf leaders not only faulted these initiatives, but they intermittently chided recipients of this support.[69]

Deaf people's critiques of special assistance programs for disabled persons were both incisive and troubling. Deaf leaders understood that schooling and the chance to demonstrate their skills were more important than cash payments that lifted recipients from poverty but left in place its root causes. Equally important, deaf leaders and some blind activists feared that state and private employers would seize upon pensions or special programs as evidence that they had no responsibility to alter discriminatory practices. However, these criticisms, although sometimes insightful and rooted in a positive ethos of "independent citizenship," failed to fully consider or appreciate the plight of workers with disabilities.[70]

Negative relations with governmental agencies also undermined innovative proposals that federal officials provide guaranteed jobs for deaf adults. In 1934 and again in 1937, newspaper publisher Willard Wood asked the president and Eleanor Roosevelt to establish a printing plant to be managed by deaf employees.[71] Marcus Kenner, NAD president from 1934 to 1940, was the most prominent proponent of mandated employment, and in 1937 he asked FDR to establish government jobs for deaf workers.[72] Similarly, in 1938, New Jersey resident David Davidowitz called for legislation to establish mandated jobs for deaf workers and for all adults with disabilities.[73] Outright opposition to these ideas circulated quickly throughout the deaf community, though, and they soon disappeared from the pages of newspapers. Most deaf leaders strongly disavowed any ties with disabled workers, and they were increasingly angry with government administrators.

As deaf people debated the possibilities and pitfalls of government employment, various state investigations revealed private employers' resistance to hiring deaf workers was growing as the Depression continued.[74] A 1937 survey, for example, indicated that 60 of 150 employers from Milwaukee would not hire deaf applicants regardless of the circumstances.[75] Furthermore, among the companies surveyed by the Indiana Association of the Deaf in 1936, one manager explained that the past successes of deaf industrial workers were irrelevant: he would turn away deaf applicants as long as there was a surplus of hearing workers.[76]

Underemployment was common among those deaf women and men who were able to find jobs in the 1930s. The decade's only national survey—a study of ten thousand hard of hearing and deaf women and men completed in 1934—indicated that nearly half of all respondents were unemployed.[77] Among job holders, however, 40 percent of men and 50 percent of women held unskilled or semiskilled positions that required no formal schooling and from which there was little chance to advance.[78]

The major thrust of efforts by deaf activists to secure more and better employment for workers during the Depression focused on expanding access to the private sector through the establishment of state-based labor bureaus.[79] They threw themselves into bureau drives in more than a dozen states.[80] Although deaf activists in New York were unable to establish a separate bureau for deaf workers, their campaign is particularly interesting because of their efforts to challenge oralist hegemony and command new communication rights for working adults. Organized by Jack Ebin and the revitalized Empire State Association, deaf people in New York state worked to establish a separate division within the Department of Labor to be staffed by professionals fluent in sign language.[81] Moreover, in an innovative effort to win recognition as a linguistic minority group—a position championed by deaf activists in the 1980s and 1990s—Ebin argued that deaf adults, by virtue of their facility in sign language, should be considered a minority-language group. Sign language, bureau proponents maintained, was indispensable to communicating with placement officers and ensuring proper job placements.

With this insistence that sign language be the medium of communication, activists implicitly rejected a role subordinate to state personnel. Deaf adults typically had been restricted to communication methods chosen by hearing professionals—for example, in the frustrating meetings individual job petitioners had with Margarette Hemle—but now they demanded the right to communicate in a language that provided them with the best opportunity for full expression. In so doing, they also challenged the legitimacy of oralist precepts. Deaf New Yorkers were able to secure legislative support for their initiatives, but they desperately needed the endorsement of leadership in the Department of Labor and the influential Temporary State Commission (TSC), then investigating the provision of state services for deaf and hard of hearing children and adults.[82] The commission had no deaf members, however, and it was dominated by hearing politicians, educators, and oralist medical personnel. Not surprisingly, the TSC dismissed the initiative. Department of Labor administrators even insisted state personnel need not learn sign language because deaf workers did not ask employers to develop such proficiency. In the end, oralist beliefs prevailed in the workplace and in the provision of state services: deaf adults had to accommodate the linguistic methods of the hearing majority.[83]

Deaf activists still remained united in their conviction that labor bureaus should undermine oralist rule and assist deaf workers, but they were increasingly divided over whether to demand independent bureaus or to align with state vocational rehabilitation services that had been developing since the World War I era. Such an association would entail closer ties to adults with disabilities and to oralist-oriented medical professionals, but it also promised access to a wider array of resources.

In the 1930s, the Michigan Association of the Deaf attempted to revitalize long-standing efforts to establish a labor bureau for the state's three thousand deaf adults. Both economic need and a desire to separate the deaf community from other adults with disabilities spurred this effort.[84] Michigan's deaf leadership opposed association with other groups of people with disabilities, one bureau proponent explained, because such a relationship undermined deaf workers' claim that they needed only the opportunity to demonstrate their abilities in the workplace.[85] The Michigan Association's strategy was politically astute. It emphasized the need to educate employers regarding deaf workers and avoided expressing dissatisfaction with current state services. In this way, campaigners gained the backing of state political and labor leaders without antagonizing state vocational rehabilitation officials. As a result, in the spring of 1937, Michigan legislators unanimously voted their support, and Michigan established a bureau for deaf workers, staffed by Jay Cooke Howard, the skilled former NAD president.[86]

High unemployment and dissatisfaction with state services also spurred Pennsylvania's deaf people into action during the Depression.[87] Organized by the powerful Pennsylvania Society for the Advancement of the Deaf (PSAD), which had an estimated one thousand members, the legislative drive was centered on expanding existing state services but at the same time accommodating state personnel. Vocational rehabilitation assistance had been available to Pennsylvania residents since 1919, but it was directed toward veterans, industrial accident victims, and groups with disabilities—not toward deaf adults. Such services were finally made available to deaf people in 1932, but relatively few deaf adults availed themselves of these opportunities.[88]

Pennsylvania's deaf leaders believed that expanding state services would provide the broadest vocational and educational training opportunities to deaf people. Unlike deaf leadership in some other states, they never contended that linkage with other disabled groups would undermine the representation of deaf people as diverse and talented workers. Instead, as in New York, they sought administrative and legislative support for hiring job placement workers fluent in sign language.

Pennsylvania's leaders engineered a vigorous campaign that drew its effectiveness from the deaf community's internal strength.[89] A cascade of letters, telegrams, and petitions produced by deaf residents at the height of the drive in 1937 impressed seasoned state politicians.[90] This demonstration of mass support overcame any opposition state bureaucrats or legislators may have harbored regarding hiring personnel familiar with sign language. In May 1937, state residents celebrated legislation that authorized the hiring of four job placement specialists for deaf and hard of hearing adults.[91] By 1938, employment specialists consulted with deaf adults across the commonwealth.[92] Working directly with state vocational rehabilitation services, deaf Pennsylvanians had established a new model that would serve as a blueprint for other states in the coming years.

By the end of the 1930s, nearly all bureaus—and a growing number of services for deaf adults—were uneasily dovetailed into state vocational rehabilitation programs for disabled groups. At the 1940 NAD convention, leaders including Marcus Kenner, Tom Anderson, Warren Smaltz, and Petra Fandrem urged deaf people to take advantage of these changes and to use vocational rehabilitation services.[93] Many adults nonetheless remained apprehensive about too strong a linkage between the deaf community and people with disabilities. Unable to control the nature or terms of much needed assistance, they continued to slight their association with other "handicapped" adults and a greater reliance on the state.

Despite the addition of two new state bureaus in the 1930s, the nation's small number of deaf labor bureaus was vulnerable. The bureaus served as poorly funded outposts that never approximated the ambitions of their supporters.[94] More important, the limited assistance provided by these bureaus could not fully compensate for the broad educational and vocational deficiencies that hampered most deaf adults in their search for meaningful and remunerative employment. At the close of the decade, few working adults thought the future looked bright.

Most deaf students and adults existed in a perilous position throughout the Depression. Many educational problems were so widespread that they seemed insurmountable. Vocational and academic instruction generally was inadequate as industrial changes and budget cutbacks frustrated the most progressive administrators. In the classroom, oralist ideology and practices were weakened but not thwarted by the episodic challenges presented by deaf adults and their few hearing supporters. Not surprisingly, amid the national economic downturn, deaf leaders and hearing professionals scarcely addressed inferior instruction for females or students of color. Even outside of these two groups, however, only a tiny percentage of such students graduated and advanced to Gallaudet College, and a small minority secured positions as trained artisans. Most female students and many of their male peers left school bound for marginal industrial, agricultural, and domestic positions.

Deaf adults also clashed with state and private employers over their rights and identity. Evidence from New Deal agencies, state labor bureaus, and private-sector surveys demonstrates that the most common obstacle deaf applicants faced may have been the refusal of government officials and private employers to hire them. Challenging private-sector exclusion presented deaf workers with often insurmountable difficulties. Constrained by their determination to rely upon strategies whose effectiveness depended upon the goodwill of prospective employers, deaf leaders had few tools at their disposal. Determined to maintain a portrait of competence among would-be employers, leaders rejected efforts to mandate either state or private employment or even to argue openly that deaf people had a right to a job. Such programs and claims, they believed, implied that deaf adults were incapable of succeeding and *needed* protections such as those provided for "handicapped" workers. Instead, most leaders worked to educate reluctant employers through labor bureaus. When existing bureaus fell short of their creators' inflated or poorly examined expectations, however, deaf workers had no effective mechanism to challenge their exclusion.

At the end of the 1930s, the ongoing unequal association between private employer and deaf petitioner remained a primary cause of unemployment and hardship among deaf women and men. This imbalanced relationship would be leveled and the status of deaf working women and men elevated—or so it seemed—during World War II.

7

"To Stand on Their Own"

Looking to the Future

World War II ushered in an era of unparalleled industrial opportunity for the nation's sixty thousand deaf workers, who were suddenly in demand.[1] As one acerbic deaf commentator noted, "[t]he deaf come into their rights only when the world is in a midst of a terrible human holocaust."[2] Almost from the outset, deaf people were aware that the war would not continue forever and looked ahead to the postwar era. In 1942, Arthur Roberts, president of the National Fraternal Society of the Deaf (NFSD) worried that industrial leaders would exclude deaf employees after the war. He asked if it would take an "interplanetary eruption" to convince future employers that deaf adults were capable workers.[3]

Between 1941 and 1946, in the midst of wartime prosperity, deaf Americans participated in a divisive debate over strategies for sustaining their economic position after the war. They contested three points in particular: (1) whether to join other citizens with disabilities who also sought a stable position in the private work force, (2) whether to support federal intervention to secure private-sector jobs, and (3) whether to have the federal government assume supervision of the nation's uneven and incomplete system of vocational training and general education for deaf people. The debates waged and decisions made during this pivotal period deeply influenced deaf students and workers for decades afterward.

Conservative deaf leaders opposed federal intervention in the private sector. Akron's Ben Schowe, chairman of the Industrial Committee of the National Association of the Deaf (NAD), argued that deaf adults put themselves at risk by relying on state or federal agencies and administrators, and noted that during the Depression government administrators had hindered deaf workers almost as much as they had helped. If deaf workers were to advance, he argued, they needed to bypass government and educate business leaders to see that it was in their interest to hire deaf applicants.[4] In short, the model of industrial employment demonstrated in Akron during World War I should be used for the nation as a whole.[5] As the United States edged toward war in 1941, Jay Cooke Howard, leader of the recently established bureau for deaf workers in Michigan, sided with Schowe, adding that federal intervention could drive away friendly employers who would misinterpret their activity as evidence that deaf adults needed state protection and were incapable of succeeding on their own.[6]

At the other end of the spectrum, a small contingent of deaf leaders and individuals demanded federal intervention on behalf of deaf workers. Leaders of New York's Empire State Association of the Deaf (ESA) were among the first to petition the Roosevelt administration, writing to the president and federal agencies to demand that training opportunities and employment programs include deaf adults.[7] In late June 1941, Roosevelt established the Fair Employment Practices Committee (FEPC), a council mandated to prohibit discrimination by all federal agencies, unions, and companies engaged in war-related work. At the same time, an entrepreneur with an all-deaf workforce urged the government to mandate that federal contracts be directed to firms with deaf workers.[8]

By the fall of 1941, another deaf adult urged the deaf community to practice the vigorous activism exemplified by A. Philip Randolph and other African Americans whose efforts had been pivotal in establishing the FEPC. Denver resident Richard Fraser wrote to NAD president Thomas Anderson urging him to mobilize members and demand that Roosevelt "open the Defense doors to the Deaf" as he had done for African Americans. However, he warned, "we can expect hard times after the war is over. No doubt of it."[9]

Several individuals from outside the deaf community also called for deaf people to align with disabled Americans and to pressure the federal government and industry into providing employment. One day before the nation entered the war, for example, Anderson received a letter from H. Jay McMahon, a private citizen who had recently lost a leg, urging him to link the NAD to workers with disabilities and to spearhead a national publicity drive.[10]

McMahon was not alone in endorsing an alliance of deaf adults and other people with disabilities. Harvey Barnes, an instructor at the residential school in Illinois, also urged Anderson to endorse a coalition of people with disabilities. He argued that only by acting in concert with other groups of marginalized workers would deaf people ever secure fair employment: "In small groups, as with individuals, we remain comparatively helpless, limited, and weak . . . but through the joining of groups we become powerful and whole."[11]

Anderson dismissed these proposals, however. He told Denver's Richard Fraser, for example, that the nation's few deaf citizens had little political power and suggested that he work with vocational rehabilitation officials rather than challenging the president.[12] His reluctance to act also reflected his ongoing involvement in contentious negotiations regarding these issues. In fact, by the winter of 1941, Anderson was determined to rely upon traditional educational approaches in any employment drive and was adamantly opposed to association with other people with disabilities.

Anderson's position was fixed during a series of negotiations with Paul A. Strachan during the fall of 1941.[13] A recently deafened political organizer, Strachan wrote to Anderson in early September to offer his services. Although he confessed "an amazing ignorance upon most matters affecting the deaf," he provided impressive references from union and congressional leaders as well as from organizations for veterans with physical disabilities. He also stated he would help the NAD build a national headquarters in Washington, D.C., and establish a federal bureau to facilitate the employment of deaf workers.[14]

Strachan's proposal greatly heartened Anderson because it seemed to resolve intractable problems. His suggestion paralleled the long-desired goal of the NAD leadership to expand the chronically weak organization. If an arrangement could be made, the NAD and deaf adults would attain an unparalleled level of influence. An introspective Anderson wrote to Marcus Kenner, a former NAD president: "You know and I know that we are next to helpless writing letters of protest, knowing so little as we do of the real ropes which a professional knows how to pull."[15]

The timing also was favorable. By mid-1941, NAD leaders including Anderson, Kenner, and Schowe had come to a dead end in their efforts to gain support for a federal labor bureau comparable to those established in Michigan and Minnesota.[16] Congressional support was nearly nonexistent, and both the Department of Labor and the Roosevelt administration opposed a federal bureau.[17] Without a regular presence in Washington or a visible national profile, the NAD had little influence.

Strachan favored the creation of a bureau for deaf workers—but only as one element in a series of measures. He called for the NAD to launch a broad campaign, including a national publicity drive, a congressional investigation of government hiring policies, and an alliance with other organizations that represented hard of hearing adults.[18] As a seasoned insider, he understood that only a comprehensive, vigorous drive had any chance of being taken seriously in a capitol increasingly fixated upon the international conflict. If the NAD was to achieve its goals, he explained to Anderson, it would have to "run like hell just in order to stand still."[19]

The wary Anderson tried to rein in the zealous organizer. Although he did not question Strachan's political acumen, he knew the threadbare NAD had neither the money nor people to initiate any bold measures. Besides, he would not commit any of the NAD's meager resources without learning more about Strachan. He arranged a meeting between the organizer and NAD leaders and advisors, where Strachan advanced even more ambitious proposals, including an expansion of the NAD to serve all adults with hearing losses and a provision that the proposed national labor bureau monitor educational practices at all state schools.[20] These proposals, if enacted, would transform the venerable organization and improve schooling nationwide.[21]

Strachan's visionary arguments spurred hurried consultations between Anderson and meeting participants. Percival Hall and Ignatius Bjorlee, both hearing educational administrators, opposed federal oversight of schools, claiming that school superintendents were better judges of educational affairs.[22] Moreover, Hall worried that the "independence" of deaf adults was at risk if they relied upon broader federal assistance. Only New York's Kenner supported Strachan, describing the potential expansion of the NAD as a "stupendous undertaking" and the association with hard of hearing adults as positive.[23]

From Washington, D.C., Strachan besieged Anderson with lengthy defenses of his claims, criticisms of his detractors, and dramatic entreaties that Anderson rally deaf adults. He condemned Hall's views as unduly conservative, explaining that federal assistance had already strengthened the economic base and personal independence of women, farmers, and union members. It was time, he asserted, for deaf adults to claim their due.[24] Strachan was right: the international conflict created a labor shortage that temporarily provided deaf and other disabled workers with heightened leverage to demand measures that would prohibit employment discrimination. Finally, Strachan conveyed a prescient warning, since affirmed by history: "If we do not do this, now while the cards are stacked favorable to us," he cautioned, "we probably will not be able to do it, in the next fifty years."[25]

Ironically, Strachan's demands hardened Anderson's resolve to move cautiously. Although he admired Strachan's grand visions, he showed little independent enthusiasm to enlarge the NAD so quickly. Rather than expand his vision to complement Strachan's, Anderson simply shelved the campaign to expand the NAD and asked the organizer only to help establish a national labor bureau—the NAD's original goal.[26]

Once again, Strachan leaped ahead of Anderson to advance even more ambitious proposals. He angrily lashed out, charging that Anderson's failure to revamp the NAD would deeply hurt deaf workers because Congress would block any effort to establish a labor bureau that did not embrace all organizations and individuals with hearing losses. He charged that even broader coalitions were in fact necessary for deaf and other minority groups to advance. He asked Anderson to help promote a National Advisory Council that would include representatives from industry, union, veterans', and women's groups. Finally, he explained that he was determined to organize not only deaf adults, but all the "physically handicapped" of the country, explaining he would forge ahead, "come hell or high water"—with or without the NAD.[27] That was enough for Anderson, who by early November notified supporters that he had severed ties with Strachan and abandoned the labor bureau drive.[28]

What went wrong? Why had a seemingly promising association turned sour? Most important, why did Anderson turn away from the chance to build the NAD and likely strengthen the status of deaf workers? Certainly Strachan's forceful manner complicated relations with him. Arrogant and impatient, Strachan openly criticized Anderson and past NAD leaders within weeks of their initial exchange. Yet although these outbursts angered Anderson, they did not cause their split.

As noted previously, financial pressures and organizational problems impeded the NAD's ability to assume any new responsibilities.[29] Composed of shifting local branches with an uncertain membership, the NAD was overshadowed by several more powerful state organizations.[30] Moreover, the scale and speed of Strachan's proposals had unsettled the politically inexperienced leadership.

Profound strategic and historical differences also divided Anderson and Strachan. Anderson understood that expanding the NAD to include hard of hearing individuals and their organizations likely threatened the organization's rationale and identity. Since its inception in 1880, the primary issue uniting NAD members and deaf adults had been their defense of sign language and their identity as an extended community. Oralist proponents, on the other hand, dominated organizations for hard of hearing people. Not surprisingly, Anderson thought it utterly illogical to invite likely adversaries into the already weak NAD.

The recently deafened Strachan apparently was unaware of these underlying differences. In a final letter to Strachan, Anderson explained he simply could not lead the NAD into a coalition in which a larger group unsympathetic to their interests could dominate them.[31] The NAD was, at its core, a cultural organization. By refusing to have the venerable group become one part of a larger political entity, Anderson sought to protect the language and autonomy of the deaf community and the wellspring of deaf culture—safeguarding, if only through inaction, the unifying principles embraced by nearly all deaf leaders before him.

Strachan and Anderson also held incompatible views regarding the responsibilities of deaf adults and the proper role of the state in assisting adults to find work. Neither leader accepted the right of private employers to exclude deaf workers, yet Anderson never endorsed Strachan's demand that the federal government define rights for deaf workers and outlaw discrimination. Instead, Anderson, like Schowe, maintained that repeated demonstrations of ability by deaf workers could convert discriminatory employers. More important, he believed that most groups turned to the state only when they were unable to "stand on their own."[32] In other words, he worried that establishing additional federal assistance could undermine the commitment of individuals to be "independent," self-supporting citizens. In a frank and angry letter to Kenner, written after he severed ties with Strachan, Anderson confided that it was best for the NAD to simply "forget the Government hand-out."[33]

Finally, in December 1941, Anderson believed that legislation to protect the rights of deaf workers was unnecessary. As the country went to war and hundreds of thousands of men enlisted or were drafted, private industry desperately looked to fill the nation's depleted work force. Strachan's demands that activists promptly secure legislation seemed alarmist.[34] World War I had enabled deaf men and women in Akron to enjoy unparalleled advances. In a terrible and even tragic irony, perhaps World War II would provide comparable opportunities to deaf adults nationwide. At the onset of war, observers once again looked to Akron, Ohio, where deaf adults soon reconstituted a thriving community whose employment and social opportunities attracted migrants from around the nation.

At first, only a small number of deaf adults secured positions at Goodyear and Firestone.[35] By the winter of 1942, some 300 deaf men and women produced war-related products.[36] The Goodyear Corporation then launched a national drive for deaf workers in the spring of 1942. Managers at Goodyear Aircraft Corporation (GYAC), a newly created adjunct branch industry, needed one thousand workers— hearing and deaf, male and female—each month. While company officials recruited students at Gallaudet College, Kreigh Ayers, prominent among workers during the World War I era, recruited more workers from the Midwest and elsewhere.[37] By 1944 more than one thousand deaf people had joined more than seventy thousand hearing workers in rubber and another thirty thousand in GYAC-related production.[38]

Managers at Firestone and Goodyear employed special but simple measures to ensure the rapid and successful training and integration of their deaf employees. Instead of spoken lectures poorly suited for deaf employees, staff relied upon thorough demonstrations at the job site. At Goodyear, sign language interpreters helped train groups of deaf workers to assume positions in manufacturing and assembly, and hearing supervisors were informed in advance when deaf workers were to be integrated into their units. Goodyear's director of training concluded that deaf applicants possessed an "unusual ability" to understand new material and methods, and apart from the changes in the "break-in" period, deaf workers neither requested nor received special attention.[39]

Deaf men and women demonstrated their skills at a wide array of semiskilled, skilled, and professional positions, and they earned positive appraisals from their supervisors.[40] Like their hearing counterparts, most of the deaf employees labored at semiskilled manufacturing and assembly positions and men enjoyed better access to a greater range of positions than women.[41] A small number of deaf adults also worked in professional positions as machinists, business researchers, draft persons, and scientists. A few deaf adults—including Fred Schreiber, who would go on to lead the NAD—overcame the resistance of hearing managers and became successful supervisors.[42] After all, graduates of Gallaudet College often enjoyed more formal schooling than their hearing peers.[43]

Akron's deaf residents again created a flourishing community of social, cultural, civic, and recreational organizations outside the workplace. An overflow meeting at a local auditorium prompted deaf residents to build a social club whose benefits, dances, and film presentations often drew several thousand deaf adults from across the state and region.[44] In addition to social activities, deaf citizens launched a wide range of civic enterprises. Deaf women, in particular, formed clubs and led numerous efforts that brought together the city's residents; many citizens attended charity events to support the nation's only facility for sick and elderly deaf adults owned and managed by

Firestone offered men and women of all skill levels and ages the opportunity for career training and advancement during World War II. Opposite page at top, Ruby T. Corey manufactures parts for anti-aircraft guns. Opposite page, bottom, a Firestone advertisement encouraging deaf workers to apply for jobs in Akron. Above, students at the Ohio School for the Deaf fingerspell v-i-c-t-o-r-y.

deaf citizens; Lois Hume's persistent and persuasive efforts brought hundreds of new members into the NAD; graduates of Gallaudet College built up their alumni organization; and the local NFSD branch grew in size.[45] Furthermore, Art Kruger presided over a basketball tournament that drew players from around the country and culminated in the first national organization open to African American as well as white deaf participants.[46] As an illustration of their diversity, pride, and humor, residents quipped that ASL was an abbreviation for *Akron Sign Language,* not American Sign Language.[47]

The advances enjoyed by deaf workers in Akron were not unique. After decades of complaints about inadequate placement assistance at schools, many deaf students and adults attended federally-funded training and placement programs at residential schools. Indeed, in 1940, children and adults in Michigan and New York attended school-based training programs organized by the Office of Education and the

United States Employment Service (USES).[48] By January 1942, observers in Alabama reported that all deaf students had jobs before they completed school;[49] at Ohio's residential school, deaf teachers consulted with officials from local industries in order to assure the entry of deaf students and adults into their establishments.[50]

Moreover, in a reversal of positions scarcely conceivable before the war, deaf adults—like hearing women—found themselves recruited by employers. Listeners were likely surprised at a radio announcement that hundreds of jobs were available to "handicapped women" as well as women "completely sound of limb, sight, and hearing."[51] Although that announcer asked listeners to convey this information to their deaf acquaintances, Loy Golladay, a deaf leader in Connecticut, could not help wondering whether newspapers would soon print advertisements recruiting *blind* workers.[52]

Thousands of deaf adults congregated around large industries scattered around the country as the war continued through 1942 and into 1943. In some instances, they labored with other workers with various disabilities—as, for example, in one Chicago-based business co-managed by a deaf graduate of Wisconsin's residential school.[53] Most deaf people, however, pursued positions in the mainstream workforce.[54] Gordon Kannapell, a leader in the deaf community of Louisville, Kentucky, hastened the hiring of more than 150 deaf adults in one plant.[55] Hundreds of deaf men and women in Connecticut labored at aircraft plants across the state by 1942.[56] Amid these changes, industrialist Henry Kaiser praised the versatility and industry of the numerous deaf employees working in his shipyards.[57]

Hearing employers, like managers at Goodyear and Firestone, found that simple alterations in training procedures and communication ensured the successful integration of deaf workers into their larger work forces. One company established a policy to convey precise information through written instructions.[58] In order to ensure the safety of their deaf workers, another firm established a series of light signals for communication.[59] A third company recognized that hearing workers, such as truck drivers, needed to be able to visually recognize deaf employees, and potential safety problems were averted when deaf workers agreed to wear red caps.[60]

The use of sign language typically was the vital element in training and retaining deaf employees, however. An Iowa-based ordnance plant employed a hearing woman knowledgeable in sign language to supervise a crew of deaf women who outproduced their hearing peers. The principal of the state residential school served as an interpreter for new workers at an aviation plant in Kansas, where hearing coworkers and supervisors also studied sign language.[61] And in California, a deaf technician taught deaf recruits at an aviation plant whose four hundred resourceful deaf employees quickly invented new signs to represent their specialized tasks.[62]

These straightforward changes, especially the use of signed communication, had important implications. In the short term, they ensured the success of deaf workers and likely facilitated their movement into a broader range of positions. For most of the century, the integration of deaf workers—as at Automatic Electric and Ford—had depended upon deaf people to minimize their differences from their hearing coworkers. Yet the acceptance of sign language during the years of World War II enabled deaf workers to communicate more freely and maneuver more fully through their working environment.

Management's effort to include deaf workers by accommodating their needs seemed to affirm the arguments of conservative deaf activists.[63] Certainly, businesses never ceded control of the hiring and allocation of workers, or ceased excluding some deaf people.[64] Moreover, individuals with disabilities, African Americans, and women continued to face systematic restrictions and outright rejection. Still, the number of firms interested in hiring deaf employees exceeded the number of deaf adults looking for work during the war. Although no national study was undertaken by deaf organizations, the government, or industry, evidence from various state bureaus and word of mouth led most leaders to believe that for the first time in history nearly all interested deaf adults were employed.[65] Although there is little evidence regarding the employment status of deaf African Americans, this era was one of singular prosperity for nearly all deaf workers.

Deaf people hoped that their good fortune would continue beyond the war. In a newspaper essay entitled "Goodbye Old Man," and published in December 1942, Wisconsin resident Arthur Leisman, a state employee who assisted deaf adults in finding work, celebrated the apparent defeat of discrimination: "In your affluent days you brought us broken homes, forced us on the relief line, made our children go to school in rags . . . [now] the tables are turned and you are on the run. . . . Good-bye old man—and no regrets!"[66]

Yet there was no extended period of harmony either between workers with disabilities and employers or among deaf citizens themselves. In the summer of 1942, NAD leaders warily noted the establishment of a new national group: the American Federation of the Physically Handicapped (AFPH), led by the indefatigable Paul Strachan.[67] The AFPH program was modeled on recommendations he had reviewed earlier with NAD leaders, including a congressional investigation of the problems of citizens with disabilities; establishment of a Federal Bureau for the Physically Handicapped to oversee services for adults with disabilities; institution of distinct divisions for applicants with disabilities in Civil Service and United States Employment Service (USES) offices; and passage of legislation initiating a national promotional campaign to encourage the hiring of workers with disabilities.[68]

Thus, where NAD leaders sought distance from the federal government, the AFPH program demanded federal oversight of services for adults with disabilities; where NAD leaders opposed ties with other groups with disabilities, AFPH members sought a dynamic national confederation of *all* Americans with disabilities.[69] From these conflicting positions, NAD and AFPH leaders vied for the allegiance of the nation's deaf people.

The systemic exclusion and marginalization of disabled veterans and civilians from the nation's expanding industrial army was likely the primary impetus for the AFPH's growth. In early 1941, out of one hundred thirty million American citizens, roughly five hundred thousand were employed in civilian-based war industries.[70] By 1942, federal officials estimated the country would need to mobilize a vast workforce, potentially ranging as high as sixty-five million civilians. These trends permitted women and African Americans to fight for positions in industry from which they had long been blocked by employers, union officials, and white male workers.

Employers quickly snapped up deaf workers, too, but the nation's citizens with other disabilities enjoyed no such popularity. In May

1942, for instance, a small but spirited corps of people with disabilities staged a sit-down strike in the offices of Federal Security Administration (FSA) administrator Paul McNutt and demanded the FSA help them find work.[71] Although these activists ended their peaceful occupation, the problem they publicized remained unsolved: hundreds of thousands of disabled citizens—including civilians, newly disabled war-industry workers, and discharged soldiers—were unemployed.

President Roosevelt moved to reduce these problems in the spring of 1942 by establishing the War Manpower Commission (WMC), led by Paul McNutt, the former head of the FSA. According to the president, the WMC was to oversee the development of the nation's industrial workforce. McNutt proved to be a consistent and articulate advocate for disabled workers as well as for women and African Americans. At the outset, for example, he increased the access of these groups to supervisory and technical jobs, generally the domain of white males with no disabilities. Unfortunately, he had little explicit power to implement his broad directives. Like the FEPC, the WMC relied on voluntary employer compliance to achieve its goal of a larger and more diverse workforce.[72]

Statistics underscored the systemic discriminatory barriers and vocational bottlenecks limiting workforce integration of individuals with disabilities. From the inception of the WMC in 1942 through the spring of 1943, approximately fifteen million workers overall entered various war-based industries and federal officials estimated that another five million would be needed by the end of the year. At the same time, as many as seven million unemployed workers with disabilities were ready to work, with an additional two million ready after they received vocational rehabilitation assistance.[73]

Grossly inadequate state and federal vocational rehabilitation facilities greatly restricted the movement of these citizens into the workforce. In 1941, for example, only fifteen thousand civilians with disabilities received employment assistance, and in 1942, only twenty-two thousand.[74] These numbers were scarcely enough to begin to lessen the needs of either industry or workers with disabilities, and ongoing discrimination by private employers further restricted employment of these workers. Firms advertised for help even though hundreds of thousands of eager adults with disabilities sought jobs.[75]

Strachan was determined to resolve this situation as well as strengthen the rights of disabled workers in the postwar era.

The founding of AFPH and Strachan's appearance created fissures in the national deaf community, however. Beginning in the summer of 1942, a small number of individuals and local organizations aligned with the AFPH. By October 1942, deaf members joined the first AFPH lodge in Washington, D.C.; within a year, deaf members had joined lodges in Baltimore and Detroit. The Empire State Association, as well as the publishers and writers of the *Detroit Sign-Post* and the popular *Silent Cavalier,* a newspaper based in Washington, D.C., supported the nascent organization.[76] Other deaf leaders who joined the AFPH included Alice Terry, Jay Cooke Howard, Harvey Barnes, and Alan B. Crammatte.[77]

A small corps of deaf leaders and writers quickly challenged the AFPH, replaying the earlier debates between Strachan and Anderson. As the organization grew in the winter of 1942–43, critics argued that deaf adults were capable workers and claimed that affiliating with "physically handicapped" workers would weaken their reputation. An NFSD official asserted that any such association would "instill and intensify" the public perception that deaf adults deserved pity.[78] Once again, some writers proudly contended that deaf citizens were not handicapped. As the editor of the Minnesota-based *Companion* explained, "We are deaf; not ashamed of it."[79]

As the debate between AFPH supporters and critics continued through 1943, federal officials moved to strengthen overstretched and uneven vocational rehabilitation services. The status of adults with disabilities nonetheless remained precarious: 30,000 civilians graduated from vocational rehabilitation programs, and 200,000 entered private industry, but unknown tens of thousands of adults remained unemployed and in need of vocational rehabilitation assistance.[80] Moreover, the rate of loss of industrial workers injured in accidents exceeded the rate of worker entrance to industry. To make matters worse, each month the Army discharged an additional 3,500 soldiers with recently acquired disabilities.[81]

In July 1943, almost two years after the country entered World War II, Congress moved to strengthen federal support and funding for state vocational rehabilitation programs. The federal government also subsidized the provision of "restorative" medical services to civilians, a change designed to speed the entry of adults with disabilities into the workforce. Furthermore, the new legislation established an Office of Vocational Rehabilitation (OVR) in the FSA and set up an independent Veterans Bureau.[82] Overall, however, these changes were intended more to aid the war drive rather than to resolve the complex needs of people with disabilities. As Paul McNutt explained in testimony supporting the legislation, the expansion of vocational rehabilitation was vital "not as a social gain, but as a wartime necessity."[83]

AFPH supporters and detractors provided opposing interpretations of these legislative changes. Now employed as a vocational rehabilitation agent for Texas, a pleased Tom Anderson encouraged deaf adults to turn to state vocational agents for job placement assistance.[84] Strachan, on the other hand, was disappointed. During the course of legislative hearings, he restated the AFPH's founding demands that the federal government provide broader services.[85] In the following year, he would present more ambitious recommendations.

Whatever its benefits, this legislation did not allay the concern of deaf workers regarding their future employment status. In the fall of 1943, Loy Golladay expressed the anxiety of many deaf people that the majority population would demand that deaf workers relinquish their positions after the war. He wrote that a "return to normalcy" would mean that women, the elderly, and workers with disabilities would be forced to surrender jobs to veterans.[86]

A small but vocal corps of deaf AFPH opponents also continued to oppose any identification with "handicapped" people. Wesley Lauritsen, the editor of the *Companion* and a teacher at the Minnesota residential school, maintained that deafness was more an inspiration than an impediment, so he proposed a national campaign against the use of the word "handicap."[87] Not all such comments were as well meaning, though. A few deaf opponents of affiliation with the AFPH were driven by antipathy to adults with other disabilities as much as by pride in the deaf community. In one such attack upon Strachan and the AFPH, Ohio's Roy Conkling relied upon demeaning stereotypes that reduced people with disabilities to helpless beggars: "Who of us wants to stand on America's Main Street, and howl to the world: 'Pity me, I am deaf, I am physically handicapped. Give me a job because I am so physically handicapped.' "[88] Some deaf leaders thus had internalized and redirected at other groups the prejudice that had long racked *their* community. In other words, the ongoing debate over affiliation with the AFPH brought into the open many deaf people's fears and anger as well as their accomplishments and pride.

As these public debates continued, Anderson sought to strengthen the ties between deaf adults and the vocational rehabilitation system. He worried that the more prominent AFPH would draw support away from the inactive NAD, which then might not survive. He confided to NAD vice president Winfield Runde, "we can only hope to hold the deaf as we deliver the goods, and we are not delivering the goods, so what is the inevitable answer?"[89] And in a frank letter to NFSD president Arthur Roberts, he conceded a fact that few deaf people had been willing to acknowledge: "despite all pretensions of complete independence," deaf citizens *were* entitled to assistance from the state—such as that provided under vocational rehabilitation.[90] Some deaf leaders wanted more than anything to remain separate from the larger community of people with various disabilities, but they had never been fully independent of the state.

In pivotal congressional testimony arranged by Representative Augustine Kelley in late 1944, deaf leaders proposed sharply contrasting strategies for the future of the deaf community.[91] Between August and December, Kelley held hearings to investigate services to civilians with disabilities, one of the AFPH's original demands. Testimony from more than seven hundred witnesses was reviewed. Groups representing people with disabilities joined leaders from business, federal and state governments, and social service agencies. Alan B. Crammatte appeared for the AFPH, representing one segment of the deaf community. Marcus Kenner testified for the NAD, Arthur Roberts for the NFSD, and Ben Schowe as an independent citizen.

The most conservative deaf leaders expressed only slight concern about discriminatory employers. Roberts claimed that discrimination was "quickly removed" once deaf workers demonstrated their abilities, and he argued against any legislative measures to assist deaf workers.[92] Similarly, with deaf adults currently fully employed and vocational rehabilitation services expanding, Anderson claimed additional legal steps were unnecessary. In a cursory letter sent to the Kelley

Committee summarizing the NAD position, he asked: "What do the deaf ask of government? Precisely this: a framework of laws regulating a system of free enterprise providing the opportunity for steady employment. . . . Nothing more. No less."[93]

Others, however, recommended the continuation of traditional efforts to reduce employment discrimination. Schowe, Kenner, and Crammatte all implicitly acknowledged that discrimination against deaf workers was widespread, and they endorsed broadened efforts to educate the public, industry, and unions. Schowe favored federal funding for a research-based office to provide employers with data on employment trends among deaf and other workers with disabilities. Crammatte endorsed the AFPH-sponsored national promotional campaign.[94] Interestingly, all of these proposals were based upon long-standing claims that information alone would induce recalcitrant parties to hire workers with disabilities.

Deaf leaders were also divided in their appraisal of vocational rehabilitation services. Several downplayed these services out of deference to employers. Roberts asserted that rehabilitation services were needed only by a small number of deaf workers and that existing services were adequate.[95] Schowe was even more reticent. Wary of sending a message to employers that deaf workers needed elaborate training, he explained that they had been easily integrated into the workforce at Goodyear and Firestone without additional vocational training. Vocational programs at residential schools, he stubbornly maintained, adequately prepared most students for positions in industry.[96]

On the other hand, Anderson, Kenner, and Crammatte maintained that the expansion of vocational rehabilitation services was vital. Anderson, in particular, contended that these services could compensate for the failures of schools to offer up-to-date vocational training, and Kenner recommended that assistance be extended into rural areas. Yet neither recommended substantive changes in the system itself. Crammatte alone insisted that a substantive expansion of federal vocational services was necessary.[97] He repeated the AFPH's demands that included federal oversight of job placement services, including establishment of a Division for the Deaf in OVR as well as establishment of a Bureau for the Handicapped to consolidate all federal programs.[98]

These men were also divided regarding the schooling of deaf students. Crammatte offered a sweeping indictment of the educational system comparable to Anderson's critiques of oralist practices. A Gallaudet graduate, Crammatte had taught at several schools for deaf students and had noted that most residential school students never advanced beyond fifth grade.[99] Inadequate vocational training, excessive reliance on oralist practices, and the lack of advanced classes prepared graduates "for little more than menial labor," he charged. Less than 2 percent of the twenty-one thousand students attending residential, private, and day schools nationwide went on to Gallaudet College. The majority became artisans, factory workers, and laborers.[100] Crammatte had revealed the deaf community's deepest problems.

Crammatte recommended substantive, if familiar, measures to improve education. He called for school administrators to reduce oral training, strengthen vocational instruction, and establish programs for adults. Moreover, he urged construction of another postsecondary educational facility, separate from Gallaudet College. He broke from his predecessors, however, in requesting federal oversight of education for deaf people.[101]

The others, unlike Crammatte, defended the nation's schools. Indeed, Kenner and Roberts avoided any discussion of the long-standing conflicts over oral practices, assuring the committee that the U.S. system of education was the most advanced in the world. Only Connecticut's Edmund Boatner conceded that many schools did not have the financial resources to keep pace with industrial changes.[102] Both Kenner and Roberts thought it unwise to use this unprecedented opportunity to reveal the vast problems of the nation's deaf schools. Crammatte was not alone in believing that systemic changes were necessary to upgrade the schools and break the pattern of underemployment that beset the deaf community, but Kenner, Roberts, and Anderson likely believed that disclosure of school-based problems before the Kelley Committee would lend credence to the AFPH contention that federal control was necessary to upgrade education.[103] Although congressional records do not reveal the exact rationale for their opposition, it is likely they worried that centralized management would unduly empower government officials who might also support oral practices.

The Kelley Committee itself sharply criticized the nation's network of vocational rehabilitation services but stopped short of endorsing federal oversight. In their final report, members described existing services as arbitrary and inadequate, but despite their condemnation recommended that states merely strengthen and coordinate existing programs. They supported four additional measures: strengthening the OVR; establishing a national promotional campaign, such as the AFPH-sponsored legislation; increasing financial support for state schools; and either expanding Gallaudet College or establishing a second college for deaf students.[104] In short, the committee affirmed Crammatte's critique but did not recommend the oversight measures opposed by more conservative deaf leaders.

Anderson quickly distanced himself and the NAD from the Kelley Committee. In a letter to Schowe written near the close of the hearings, he angrily caricatured Representative Kelley as "little more than a stooge" for Strachan. He was even more dismissive of other adults with disabilities. "What I want to do most of all," he explained, "is to get the deaf out of this conglomeration of black-and-whites, diseased and maimed, for it is a godammed [sic] lasting disgrace to be deaf if we are to be considered as lumped with these and seeking governmental 'aid.'"[105]

The winter of 1944–45 brought a brief lull to the battle that divided the nation's deaf citizenry. Employment of deaf workers remained at an all-time high, but unemployment continued to plague workers with disabilities. On the one hand, in 1944 industry hired three hundred thousand disabled civilians and veterans, 50 percent more than in 1943.[106] On the other hand, inadequate vocational rehabilitation services continued to restrict the advance of other workers with disabilities: by the end of 1943, fewer than fifty thousand adults with disabilities had received vocational assistance.[107]

As the war in Europe drew to a close in the spring of 1945, deaf AFPH members in Michigan promoted an employment initiative they hoped would become a national blueprint. Working to guarantee the employment of that state's disabled civilians and veterans, a coalition including the Congress of Industrial Organizations (CIO) and the

AFPH endorsed the Disability Employment Act that would *require* businesses with eight or more employees to hire quotas of disabled civilians and veterans whenever unemployment rose to predetermined levels among these groups.[108] As introduced to the state legislature, this legislation embodied three new positions: that voluntary, education-based approaches would not alone ensure the adequate employment of disabled adults; that disabled civilians and veterans had a *right* to a job in much the way they had a right to a public education; and that the right of adults with disabilities to be employed superseded any rights private employers had to control the composition of their work-force. These positions represented a decisive, even radical, departure from past philosophy, practices, and expectations.

Deaf proponents argued that this legislation was vital to protect the hard-earned, wartime advances of the state's deaf workers. In the spring of 1941, as director of the Michigan Bureau for Deaf Workers, Jay Cooke Howard had proudly announced that all deaf adults in the state were fully employed, and he had forcefully opposed state inter-vention on their behalf. Four years later, however, a worried Howard reversed course, now claiming that state involvement was vital if deaf and other adults with disabilities were to retain their recent gains. "The handicapped of this country now have a war on their hands," he asserted. "It is a war of survival of the right to employment attained in the past three years."[109]

Few Michigan legislators agreed with Howard's assessment or with the inventive and bold initiative, which was handily defeated within months of its introduction. In the House, opponents eliminated civil-ians from the bill's protections, senatorial opponents then dismissed the bill as unnecessary, because veterans would be served by the Veter-ans' Bureau.[110] After the bill's defeat, Howard feared that without spe-cific protections deaf workers would be consigned to menial positions. "There is doubt and uncertainty in the hearts of us all," he confided.[111]

The AFPH bounced back quickly from its setback in Michigan with a long-sought federal legislative victory, however. Several days after the end of the war in August 1945, President Harry Truman signed legislation that would establish the President's Council on Em-ployment of the Handicapped (PCEH). Strachan and the AFPH had secured a prominent national victory after three years of intense lobbying in Washington and Congress. The President's Council was comprised of representatives of unions, business, the military, veterans, and the federal government. The council developed educational activities and used a week-long national drive to educate the public, industry, and union employers about hiring civilians and veterans with disabilities. In the coming decades, Strachan and the PCEH would proudly assert that the educational campaign produced noteworthy increases in the hiring of disabled workers around the nation.[112] A pleased Strachan pressed ahead.

In January 1946, Representative John Sparkman of Alabama, known for his interest in veterans' and workers' rights, proposed comprehensive federal legislation designed to transform the working lives of the nation's disabled civilians. Sparkman's proposal had several distinctive features, including the establishment of training facilities for disabled workers and their teachers; an expansion of "sheltered industries"; an increase in direct payments to disabled adults unable to work in the private market; the establishment of a division for workers with disabilities in the civil service; the mandatory provision of rehabilitation and training assistance to workers with disabilities by private firms themselves; and, most important, the *mandated* hiring of disabled workers by firms contracting with the federal government.[113] Sparkman sought nothing less than the conversion of the nation's programs from a philanthropic to an explicit rights-based system.

Strachan naturally supported Sparkman's proposals, passionately defending them before a congressional hearing. Mandatory hiring, he noted, simply provided "belated justice" to workers with disabilities. He estimated that the majority of employers would willingly abide by these directives, as they were similar to edicts in place in Great Britain. Then, in a final angry outpouring, he demanded that Congress "[e]ither provide an actual means of opportunity for employment, or let us start a 'euthanasia league' and do what Hitler did to the handicapped—get rid of us by killing us off."[114]

Most deaf leaders did not share Strachan's enthusiasm and vigorously opposed the legislation. Pennsylvania's Warren Smaltz provided a typical brief against the bill, reasoning that deaf workers would fare better if they were not linked to groups that needed workplace protections and if hiring decisions remained in the purview of employers.[115]

This traditional approach had brought remarkable employment gains during the war, and therefore individuals and groups clung to it, echoing the criticisms offered by deaf spokesmen. Congressional leaders and representatives from the FSA, USES, and the Civil Service all disapproved of the bill.[116] Medical administrators and insurance company leaders were also critical, and state vocational rehabilitation officials registered their aversion.[117] Most were against mandated hiring, often repeating deaf leaders' positions: employers would be angered; workers would be locked into dead-end jobs; and, in short, quotas amounted to preferential treatment and were wrong.[118] The National Federation of the Blind (NFB), an independent, vigorous critic of paternal state-based services, stood almost alone in its endorsement of the bill, maintaining that quotas were unavoidable given the usual employer's belief that it was either expensive or a burden to employ workers with disabilities.[119] Congressional support was marginal: apart from Sparkman, only Representative Jerry Voorhis of California testified on behalf of the bill.[120]

In light of this widespread opposition, Sparkman's proposals suffered the same fate as their Michigan-based predecessors, and the last of the great conflicts between AFPH supporters and detractors in the war era came to an uneasy end.[121] Strachan and the AFPH had suffered a stinging legislative defeat. With the war ending, though, still to be tested were Strachan's predictions that unprotected deaf workers and those with various other disabilities would face widespread unemployment.

Deaf leaders generally were heartened by immediate postwar trends. A detailed study in the *American Annals of the Deaf* that closely evaluated the status of industrial workers at one plant was especially encouraging. Managers agreed that deaf employees were equal or superior to hearing workers with regard to safety, productivity, efficiency, and rapport. An extended examination by the Bureau of Labor Statistics offered comparable conclusions.[122] Labor bureaus in Minnesota and Michigan reported promising news, as did residents of Akron: most male deaf workers retained their positions a year after the close of the war.[123]

Not considering any new legislative approaches, deaf leaders increasingly endorsed the expansion of vocational rehabilitation services. At the August 1946 NAD convention, outgoing President Tom Anderson announced a cooperative agreement between the federal OVR, the NAD, the NFSD, and the Convention of American Instructors of the Deaf (CAID). He assured his audience that these services, like the aid long offered by labor bureaus, was neither a "handout" nor "charity" but would enable deaf men and women to become self-reliant.[124]

Vocational services provided much needed assistance to deaf adults beyond that available in residential or day schools. At the 1946 NAD convention, Boyce Williams, a graduate of Gallaudet College recently hired by the OVR to assist deaf workers, explained that adults were eligible for assistance, such as counseling, assessment, job training, and placement.[125] Vocational rehabilitation, proponents believed, would enable recent graduates and unemployed adults to find work and remain independent.

Despite employment advances brought about by the wartime labor shortage, educational shortcomings that had hampered deaf students throughout the century remained at the end of the war. Vocational training was often outmoded at residential schools and completely unavailable at day schools; academic instruction lagged far behind that available to hearing students; tedious speech and lipreading practice took up valuable time but aided few students; many administrators continued to ban or restrict sign language; and admission to Gallaudet College remained limited to a small segment of the national deaf community.

The economic gains of the war era had not provided deaf leaders any additional power to alter the educational circumstances. Activists remained united by an unwavering support for sign language and the need for deaf teachers, opposition to oral-centered instruction, and a belief that they were entitled to review, if not oversee, the schools, which were the vital institutions in their community. Unfortunately, the divisions between AFPH and NAD supporters had—temporarily at least—fractured deaf leadership. A united front among deaf leaders and organizations for the deaf community might have produced a more influential coalition to advocate for a prominent place for sign language within the schools.

At the close of the war, most deaf leaders continued to embrace the values of their nineteenth-century predecessors regarding the rights and identity of deaf people in the workplace. They had argued against federal intervention that would have established a right to employment, interpreting any demand for such prerogatives as either an unnecessary request or a confession of weakness that undermined the independent character of the deaf community. They did not advocate for bilingual communication rights, either. In Akron and other locations, for example, activists never broadly publicized the fact that their employment advances had been hastened by the use of sign language and interpreters. In fact, in a speech before school executives in 1944, Tom Anderson explained that he did not want employers to think that deaf workers needed either sign language or interpreters to succeed in industry.[126]

Deaf leaders and workers sought to deemphasize their identity as deaf people in order to avoid differences with employers and to assure their integration into the mainstream workforce. Thus, if deaf workers were to remain within the mainstream economy, it would be on terms established by hearing employers and employees for their convenience. Little had changed since deaf leaders first promoted these precepts seventy-five years earlier.

In this formative period between the mid-nineteenth and mid-twentieth centuries, deaf leaders centered their efforts on a strategy rooted deep in the experiences of an earlier generation of deaf leaders. Akron's Ben Schowe best articulated this approach. The example of excellence established by working men and women in Akron and around the country, Schowe maintained, was the most effective method to combat discrimination and secure opportunities for deaf workers in the second half of the twentieth century. "Each deaf workman of this sort," Schowe explained, "is like a man with a lantern on a moonless night. He dispels the gloom of prejudice all around him and others can see the gleam of his light from afar." These working men and women, he concluded, "are the unsung heroes we must depend on."[127]

Epilogue

The material prosperity and optimistic expectations that characterized most of the national deaf community at the close of World War II did not last. In the half-century since the end of the war, deaf workers and leaders have continued to labor against formidable systemic obstacles in the workplace, the classroom, and society at large.

The continued vulnerability of deaf adults has been most powerfully demonstrated in the workplace. Many, if not most, deaf adults complete their formal schooling ill-prepared to advance through an increasingly demanding economy. Although most states now provide greatly expanded vocational rehabilitation services, these initiatives are neither sufficient to reach all eligible adults, nor are they able to provide the sustained academic and vocational instruction needed by the most vulnerable adults. Equally worrisome has been the unabated automation of businesses and industry that has especially hurt deaf workers in semiskilled positions typically prone to contraction or elimination. Finally, employers' continuing resistance to hiring or promoting qualified deaf workers has further isolated even the most well-prepared working adults. Together, these trends have contributed to the disproportionate representation of deaf adults in manual labor and service industries.[1]

In response to these disturbing conditions, deaf leaders have been modestly successful at upgrading existing educational institutions and promoting additional postsecondary educational facilities. Within the past several decades, for example, Gallaudet University has matured into an internationally respected institution, while the development of varied college-based programs in New York, Minnesota, California, and elsewhere has greatly increased the number of deaf adults who have received advanced academic and vocational schooling.[2]

At the same time, deaf leaders have sustained their long-standing tradition of advocacy in the schools they helped create. This tradition of activism was powerfully illustrated in 1988 when Gallaudet students commanded sustained national attention with bold protests that spurred the appointment of the university's first deaf president.[3] Less visible, but no less important, have been deaf adults' efforts—typically organized through alumni and state associations—to influence local, state, and national educational practices.[4] In addition to questioning whether "mainstreaming" best serves the academic, vocational, and cultural needs of deaf students, leaders have continued to advocate broader acceptance of sign language and the hiring of more deaf teachers and administrators.

Throughout these postwar decades, deaf activists and workers have also labored to diversify the membership and activities of their own community. State and national institutions, including the National Fraternal Society of the Deaf, the National Association of the Deaf, and Gallaudet University, have opened their doors to African Americans and women, increasing numbers of whom have gone on to assume leadership positions within these establishments.[5] Many state associations of deaf adults have worked, typically with little fanfare and scarce public attention, to challenge workplace discrimination.[6] Other deaf leaders have established advantageous working alliances with organizations representing people who are hard of hearing or those with other disabilities. These strategies have spurred social and legal changes that have advanced the rights of deaf workers as well as other adults identified as disabled.[7]

Among these varied social and legal changes, the 1990 passage of the Americans with Disabilities Act (ADA) most clearly illustrates the complexity of the situation facing deaf workers and activists.[8] By limiting the power of employers to arbitrarily exclude deaf applicants, the ADA can, in the short term, broaden the opportunities for deaf adults to demonstrate their talents and training. At the same time, some deaf leaders remain ambivalent about, if not averse to, associating with the ADA—whatever its legal protections. After all, for more than one hundred years, deaf adults have uniformly rejected claims that they are handicapped or disabled, and instead have focused on their many talents and skills. From this perspective, the ADA's emphasis on "disability" appears inappropriate. Nevertheless, by its underlying philosophical insistence that diversity and difference are the only constants in human societies, the ADA may help enlighten mainstream culture regarding the varied abilities of *all* individuals, groups, and communities long misidentified as "disabled."

Notes

Introduction

1. American Sign Language (ASL) is not a "simplified" language but a complete language with its own morphology, symbol system, and syntax. Signed languages resemble spoken languages in all central aspects, despite the different (spatial) modality in which they are expressed. ASL is the primary language of an estimated two hundred thousand to five hundred thousand Americans, including deaf native signers, hearing children of deaf parents, and late-deafened adults. Because of its visual system of representation, some laypersons have incorrectly assumed that ASL is fundamentally different from spoken languages or that it is a representational system for English. ASL contains structures and processes not found in English that are comparable in complexity, range, and richness to any other written or oral language. See Stokoe, *Sign Language Structure,* 1–78 passim.

2. For a discussion of membership in the deaf community see Padden and Humphries, *Deaf in America* (Cambridge, Mass.: Harvard University Press, 1988), 2–6. Padden and Humphries use the uppercase notation Deaf when referring to Deaf individuals. For articles that explore the American deaf community, see Andrew Solomon, "Deaf Is Beautiful," *New York Times Magazine* (28 August 1994): Section 6, 38–45; Edward Dolnick, "Deafness as Culture," *Atlantic Monthly* 272 (September 1993): 37–53. For an engrossing portrait of contemporary deaf high school students as they craft their identities and negotiate between the deaf and hearing worlds, see Cohen, *TRAIN GO SORRY,* 3. For a current study that documents the formative educational experiences of an African American deaf woman, see Wright, *Sounds Like Home.*

Chapter 1. "For the Deaf of the Land" Building Independence

1. For a case study that counters this trend, see Nora Groce, *Everyone Here Spoke Sign Language.* See also Nora Groce, "Everyone Here Spoke Sign Language," *Natural History* 89 (June 1980): 10–16.

2. Schein and Delk, *The Deaf Population,* 18. For an overview, see Jack Gannon, *Deaf Heritage,* 1–92.

3. For the definitive narrative account of the schooling, see John W. Jones, "One Hundred Years of History in the Education of the Deaf in America and Its Present Status," *American Annals of the Deaf* 63 (January

1918): 1–47 passim (hereafter *Annals*). For the definitive interpretative account, see Harlan Lane, *When the Mind Hears,* chaps. 8–12. Lane's study describes the development of a deaf community and its subsequent conflict with oralist professionals.

4. On Thomas H. Gallaudet, see Barnard, *Tribute to Gallaudet*; Gallaudet, *Life of Thomas Hopkins Gallaudet*; Humphrey, *Life and Letters of Gallaudet.*

5. "Laurent Clerc," in Barnard, ed., *Tribute to Gallaudet,* 109, 106–16. See Guilbert C. Braddock, "Laurent Clerc," in Braddock, *Notable Deaf Persons* (Washington, D.C.: Gallaudet College Alumni Association, 1975), 3; Angeline Fuller Fischer, "The Three Immortals," comp. Edwin Isaac Holycross, *The Abbé de l'Épée,* 62.

6. See Berg and Buzzard, *Thomas Gallaudet,* 24.

7. Thomas H. Gallaudet, "The Natural Language of Signs II," *Annals* 1 (January 1848): 82, 88. See also James J. Fernandes, "Thomas Hopkins Gallaudet," in *Gallaudet Encyclopedia of Deaf People and Deafness,* ed. John V. Van Cleve, 444–47 (hereafter *Gallaudet Encyclopedia*).

8. For an excellent analysis of the role of religious pedagogy on the character of early schools, see Douglas Baynton, " 'A Silent Exile on This Earth,' The Metaphorical Construction of Deafness in the Twentieth Century," *American Quarterly* 44 (June 1992): 220.

9. On vocational instruction at the Hartford School, see Williams, *History of the American Asylum,* 15–19; Maxine Tull Boatner, "Vocational Education under the Gallaudets," *Annals* 102 (May 1957): 300–11.

10. Seth Terry, *Third Report of the Directors of the Connecticut Asylum for the Education and Instruction of Deaf and Dumb Persons* (Hartford, Conn.: Hudson, 1819), 6. Four modes of communication were employed, American Sign Language (ASL), methodical sign, fingerspelling, and writing in English. For a summary of Gallaudet's views on sign language, see Thomas Gallaudet, "The Natural Language of Signs I," *Annals* 1 (October 1847): 55–59 and "The Natural Language of Signs II," 79–92. See also Van Cleve and Crouch, *A Place of Their Own,* 45.

11. Henry C. Rider, "The Northern New York Institution," in *Histories,* vol. 2, ed. Fay; Gannon, *Deaf Heritage,* 48–49.

12. Braddock, *Notable Deaf Persons,* 150–51; Gannon, *Deaf Heritage,* 19; Edmund Boatner, "Deaf Teachers of the Deaf," *Silent Worker* (in Deaf Biographical Files and Deaf Subject Files, "Deaf Education," Gallaudet University Archives, Gallaudet University, Washington, D.C. [hereafter GUA]).

13. Regarding this presumption of state support, see John M. Francis, "The Claims of the Deaf and Dumb upon the State," *Annals* 7 (January 1855): 90–100. On the American School, see Job Williams, "The American Asylum," in *Histories*, vol. 1, ed. Fay. Regarding the number of states and schools, see Jones, "One Hundred Years," 181–92. On schooling in New York, see Thomas Francis Fox, *A Chronology of the New York School for the Deaf* (New York: New York School for the Deaf, 1935). Regarding Minnesota, see "Minnesota School for the Deaf," *Companion* (11 February 1925): 1–11. Regarding the number of teachers, see Jones, "One Hundred Years," 181–92.

14. For discussions concerning compulsory attendance, see James L. Smith, "Compulsory Education of the Deaf," *Proceedings of the Third Convention of the National Association of the Deaf* (New York: Office of the *Deaf Mute's Journal* (1890), 53–57 (hereafter, *Third NAD*); Olof Hanson, "How the National Association of the Deaf May Be Made More Useful," *Proceedings of the Sixth Convention of the National Association of the Deaf* (Paola Kansas, J. T. Trickett, 1900), 17–20 (hereafter, *Sixth NAD*); James L. Smith, "Where Are We At?" *Sixth NAD*, 60–64. Regarding compulsory attendance drives in Minnesota, see *Proceedings of the Sixth Convention of the Minnesota Association of the Deaf* (Faribault, Minn.: Minnesota State School for the Deaf, Printing Office, 1901), 18–19.

15. Reverend Collins Stone, "Report on the Subject of Trades For the Deaf and Dumb," *Proceedings of the Fifth Convention of American Instructors of the Deaf* (Alton, Ill.: Courier Steam Book and Job Printing House, 1859), 127 (hereafter, *Fifth CAID*).

16. According to Carlin, these schools provided instruction in book-binding, cabinet making, and tailoring. John Carlin, "On The Mechanical and Professional Occupations of Deaf-Mute Graduates," *Proceedings of the Third Convention of American Instructors of the Deaf and Dumb* (Columbus, Ohio, Steam Press of Smith and Cox, Statesman Office, 1853), 204 (hereafter, *Third CAID*). On the origins of CAID, see Edward A. Fay, "The Conventions of American Instructors of the Deaf," in *Histories*, vol. 3, ed. Fay.

17. Carlin, "On the Mechanical," 200–214. For background on Carlin, see Guilbert Braddock, "John Carlin," *The Frat* (July 1937): 2–3.

18. Edward A. Hodgson, "Industrial Education of Deaf-Mutes," *First National Convention of Deaf Mutes* (New York: New York Institution for the Deaf and Dumb, 1880), 10–13. On Hodgson's contributions as an educator and intellectual, see Isaac Lewis Peet, "General View of the Education of the Deaf and Dumb in the United States," *Annals* 29 (January 1884): 1–17.

19. Editorial, "Plain Facts," *Deaf Mute's Journal* (20 March 1884): 2 (hereafter *DMJ*). See also, Editorial, *DMJ* (15 September 1881): 2, and (24 September 1885): 2.

20. On students being used to defray operating expenses, see Thomas Francis Fox, "Social Status of the Deaf," *Proceedings of the Second National Convention of Deaf Mutes* (New York: New York Institution for the Deaf and Dumb), 12–16.

On students being rushed through school, see Francis D. Clarke, "Trades For the Deaf, and Industrial Training Schools, How to Improve Them," *Proceedings of the World Congress of Instructors of the Deaf and of the Thirteenth Convention of American Instructors of the Deaf* (Washington, D.C.: Published as a supplement to the *Annals,* 1893): 212–14.

On students needing agricultural and industrial training, see Fort Lewis Seliney, "Presidential Address," *Proceedings of the Thirteenth Convention of the Empire State Association of Deaf-Mutes* (Rome, N.Y.: Register Office, 1890), 3–5.

On the need for state associations to strengthen school programs, see Olof Hanson, "Presidential Address," *Report of Proceedings of the Fifth Convention of the Minnesota Association of the Deaf* (Faribault, Minn.: Minnesota State School for the Deaf, Printing Office, 1899), 4–6; James L. Smith, "A Review of the Education of the Deaf in Minnesota," *Fifth Convention of the Minnesota Association of the Deaf,* 12–17.

On the need to provide deaf students with complete training, see Warren Robinson, "Manual Training from a Preparatory Point of View," *Proceedings of the Fifth National Convention of the National Association of the Deaf* (Fulton, Mo.: Henry Gross, 1898), 32–34.

21. James Lewis Smith, "Presidential Address," *Proceedings of the Second Convention of the Minnesota Association of the Deaf* (Faribault, Minn.: Minnesota State School for the Deaf, Steam Print, 1890), 2–5.

22. See Helen S. Ohnstad, "What Manual Training Has Done For Our Girls," *Proceedings of the Fourteenth Convention of American Instructors of the Deaf* (Flint, Mich.: Michigan School for the Deaf, 1895), 182–85 (hereafter, *Fourteenth CAID*).

23. For an example of a well-developed program, see Richard O. Johnson, "The Indiana Institution," in *Histories,* vol. 1, ed. Fay. Indiana offered female students a two-year program in various sewing trades. Male students pursued six-year programs.

24. Superintendent Robert Mathison of the Ontario School for the Deaf called for greater attention upon trades for girls in "Convention of Principals," *DMJ* (24 July 1884): 1.

25. Angie Fuller, a leader of the drive to admit women to Gallaudet College, firmly believed that traditional programs aided female students. See Angie Fuller, "The Apportionment of Labor," *Annals* 27 (July 1882): 158–60; Angie Fuller, "Laundry Work in Institutions for the Deaf and Dumb," *Annals* 27 (October 1882): 244–48.

26. *Fourth National Conference of Principals of Institutions for Deaf-Mutes* (Northampton, Mass.: Gazette Printing Company, 1880), 89.

27. Clarke, "Trades for the Deaf," 204. For a defense of training, see *Proceedings of the Fifteenth Meeting of the Convention of the American Instructors of the Deaf* (Washington, D.C.: Government Printing Office, 1899), 256 (hereafter, *Fifteenth CAID*).

28. The NAD and the Virginia Association of the Deaf supported the efforts of a white deaf man to establish a school for African American children in Virginia. See "Synopsis of the Fight Made by a Deaf Man for the Establishment of a School for the Colored Deaf and Blind," *Silent Worker* (January 1909): 59, 69; William Ritter to *DMJ* (4 April 1912): 2; Editorial, *DMJ* (17 August 1902): 2; *Proceedings of the World's Congress of the Deaf and the Report of the Seventh Convention of the National Association of the Deaf* (n.p. 1904), 176 (hereafter, *Seventh NAD*).

29. In Maryland, school administrators promoted the integration of African American students. See M. A. Morrison, "The Maryland School for the Colored Blind and Deaf, Baltimore Maryland, 1872–1893," in *Histories*, vol. 2, ed. Fay, xxxv. In South Carolina, school officials fiercely resisted efforts at integration. See Newton F. Walker, "The South Carolina Institution," in *Histories*, vol. 1, ed. Fay, xii.

30. Jacob Van Nostrand, "Necessity of a Higher Standard of Education for the Deaf and Dumb," *Annals* 3 (July 1851): 196–97. John Carlin, "Advantages and Disadvantages of the Use of Signs," *Annals* 4 (October 1851): 49. John Carlin, "The National College for Mutes," *Annals* 6 (April 1854): 176–77. See also Empire State Association of Deaf Mutes, *Third Biennial Convention*, 263–69, *Deaf Mute's Friend* (September 1869), vol. 1, no. 9.

31. Since its inception, the leadership of the National Association of the Deaf has been drawn almost exclusively from graduates of Gallaudet College. See Edward M. Gallaudet, "The First Decade of the National Deaf-Mute College," *Annals* 19 (July 1874): 154–58; Edward M. Gallaudet, "The Columbia Institution for the Instruction of the Deaf and Dumb, 1857–1893," in *Histories*, vol. 2, ed. Fay, xx; Dr. John Hotchkiss, "Gallaudet College," *Silent Worker* (October 1919): 4–8; Atwood, *Gallaudet College*; Gannon, *Deaf Heri-*

tage, 38–39; Van Cleve and Crouch, *A Place of Their Own,* 83–86. On Gallaudet, see Boatner, *Voice of the Deaf.*

32. For an overview, see Carolyn Jones, "Don't Take Any Aprons to College! A Study of the Beginning of Co-Education at Gallaudet College" (master's thesis, University of Maryland, 1983). For background, see Edward C. Merrill, "Gallaudet College," in *Gallaudet Encyclopedia,* vol. 1, ed. Van Cleve, 448; Van Cleve and Crouch, *A Place of Their Own,* 85–86.

33. Editorial, *DMJ* (2 February 1882): 2.

34. Laura Sheridan, "The Higher Education of Deaf-Mute Women," *Annals* 20 (October 1875): 248–51.

35. Editorial, *DMJ* (4 November 1886): 2; Holcomb and Wood, *Deaf Women,* 110–11; *First National Convention of Deaf Mutes,* 28–29; Angie Fuller to *DMJ* (19 October 1880): 2, and (4 November 1880): 2.

36. College policy admitted deaf African Americans, but college officials actively discouraged their entrance until the rise of the Civil Rights movement. For critical commentary, see Oliver J. Whilden, "Reminiscences," *The Frat* (May 1941): 5; "Negroes at Gallaudet," *Cavalier* (September 1950): 2; Ernest Hairston and Linwood Smith, *Black and Deaf in America,* 11. For an illustration of this policy, see Charles A. Bradford, superintendent of New York School for the Deaf, to Percival Hall, president of Gallaudet College, 24 November 1943; Percival Hall to Charles A. Bradford, 26 November 1943, in box 95, Correspondence A–F, July-June 1943–1944, folder, Charles A. Bradford, Presidential Papers of Percival Hall, GUA. By the 1950s, however, administrators apparently relaxed this policy. Two African American students graduated from Gallaudet College in 1954 and 1955. See folder "Admission of Blacks to Gallaudet College and Kendall School," GUA.

37. ESA, *Third Biennial Convention,* 265.

38. Hartwell M. Chamberlayne, "Vagrancy among Deaf-Mutes," *Annals* 11 (April 1859): 86–88. For background on Chamberlayne, a graduate of the New York School and an instructor at the Virginia School, see Gannon, *Deaf Heritage,* 10. For a comparable argument, see J. A. Jacobs, "Importance of Teaching Deaf-Mutes Self-Reliance," *Annals* 10 (July 1858): 161–63.

39. For examples, see "Deaf and Dumb Laborers," *New York Times* (27 August 1881): 5; Editorial, *DMJ* (19 October 1882): 2.

40. James L. Smith, "The Progress of the Deaf," *Second Convention of the Minnesota Association,* 26–28. For background on Smith, see "James Lewis Smith," *Companion* (20 April 1933): 1–26 (reprint, *Nebraska Journal,*

May 1930); Editorial, "Fifty Years a Teacher and Editor," *Companion* (3 October 1935): 6–7.

41. Jersey Blue (pseud.) to *DMJ* (29 September 1881): 4.

42. *Second National Convention of Deaf-Mutes,* 16–19. For background on Thomas Brown, see "Biographical Sketch of Thomas Brown," *DMJ* (21 January 1880): 2; William Martin Chamberlain, "Thomas Brown," *Annals* 31 (July 1886): 204–10.

43. For background on Flournoy, see Gannon, *Deaf Heritage,* 26; Van Cleve and Crouch, *A Place of Their Own,* 61. For two contrasting treatments of Flournoy and his proposal, see Margret Winzer, "Deaf Mutia, Responses to Alienation by the Deaf in the Mid-Nineteenth Century," *Annals* 131 (March 1986): 29–32; Barry Crouch, "Alienation and the Mid-Nineteenth Century American Deaf Community, A Response," *Annals* 131 (December 1986): 322–24.

44. William W. Turner to J. J. Flournoy, 6 December 1855, in "Scheme for a Commonwealth of the Deaf and Dumb," *Annals* 8 (January 1856): 118.

45. Edmund Booth to John J. Flournoy, 6 September 1857, in "Mr. Flournoy's Plan for a Deaf-Mute Commonwealth," *Annals* 10 (January 1858): 40–42.

46. P. H. Confer to Samuel Porter Chamberlain in "Mr. Chamberlain and Others," *Annals* 10 (April 1858): 87–88.

47. E. P. Holmes, "Plea For A Deaf-Mute Colony," *First National Convention of Deaf Mutes,* 36–39.

48. "E. C. Rider's Address," *DMJ* (15 September 1881): 3.

49. Granger (pseud.) to *DMJ* (6 April 1882): 4.

50. Gatesby (pseud.) to *DMJ* (6 July 1882): 1.

51. Harry White, "Deaf-Mutes in Politics," *Second National Convention of Deaf-Mutes,* 22–29. Note that although the document cites Harry White, the Gallaudet University Student Records only list Henry White, so these men are most likely one and the same.

52. Thomas F. Fox, "The Federation of the Deaf," *Third NAD,* 14–17.

53. Thomas F. Fox, "Social Status of the Deaf," 12–16. See "Convention," *DMJ* (3 September 1885): 2. For background on Fox, see Thomas Francis Fox, "An Autobiography," *Fanwood Journal* (15 May 1933): 4–8; Gallaher, *Representative Deaf Persons,* 152–55.

54. Henry Rider, "Oration," *DMJ* (9 September 1875): 2. On Rider, see Editorial, *DMJ* (5 June 1913): 2; Braddock, *Notable Deaf Persons,* 13–14.

55. For background on Hodgson, see Gallaher, *Representative Deaf Persons*, 159–61; "Editor Hodgson," *DMJ* (24 August 1933): 2; Leon Auerbach, "Looking Back," *NAD Broadcaster*, (September 1989): 12; Leon Auerbach, "The National Association of the Deaf Then and Now," *Deaf American* (September 1978): 15–16.

56. Editorial, *DMJ* (2 June 1881): 2.

57. On Hypatia Boyd, see "Prominent Deaf Persons," *Silent Worker* (December 1899): 55.

58. Hypatia Boyd, "The Business Girl," *Silent Worker* (October 1899): 27.

59. Van Cleve and Crouch, *A Place of Their Own*, 100–101. The authors describe this approach as cultural guidance. I argue that this code was of fundamental significance in the nineteenth and twentieth centuries. Deaf leaders described it in rhetoric, speeches, and writing. More important, I maintain that they incorporated the precepts of personal responsibility in their individual and collective actions as leaders.

60. Statement of Thomas Gallaudet, 21 June 1897, Box 44, folder, Correspondence Thomas Gallaudet, 1896–1897, Diocese of New York of the Episcopal Church Archives, St. Ann's Church for the Deaf Collection, New York, New York (hereafter, St. Ann's Church Collection).

61. On Thomas Gallaudet, see Berg and Buzzard, *Thomas Gallaudet*; Berg, *A Missionary Chronicle* (41–59, 60–67; Patten, *Lives of the Clergy*, 217–19; Gannon, *Deaf Heritage*, 181; Amos Draper, "Thomas Gallaudet," *Annals* 47 (November 1902): 393–403.

62. Draper, "Thomas Gallaudet," 399. Draper spoke after the death of Gallaudet.

63. Clarke, comp., *An Account of St. Ann's*, 9.

64. "1880 Report of the General Manager to the Trustees of the Church Mission to Deaf-Mutes, New York," series 5, box 3, folder 7, St. Ann's Church Collection. See also "Help Needed for Deaf-Mutes," *New York Times* (5 June 1893): 5.

65. "Employment for Deaf Mutes," *New York Times* (30 March 1868): 8.

66. On a free night school offered by James S. Well, see "General Manager Report to the Trustees of the Church Mission to Deaf-Mutes, New York, 1876," series 5, box 3, folder 7, St. Ann's Church Collection.

On related classes for parishioners, see Berg and Buzzard, *Thomas Gallaudet*, 53; Henry Buzzard Papers, unprocessed folder, GUA. For background on Well, see Berg, *A Missionary Chronicle*, 23, 34, 45–46; Berg and Buzzard, *Thomas Gallaudet*, 33.

67. Gallaudet explained, "We ask them [deaf parishioners] especially to aid us in our attempt to improve the condition of their less fortunate brethren." See "General Manager Report to the Trustees of the Church Mission to Deaf-Mutes, New York, 1878," series 5, box 3, folder 7, St. Ann's Church Collection.

For examples of the deep difficulties confronting unemployed deaf workers, see "1880 Report of the General Manager to the Trustees of the Church Mission to Deaf-Mutes, New York," series 5, box 3, folder 7, St. Ann's Church Collection; "Help Needed For Deaf-Mutes," *New York Times* (5 June 1893): 5.

See also Reverend Thomas Gallaudet, "St. Ann's Church For Deaf Mutes, New York," *Annals* 10 (January 1858): 163; Reverend Thomas Gallaudet, "St Ann's Church for Deaf-Mutes, New York," *Annals* 12 (October 1860): 243–48.

68. Edward M. Gallaudet, "The First Decade of the National Deaf-Mute College," *Annals* 19 (July 1874): 157.

69. "Convention," *DMJ* (3 September 1885): 2; *Sixty-seventh Annual Report New York Institute for Instruction of the Deaf and Dumb For the Year 1885* (New York: New York Institute for Instruction of the Deaf and Dumb, 1886).

70. Edward Allen Fay, "The Civil Service Requirements," *Annals* 30 (October 1885): 300–301.

71. Editorial, *DMJ* (1 October 1885): 2.

72. George E. Reynolds to *DMJ* (30 August 1888): 2.

73. "Deaf-Mutes in Government Positions," *Silent Worker* (31 March 1892): 4 (reprint, *Deaf-Mute Critic*, n.d.).

74. *Proceedings of the World's Congress of the Deaf and the Report of the Fourth Convention of the NAD*, (Chicago, 1893), 206–7.

75. John T. Doyle to James Lewis Smith, 8 August 1893, in James Lewis Smith, "The Deaf and the Civil Service," *Annals* 38 (October 1893): 274–77.

76. United States Civil Service Commision, *Ninth Report of the United States Civil Service Commission* (Washington, D.C.: Government Printing Office, 1893), 90. The report notes that the general superintendent of the Rail-

way Mail Service concluded it was "very dangerous" for deaf individuals to be employed on the railroad. For this "and other reasons" he banned deaf candidates.

77. Ibid., 20. See also General Rule IV, Clauses 2 and 3.

78. F. P. G., "Deaf Not Barred from the Civil Service," *DMJ* (11 March 1897): 2; J. S. R., "Philadelphia," *DMJ* (18 March 1897): 3; Moses Smith to *DMJ* (25 March 1897): 1.

79. Out of 1,428 deaf respondents to the 1890 census, 243 (163 males and 80 females) were at school, according to Edward Allen Fay, "The Eleventh Census II," *Annals* 43 (November 1898): 350–51. On the other hand, Fay estimated that approximately one-half of all white children and adults between five and twenty-five years of age in 1890 were at school in 1890; see Fay, "The Eleventh Census I," *Annals* 43 (June 1898): 240–47. See also Jack Gannon, *Deaf Heritage*, 14. It is also worth noting that Van Cleve and Crouch caution that the 1890 and 1900 censuses included older adults with severe hearing losses; see Van Cleve and Crouch, *A Place of Their Own*, 158–59.

80. Fay, "Eleventh Census II," 354. Skilled trades included carpentry, cabinetmaking, printing, and shoemaking. Only 3 percent, or 30 individuals, worked in these fields, compared to 11 percent of white respondents. Of 680 women, 216 (32 percent) were farmers or farm laborers; 166 (24 percent) were servants; 29 (4 percent) were laundresses.

81. On racism within the deaf community, see Glenn Anderson and Frank Bowe, "Racism Within the Deaf Community," *Annals* 117 (December 1972): 617–19; Hairston and Smith, *Black and Deaf in America*.

82. "Employment of the Deaf," *Annals* 31 (October 1886): 290–92.

83. Harvey P. Peet, "Statistics of the Deaf and Dumb and the State Census of New York for 1855," *Fourth CAID*, 181–90. Of 113 graduates from the New York School, 59 were farmers and the rest distributed through varied trades. This diversification is borne out by surveys from schools and deaf organizations but not the 1890 national census. School surveys likely overreported the most prominent graduates and underreported former students in agricultural labor. The 1890 census likely overreported the number of men in agriculture—and other fields—because it included men who were deafened late in life and would not consider themselves members of the deaf community. See Fay, "Eleventh Census II," *Annals* 43 (November 1898): 353; Fay, "Reports of American Institutions for the Deaf and Dumb Occupations of Ohio Graduates, 1870," *Annals* 16 (October 1871): 248. For Connecticut, see "Employment of the Deaf," *Annals* 31 (October 1886): 290–92.

For New York, see E. H. Currier and Thomas F. Fox, "New York Institute for the Instruction of the Deaf and Dumb," in *Histories*, vol. 2, ed. Fay, ii. For additional background, see "Occupations of the Deaf," *Annals* 33 (April 1888): 160; *New York School for the Deaf, Seventy-first Annual Report* (New York, Fanwood School, 1889), 90–91; Job Williams, "The American Asylum," in *Histories*, vol. 1, ed. Fay, i.

84. "Tabular Statements of American Schools for the Deaf," *Annals* 63 (January 1918): 38–39. Regarding pay, see James E. Gallaher, "Deaf-Mutes as Printers," *Annals* 25 (April 1880): 135–37. For background, see Editorial, *DMJ* (10 April 1884): 2; Anthony Capelli to *DMJ* (28 February 1890): 1; Van Cleve and Crouch, *A Place of Their Own*, 164–68.

85. For a contemporary view of these shortcomings, see Ronald E. Nomeland, "Beginnings of Vocational Education in Schools for the Deaf" (master's thesis, University of Maryland, College Park, 1967), 32.

Chapter 2. "Our Claims to Justice" Challenging Oralism

1. Bell, *Memoir*, 41, 3, 4. See also "A Deaf Mute Community," *DMJ* (31 December 1884): 3; "A Deaf-Mute Community," *New York Times* (11 January 1885): 3.

2. See also Lane, *When the Mind Hears*, xiii, 283–85, in which Lane properly argues that these efforts reflected a broader tendency of majority citizens to suppress minority languages. On the impact of Bell, see Sue Mitchell, "The Haunting Influence of Alexander Graham Bell," *Annals* 116 (June 1971): 349–56.

3. Robert McGregor, "Deaf Teachers," *Fourth NAD*, 165.

4. "The Twenty-second Convention of the Empire State Association," *DMJ* (18 July 1901): 2.

5. Edward Miner Gallaudet, "'Deaf-Mute' Conventions, Associations and Newspapers," *Annals* 18 (July 1873): 200, 202, 203–6. Edward Miner Gallaudet, "Deaf-Mutism," *Proceedings of the Eighth Convention of American Instructors of the Deaf and Dumb* (Toronto: Hunter, Rose and Company, 1876), 144–46 (hereafter, *Eighth CAID*).

6. Harvey Peet, "Discussion," *Proceedings of the Ninth Convention of American Instructors of the Deaf and Dumb* (Columbus, Ohio: Nevins and Meyers, 1879), 138–39, 134–37, 156–58 (hereafter, *Ninth CAID*). Peet urged deaf leaders to establish collective farms, workhouses, and even factories.

7. For an example of this paternal view, see Benjamin Talbot, "The Development of the Social Capacities of the Deaf and Dumb," *Fifth CAID*, 38.

8. Prominent among the small number of dissenters was Olof Hanson, a graduate of Gallaudet College. As late as 1884, Hanson questioned the value of national associations and conventions. See Olof Hanson, "The Tendency among the Deaf to Exclusive Association with One Another," *Annals* 29 (January 1884): 28–32. For background on Hanson, see "Olof Hanson, An Autobiography," *Companion* (5 May 1932): 1. See also *Empire State Association of Deaf-Mutes, Third Biennial Convention,* 258.

9. Henry Winter Syle, "Societies and Periodicals for the Deaf," *Annals* 18 (October 1873): 257–58. For biographical information on Syle, see Braddock, *Notable Deaf Persons,* 110–12; Robert C. Sampson, "Henry Winter Syle," in Berg and Buzzard, *Thomas Gallaudet,* 133–59. The sharpest criticism of Gallaudet's charges came from Harvey Peet, principal of New York's Fanwood School. At the 1878 CAID convention, Peet claimed that deaf adults ought to do more to live and work together as an extended family. See Peet, "Discussion," *Proceedings of the Ninth Convention of American Instructors of the Deaf and Dumb* (Columbus, Ohio: Nevins and Meyers, 1879): 138–39, 134–37, 156–58 (hereafter, *Ninth CAID*).

10. Best, *The Deaf,* 91–98; Gannon, *Deaf Heritage,* xxvii–xxviii. Indeed, by the 1890s, Edward Gallaudet reversed course and endorsed these associations. Edward Miner Gallaudet, "What the Educated Deaf Can Do for the Deaf," *Annals* 39 (January 1894): 78.

11. Frank R. Wheeler, "Growth of American Schools for the Deaf," *Proceedings of the Twenty-second Meeting of the Convention of the American Instructors of the Deaf.* (Washington, D.C.: Government Printing Office, 1921), 129–33 (hereafter, *Twenty-second CAID*). See also Jones, "One Hundred Years," 1–9. The first oral school was a short-lived experiment in Virginia in 1812; the second, established in Kentucky, operated between 1844 and 1854.

12. Horace Mann, secretary of the Massachusetts Board of Education, and Samuel Howe, superintendent of the Perkins Institute for the Blind, returned from Germany to publish laudatory reports and secure state support for the establishment of an oral school in Boston. On the other hand, administrators from the American School and the New York School visited Europe and returned to argue that students' speech had been useless. For overviews of these early differences see Powrie V. Doctor, "The American Annals of the Deaf, 1847–1947," *Annals* 92 (November 1947): 367–438. Collins Stone, "Articulation as a Medium of Instruction of the Deaf and Dumb," *Annals* 2 (January 1849): 105–12, *Annals* 2 (July 1849): 232–42.

13. For a representative presentation, see Reverend John R. Keep, "On the Best Methods of Teaching Language to the Higher Classes in our Institutions for the Deaf and Dumb," *Third CAID,* 2–31.

14. On New York, see D. Greene, "The New York Institution for Improved Instruction," in *Histories*, vol. 2, ed. Fay, xxvi; on the Clarke School, see Gardiner G. Hubbard, Frank B. Sanborn, Lewis J. Dudley, and Caroline A. Yale, "Clarke Institution for Deaf-Mutes, Northampton, Massachusetts, An Historical Sketch," in *Histories*, vol. 2, ed. Fay, xxvi; on Boston's school, see Sarah Fuller, "The Horace Mann School for the Deaf, Boston, Massachusetts," in *Histories*, vol. 2, ed. Fay, xxxi.

15. Caroline A. Yale, "From the Report of the Principal," in *Histories*, vol. 2, ed. Fay, 24; "Notices of Publications," *Annals* 19 (April 1874): 107.

16. On the development of instruction in Europe through the nineteenth century, begin with Lane, *When the Mind Hears*, 67–154. See also John R. Burnet, *Tales of the Deaf and Dumb*, 51–72; Van Cleve and Crouch, *A Place of Their Own*, 10–20.

17. The term "combined instruction," despite its prevalence, has not referred to any one method. Deaf activists generally favored signed communication as a common medium for both instruction and communication, with oral instruction for students who demonstrated promise in developing their skills in speaking or lipreading. In practice, however, the combined approach has included oral instruction (articulation, speech, and lipreading —of which there are several variants) with manual communication (fingerspelling and sign-based communication—of which there are several methods, including English-based signing and American Sign Language). For example, teachers have employed a range of approaches including oral instruction and fingerspelling without signed communication; oral instruction in classrooms and signed communication outside the class; oral instruction for all students; and signed instruction for students deemed incapable of advancing under oral tutelage. Moreover, anecdotal accounts from deaf students indicate that some teachers relied upon signed communication even when it was prohibited. For background, see Dennis Berrigan and Kenneth Rust, "Sign Language Teaching," in *Gallaudet Encyclopedia*, vol 3, ed. Van Cleve, 23–26.

18. Edward Miner Gallaudet, "The American System of Deaf-Mute Instruction, Its Incidental Defects and Their Remedies," *Sixth CAID*, 47–59, 66, 72, 119.

19. For this vigorous and vital discussion, see *Proceedings of the Seventh Convention of American Instructors of the Deaf and Dumb* (Indianapolis, Sentinel Steam Printing and Book Binding Establishment, 1870): 56–80 (hereafter, *Seventh CAID*).

20. *Eighth CAID,* 134, 132–39.

21. Bell was the commanding leader of the oralist movement. For background on Bell, see Winefield, *Never the Twain Shall Meet;* Van Cleve and Crouch, *A Place of Their Own;* Lane, *When the Mind Hears.*

22. Edward M. Gallaudet, "The Milan Convention," *Annals* 26 (January 1881): 1–16; Van Cleve and Crouch, *A Place of Their Own,* 108–11; Gannon, *Deaf Heritage,* 359; Lane, *When The Mind Hears,* 389–96.

23. Emma Garrett, "A Plea That the Deaf-Mutes of America Be Taught to Use their Voices," *Proceedings of the Tenth Convention of American Instructors of the Deaf and Dumb* (Springfield, Ill.: H. W. Rokker State Printer and Binder, 1882), 66 (hereafter, *Tenth CAID*). Garrett taught at the Pennsylvania Institute.

24. Benjamin D. Pettingill, "The Sign Language," *Annals* 18 (January 1873): 1–12. For arguments linking early exposure to sign language and the intellectual development of deaf children, see Ben Hoffmeister, "Era of Exploration," *Annals* 115 (March 1970): 55–56; Margaret Kent, "Are Signs Legitimate?" *Annals* 115 (September 1970): 497–98; McCay Vernon and Soon D. Koh, "Early Manual Communication and Deaf Children's Achievement," *Annals* 115 (September 1970): 527–36; Jack Olson, "A Case for the Use of Sign Language during the Critical Learning Period in a Congenitally Deaf Child," *Annals* 117 (June 1972): 397–400.

25. "Proceedings of the Buffalo Deaf-Mute Convention," *DMJ* (4 September 1879): 4. See also John Burnet, "Oration," *Silent Worker* (1 October 1873): 4–5, 7. Daily instruction lasted from one to two hours per day. For insight into the time requirements and expectations of oral instruction, see Yale, "Clarke Institution for Deaf-Mutes," in *Histories,* vol. 2, ed. Fay, 21–24. Critics argued that without sign language, students could not readily communicate with each other or their teachers.

26. In New York, leaders of the ESA printed and circulated a compelling personal essay critical of oral instruction. See William M. Chamberlain, "My Experiences and Conclusions as a Lip-Reader," *Empire State Association of the Deaf, Twelfth Biennial Convention,* 18–26.

27. This section draws on Douglas C. Baynton's study, "'Savages and Deaf-Mutes,' Evolutionary Theory and the Campaign against Sign Language in the Nineteenth Century," in *Deaf History Unveiled,* ed. Van Cleve, 92–112. See also Alexander Graham Bell, "Visible Speech as a Means of Communicating Articulation to Deaf-Mutes," *Annals* 17 (January 1872): 1–21; Richard Hofstadter, *Social Darwinism.*

28. James H. Stam, *Inquiries into the Origin of Language.*

29. *Proceedings of the Fifth National Conference of Principals and Superintendents of Institutions for Deaf-Mutes,* (St. Paul, Minn.), 178; "The Fifth Conference of the Principals of American Institutions for the Deaf and Dumb," *Annals* 29 (October 1884): 289; "Convention of Principals," *DMJ* (24 July 1884): 1.

30. See S. G. Davidson. "The Relation of Language to Mental Development and of Speech to Language Teaching," *Association Review* (December 1899): 132.

31. For an oralist perspective, see J. C. Gordon, "Opening Address of the Oral Section," *Fourteenth CAID,* 96–104. Alternatively, see Edward Gallaudet, "Some Incidents in the Progress of Deaf-Mute Education in America, 1890–1895," *Fourteenth CAID,* 40–56.

32. Edward A. Fay, "Day-School for the Deaf and Dumb," *Seventh CAID,* 114–19, 120.

32. For day schools, see John V. Van Cleve, "The Academic Integration of Deaf Children, A Historical Perspective," in *Looking Back,* ed. Fischer and Lane, 336–41; Winnie, *History and Handbook of Day Schools,* 11; Wisconsin Phonological Institute, *Wisconsin System,* 5–13. For these legislative efforts and the development of Wisconsin's schools, see Winnie, comp., *History and Handbook,* 8–32; Edward Allen Fay, "Day-Schools in Wisconsin," *Annals* 30 (October 1885): 302; Lane, *When the Mind Hears,* 362–64; Van Cleve and Crouch, *A Place of Their Own,* 117–20.

33. For representative criticisms, see Olof Hanson, "Day Schools for the Deaf," *DMJ* (11 April 1901): 2. For discussion of terms under which schools are acceptable, see "Resolutions," *Report of Proceedings of the Fourth Convention of the Minnesota Association of the Deaf* (Faribault, Minn.: Companion, 1896), 29–31 (hereafter, *Fourth Convention of the Minnesota Association*). On Robert McGregor's views on day schools, see "Day Schools and Boarding Schools for the Deaf," *Thirteenth CAID,* 106–8.

34. Editorial, *DMJ* (16 May 1895): 2. For a comparable critique, see Editorial, *DMJ* (24 January 1901): 2.

35. Editorial, *DMJ* (9 April 1896): 2. Also see Lane, *When the Mind Hears,* 364–65.

36. For the oral perspective, see "Save the Deaf School," *DMJ* (8 February 1894): 2; "An Open Letter to the Parents of the Pupils of the Portland School For the Deaf," *DMJ* (15 March 1894): 4. For the views of deaf and

hearing advocates of a combined system, see "Hartford School for the Deaf," *DMJ* (8 February 1894): 2; Editorial, *DMJ* (15 February 1894): 2; Henry C. White, "Whispering Under the Rose," *DMJ* (15 February 1894): 2.

37. "Maine Deaf Mutes Congratulated," *DMJ* (29 March 1894): 4. On White, see Editorial, *DMJ* (12 January 1922): 2; Gannon, *Deaf Heritage*.

38. Best, *The Deaf,* 188, 191–93; Best, *Deafness and the Deaf,* 454. For background, see Edward Allen Fay, "Day Schools," *Annals* 44 (September 1899): 395–96; Edward Allen Fay, "Day-Schools in California," *Annals* 48 (May 1903): 304; Lane, *When the Mind Hears,* 364.

39. Regarding an unsuccessful effort to close Wisconsin's residential school, see Editorial, *DMJ* (24 January 1901): 2.

40. H. Van Allen, "The Pennsylvania Institution," in *Histories,* vol. 1, ed. Fay, iii. On Crouter, see "Albert Louis Edgerton Crouter," *Proceedings of the Twenty-fourth Convention of American Instructors of the Deaf* (Washington, D.C.: Government Printing Office, 1926), 194–95 (hereafter, *Twenty-fourth CAID*).

41. Albert L. Crouter, "Changes of Method in the Pennsylvania Institution," *Annals* 46 (January 1901): 62–68.

42. Albert L. Crouter, "Statistics of Articulation Work, in America," *Thirteenth CAID,* 284–89.

43. Editorial, *DMJ* (26 April 1894): 2.

44. James L. Smith, "A Comment on Comparison of Methods at Mount Airy," *Annals* 46 (March 1901): 224–31.

45. Edward A. Fay. "Progress of Speech Teaching in the United States," *Annals* 60 (January 1915): 115.

46. On pay differences, see John Carlin, "On the Mechanical," 200–214; John Carlin, "Wages of Deaf Mute Instructors," *Fifth CAID,* 55–59; Reverend James H. Cloud, "The Social Status of the Deaf," *Thirteenth CAID,* 44. For superintendents' views on pay differentials, see *Fifth CAID,* 56–61.

47. Several deaf adults thought the displacement of deaf teachers was not part of a larger movement. These comments were exceptional and inaccurate. See Douglas Tilden, "The Great Convention and It's Features," *DMJ* (26 August 1886): 2; Harry Fielding, "Reply to Enos," *DMJ* (21 January 1886): 3.

48. "The Fifth Conference of the Principals of American Institutions for the Deaf and Dumb," *Annals* 29 (October 1884): 307–8, 267–312; "Convention of Principals," *DMJ* (24 July 1884): 1.

49. Michigan Girl (pseud.), "Teachers of Deaf Mutes," *DMJ* (1 December 1881): 1.

50. Enos (pseud.), "Deaf Teachers and the Aristocracy of the Ear," *DMJ* (14 January 1886): 2.

51. Robert McGregor, "Deaf Teachers," *Fourth NAD*, 165, 163–66. See also Warren Robinson, "The Necessity of Technical Schools For The Deaf," *Fourth NAD*, 234.

52. Infante (pseud.), "Our New York Letter," *Silent Worker* (September 1894): 10.

53. Henry C. White, "Deaf-Mute Teachers," *DMJ* (10 December 1885): 4.

54. On the conflict at Ohio, see Editorial, "The Deaf-Mute Must Go," *DMJ* (8 September 1887): 2; "Columbus," *DMJ* (24 May 1888): 3.

55. Jones, "One Hundred Years," 7, 10–13. For precise figures for each year, see "Tabular Statements of American Schools for the Deaf," in *Annals*.

56. "Address of Miss Babcock," *Seventeenth CAID*, 18–20.

57. "Practical Value of Articulation to Deaf in Business," *Annals*, vol. 29, no. 4, 285–88.

58. *Fourth NAD*, 31.

59. Thomas Moses, W. E. Burt and J.W. Jones, "A Statement Describing the Accomplishments and Limitations of Our Schools," *Proceedings of the Eighteenth Meeting of the Convention of American Instructors of the Deaf* (Washington, D.C.: Government Printing Office, 1912), 134–36 (hereafter, *Eighteenth CAID*).

60. "Practical Value of Articulation to Deaf in Business," *Fifth Conference of the Principals*, 285–88.

61. James E. Gallaher to *DMJ* (23 October 1890): 2.

62. E. Henry Currier, *The Deaf, By Their Fruits*.

63. Ibid., 40.

64. Ibid., 12.

65. "Report of the Committee on the Industrial Status of the Deaf," *Seventh NAD*, 225–28; "Report of the Bureau of Industrial Statistics," *Proceedings of the Eighth Convention of the National Association of the Deaf* (n.p., 1907), 47–61 (hereafter *Eighth NAD*).

66. *Proceedings of the Tenth Convention of the National Association of the Deaf* (Olathe, Kan.: Independent Publishing Company, 1913), 51–54 (hereafter *Tenth NAD*).

67. These results were hand tallied from the survey and were not summarized on the original report. For the report, see "To Former Pupils and Graduates of Schools for the Deaf in the United States and Canada," *Proceedings of the Twentieth Convention of American Instructors of the Deaf* (Washington, D.C.: Government Printing Office, 1915), 211–365 (hereafter, *Twentieth CAID*).

68. "To Former Pupils And Graduates," *Twentieth CAID*, 317.

69. Robert McGregor, "Report of Committee on Statistics," *Proceedings of the Twelfth Convention of the National Association of the Deaf* (Olathe, Kan.: Register Print), 84–86 (hereafter, *Twelfth NAD*).

70. On trends at the turn of the century, see Edward Allen Fay, "Progress of Speech Teaching in the United States," *Annals* 60 (January 1915): 115. On trends in 1920, see "Statistics of Speech Teaching in American Schools for the Deaf," *Volta Review* (June 1920): 372.

71. For a compelling analysis of these trends, see Baynton, " 'A Silent Exile,' " 220.

72. Robert McGregor, "The Proscription of Signs," *Fifth NAD*, 44–45.

Chapter 3. *"Shoulder to Shoulder" Protesting Civil Service Discrimination*

1. U.S. Civil Service Commission, *Twenty-fourth Report of the United States Civil Service Commission* (Washington, D.C.: Government Printing Office, 1908), 24 (hereafter, *Twenty-fourth Report, CSC*).

2. U.S. Civil Service Commission, *Nineteenth Annual Report of the United States Civil Service Commission* (Washington, D.C.: Government Printing Office, 1902), 15, 202 (hereafter, *Nineteenth Report, CSC*).

3. U.S. Civil Service Commission, *Twenty-second Annual Report of the United States Civil Service Commission* (Washington, D.C.: Government Printing Office, 1905), 175–76 (hereafter, *Twenty-second Report, CSC*).

4. U.S. Civil Service Commission, *Biography of an Ideal*, 20, 45–66, passim.

5. U.S. Civil Service Commission, *Twenty-first Report of the United States Civil Service Commission* (Washington, D.C.: Government Printing Office, 1905), 252–56 (hereafter, *Twenty-first Report, CSC*); *Biography of an Idea*, 45–66. The law in force before the passage of the 1883 Civil Service Act gave departmental chiefs the authority to determine whether women would be accepted; this authority remained unimpaired. U.S. Civil Service Commis-

sion, *First Annual Report of the United States Civil Service Commission*, 2d edition (Washington, D.C.: Government Printing Office, 1884), 25–30 (hereafter, *First Annual Report, CSC*). For an overview, see Sondik, *Ladies and Gentlemen.*

6. U.S. Civil Service Commission, *Twenty-fifth Annual Report of the United States Civil Service* (Washington, D.C.: Government Printing Office, 1909), 123–24 (hereafter, *Twenty-fifth Report, CSC*). Conditions that would bar persons from examinations included insanity; tuberculosis; paralysis; epilepsy; blindness; total deafness; loss of speech; loss of both arms or both legs; loss of arm and leg; badly crippled and deformed hands, arms, feet, or legs; heart disease; locomotor ataxia; cancer; Bright's Disease; and diabetes. For the most complete rationale of this policy, see Civil Service Commission President John Black to Congressman Martin B. Madden, 7 January 1908, in George Veditz, "The Deaf and the Civil Service," *American Industrial Journal* (June 1909): 7, 9.

7. See also *Twenty-fourth Report, CSC*, 20.

8. Oliver J. Whildin to Henry F. Greene, 3 June 1907, in Oliver J. Whildin, "The Deaf and the Civil Service," *DMJ* (27 June 1907): 2. Regarding Whildin's work, see Berg, *A Missionary Chronicle*, 145–46.

9. Odie W. Underhill, "The Deaf Man and the Printing Trades," *Report of the Twenty-third Meeting of the Convention of the American Instructors of the Deaf* (Washington, D.C.: Government Printing Office, 1924), 176–80 (hereafter, *Twenty-third CAID*).

10. Henry F. Greene to Oliver J. Whildin, 6 June 1907, in Whildin, "The Deaf and the Civil Service," 2.

11. Ibid.

12. Veditz, "The Deaf and the Civil Service," 3–4.

13. Frederick James Neesam, "Civil Service," *American Industrial Journal* (December 1907): 12.

14. George Veditz quoted in Frederick Neesam, "Civil Service," *American Industrial Journal* (December 1907): 12. In proportion to their overall population, more than two times as many deaf as hearing workers were employed by the Civil Service. In the deaf community, 28 of the approximately 37,000 deaf citizens were so employed. In the hearing community, 25,000 out of nearly 8 million were civil servants. See John C. Black to President Theodore Roosevelt, 28 February 1908, in Edward A. Fay, "The Deaf and the Civil Service," *Annals* 53 (May 1908): 250–51.

15. Ichabod Crane (pseud.), "Some Thinks on Homes for the Deaf, Civil Service, Et Cetery," *American Industrial Journal* (December 1907): 14–15.

16. Veditz, "The Deaf and the Civil Service," 4.

17. George Veditz, "President's Address," *Eighth NAD*, 16.

18. *Eighteenth CAID*, 210.

19. Editorial, *DMJ* (7 May 1908): 2.

20. Albert Berg, "The Deaf and the Civil Service," *Silent Worker* (April 1908): 121; Editorial, *DMJ* (7 May 1908): 2. Regarding Johnson, see *Eighteenth CAID*, 163–64.

21. John C. Black to President Theodore Roosevelt, 28 February 1908, in Berg, "The Deaf and the Civil Service," 121–22.

22. Ibid.

23. Richard Johnson to Albert Berg, in ibid, 122.

24. Ibid., 121–22.

25. Fay, "The Deaf and the Civil Service," 256, 249–56.

26. Veditz, "The Deaf and the Civil Service," 12.

27. George Veditz to President Theodore Roosevelt, 17 March 1908, in ibid., 11.

28. Holy Bible, Revised Standard Version (Philadelphia: A. J. Holman, 1962), 19 Lev. 14.

29. John C. Black to George Veditz, 23 March 1908, in Veditz, "The Deaf and the Civil Service," 11.

30. Editorial, *DMJ* (30 July 1908): 2. Even as Hodgson admired the political activity of African Americans, they were excluded from the National Association of the Deaf. See "Buffalo, N.Y., 28th Convention of the E.S.A.," *DMJ* (23 July 1908): 2.

31. Veditz, "The Deaf and the Civil Service," 12–13.

32. William J. Bryan to George Veditz, 14 August 1908, in ibid., 13.

33. William H. Taft to George W. Veditz, 17 August 1908, series 8, reel 476, volume 23-P484, William H. Taft Presidential Papers, Wisconsin State Historical Society, Madison (hereafter, WSHS).

34. Eugene V. Debs to Edward Clarke (n.d.), in Veditz, "The Deaf and the Civil Service, 13.

35. Ibid.; George Veditz to William Taft, 14 August 1908, series 3, reel 92, vol. P73–5378. William H. Taft Papers, WSHS; George Veditz to William Taft, September 3, 1908, series 3, reel 93. William H. Taft Papers, WSHS.

36. Olof Hanson to Theodore Roosevelt, 18 November 1908, box 1, folder 3, Civil Service, Olof Hanson Papers, GUA. Folklore in the deaf community asserts the president was converted by Hanson's missive and signaled his change in a later meeting with Secretary of the Interior Garfield. For examples, see Editorial, *DMJ* (11 February 1909): 2, and Berg, *A Missionary Chronicle*, 74–75. There is no record in the presidential papers of Theodore Roosevelt that the president ever received Hanson's correspondence.

37. Secretary of the Interior James Rudolph Garfield to Olof Hanson, 1 December 1908, box 1, folder 3, Civil Service, Olof Hanson Papers, GUA; "The Deaf and the Civil Service," *Annals* 54 (January 1909): 113–14.

38. On Executive Order, no. 984, issued 1 December 1908, see *Twenty-fifth Report, CSC,* 123. According to the Civil Service Commission, deaf applicants were to be admitted for examinations for positions whose duties they were capable of performing.

39. Ibid.; *Ninth NAD,* 71.

40. George Veditz, "President's Address," *Ninth NAD,* 27.

41. Regarding the competitive ethos of deaf workers, see Frank M. Houck, "Prejudice against the Deaf," *DMJ* (28 July 1904). Regarding "undesirables," see Veditz, "The Deaf and the Civil Service," 4.

42. George Veditz to Warren Robinson, *American Industrial Journal* (June 1909): 8. One activist worried that deaf applicants would pass entrance examinations only to be blocked by discriminatory managers who selected appointments from a list of qualified applicants. See Freelance (pseud.), "Another Executive Order Needed?" *DMJ* (14 January 1909): 1.

43. George Veditz to William Taft, 26 April 1909, series 5, reel 343, case file 2568, William H. Taft Papers, WSHS.

44. *Twenty-sixth Report CSC,* 40–41; Edward Perkins Clarke to Edward A. Hodgson, 16 August 1909, in "The Deaf and the Civil Service," *DMJ* (19 August 1909): 2.

45. "What's the Matter with Taft?" *Deaf American* (27 May 1909): 2; Secretary of Commerce and Labor Charles Nagel, quoted in "The Deaf and the Civil Service," *Annals* 54 (September 1909): 387–89; Fred Carpenter to George Veditz, 18 May 1909, in Veditz, "The Deaf and the Civil Service," 16; "Deaf to Be Given Preference," *DMJ* (26 August 1909): 2 (reprint, *New York World*).

46. George Veditz, "President's Address," *Tenth NAD,* 26–27.

47. "Report of Committee on Civil Service," *Tenth NAD,* 86; Isaac Goldberg to Edward A. Hodgson, *DMJ* (18 April 1912): 2.

Chapter 4. "For the Deaf by the Deaf" Advocating Labor Bureaus

1. Minnesota Legislature, *General Laws of the State of Minnesota*, 330.

2. Carlin, "On the Mechanical," 200–214; Reverend Collins Stone, "Report on the Subject of Trades for the Deaf and Dumb," *Fifth CAID*, 127–44.

3. Amos G. Draper, "The Future of the Deaf in America," *Fifth NAD*, 15–22. For background on Draper, see Gallaher, *Representative Deaf Persons*, 33–36. See also Olof Hanson, "How The National Association of the Deaf May be Made More Useful," *Sixth NAD*, 17–20.

4. Editorial, *DMJ* (21 June 1900): 2.

5. May Martin, "Employments Open to Deaf Women," *Sixth NAD*, 76–81. For biographical information on Martin see Holcomb and Wood, *Deaf Women*, 19.

6. Braddock, *Notable Deaf Persons*, 188; Warren Robinson to *DMJ* (22 February 1912): 22 (reprint, *Minneapolis Journal*, 13 February 1912).

7. Warren Robinson, "Industrial Bureau for the Deaf," *Conference of Executives of American Schools for the Deaf—Eighth National Conference*, 52–55.

8. From New York, Timothy Driscoll, a member of the Empire State Association, charged in 1904 that employers were "woefully lacking" in knowledge concerning deaf employees, in "New York, Convention of the Empire State Association," *DMJ* (11 August 1904): 3.

9. Elsie M. Steinke, "Are Labor Bureaus for the Deaf Necessary?" *Seventeenth CAID*, 111–12; Warren Robinson, "Opening Address, Vocational Section," *Eighteenth CAID*, 105.

10. For background on Spear, see Gallaher, *Representative Deaf Persons*, 117–19; Guilbert Braddock, "Notable Deaf Persons," *The Frat* (February 1946): 3, 6; Douglas Bahl, "Anson Rudolph Spear, Inventor, Administrator and Advocate," *Companion* (April 1988): 1–2; Deaf Biographical Files and Deaf Subject Files, Anson Spear, GUA.

11. For a history of the North Dakota School, see Anson R. Spear, "The School for the Deaf of North Dakota," in *Histories*, vol. 2, ed. Fay, xvi. At the North Dakota School, Spear's deaf teaching staff included Alto Lowman, one of the first women to enter Gallaudet College. Regarding Lowman, see Gallaher, *Representative Deaf Persons*, 91–92; Holcomb and Wood, *Deaf Women*, 19.

12. *First Reunion of the Graduates of the Minnesota School for the Deaf at Faribault, June 24–27, 1885* (Faribault, Minn.: School for the Deaf Steam Print, 1885), 24, 31.

13. A. R. Spear, "The Deaf as Members of Society and Citizens," *Report of Proceedings of the Third Convention of the Minnesota Association of the Deaf* (Faribault, Minn.: School for the Deaf Steam Print, 1894), 19.

14. For general background on the school, see James Lewis Smith, "History of the Minnesota School for the Deaf," in *Histories,* vol. 2, ed. Fay, xxv; "Minnesota School for the Deaf," *Companion* (11 February 1925): 1–9.

15. For background on the status of students that supports Spear's position, see James L. Smith, "A Review of the Education of the Deaf in Minnesota," *Fifth Convention of the Minnesota Association,* 12–17. Smith depicts problems in industrial training for males and especially for female students. For a complementary finding, see Agatha Tiegel, "The Future of Our Girls after Leaving School," *Fifth Convention of the Minnesota Association,* 21–23. Tiegels's study of 160 women graduates noted that more than 50 stayed at home with their family. Another 21 were employed as domestics, 15 as seamstresses or dressmakers, 5 as factory workers, and 5 as teachers.

16. "Plea For the Deaf," *DMJ* (24 December 1896): 3 (reprint, *Minneapolis Tribune,* 15 December 1896).

17. A. R. Spear, "Legislation for the Deaf," *Sixth Convention of the Minnesota Association of the Deaf,* 28.

18. Ibid., 34–38. Jay Cooke Howard, *Report of Proceedings of the Seventh Convention of the Minnesota Association of the Deaf* (Faribault, Minn.: Minnesota State School for the Deaf, 1904), 23, 19–26.

19. For background on Superintendent Jonathan Noyes, see Editorial, *DMJ* (19 October 1905): 3.

20. In 1907, for example, according to the Minnesota Association of the Deaf, there were thirteen manual and no oral classes at the school. By 1912, however, Tate had reversed instruction at the school, fourteen oral classes overshadowed nine manual classes. See V. R. Spence, "Presidential Address," *Twelfth Biennial Convention of the Minnesota Association of the Deaf,* 18–21.

21. Anson Randolph Spear, May 1, 1912, to *DMJ* (16 May 1912): 2.

22. School officials readily acknowledged shortcomings in vocational instruction. Superintendent Tate and James L. Smith called for a postgraduate course in industrial training for males. See Editorial, *Companion* (22 October 1913): 8. Tate appeared before the Minnesota Association of the Deaf in 1917, where he described his efforts to secure increased funding. See also "Address," *Proceedings of the Fourteenth Biennial Convention of the Minnesota Association of the Deaf* (n.p., 1917), 11–14.

23. "A Chance for the Deaf," *DMJ* (1 February 1912): 3 (reprint, *Minneapolis Tribune*, 22 January 1912). See also *DMJ* (18 April 1912): 1, for a letter in which Spear praises B. B. Sheffield of the Board of Directors but criticizes Superintendent Tate.

24. James H. Cloud, "Minnesota's Bureau of Labor for the Deaf," *Silent Worker* (June 1913): 161–62.

25. J. Schuyler Long, 19 March 1912, to *DMJ* (18 April 1912): 3.

26. "Helping the Deaf to Find Work," *DMJ* (22 February 1912): 12 (reprint, *Minneapolis Journal*, 13 February 1912).

27. Minnestota Legislature, *Legislative Manual*, 627.

28. "Looking Backward—A review [sic] of the State Labor Department," *Fourth Report of the Industrial Commission of Minnesota, 1927–28* (n.p. 1929), 16–21.

29. "Will Ask State Jobs for Deaf," *DMJ* (22 February 1912): 2. Houk preferred that the proposed bureau also provide services to blind workers. Spear did not publicly comment on Houk's proposal. The state did not provide joint services.

30. *Legislative Manual*, 589.

31. For background on the legislative process and the early years of the bureau, see George Veditz, "A Labor Bureau," *DMJ* (22 May 1913): 1; Cloud, "Minnesota's Bureau of Labor," 161–62; "Minnesota Sets Pace in Aiding the Deaf," *Companion* (27 October 1915): 1 (reprint, *St. Paul Pioneer Press*, 26 September, 1915).

32. Ibid., 583.

33. Anson R. Spear, "The Future Work of the Minnesota Association of the Deaf," *Twelfth Convention of the Minnesota Association*, quote 23, 21–27.

34. *General Laws of the State of Minnesota*, 330.

35. James H. Cloud, "Minnesota's Bureau of Labor for the Deaf," *Silent Worker* (June 1913): 161–62.

36. Veditz, "A Labor Bureau," 1.

37. *Twentieth CAID*, 67.

38. Spear, "The Future Work," 24–25, quote 27.

39. Ibid., 21–27.

40. *Twelfth Convention of the Minnesota Association*, 30–32.

41. Anson Rudolph Spear, "The Minnesota Labor Bureau for the Deaf," *Proceedings of the Tenth Convention of the National Association of the Deaf* (n.p., 1915), 106–7.

42. *Companion* (5 May 1915), 6; *Companion* (29 September 1915): 7. In 1917, the budget was increased to $1,500.00. See *Companion* (25 April 1917): 6.

43. For background on Petra Fandrem, see "The Labor Bureau," *Companion* (29 September 1915): 7; Wesley Lauritsen, "Mrs. Petra F. Howard Honored Upon Retirement," *Silent Worker* (February 1960): 5–6; Deaf Biographical Files and Deaf Subject Files, Petra Howard, GUA. For an early interview with Fandrem, see "Minnesota Sets Pace," 1, 2.

44. Petra Fandrem, "Division for Deaf in the Department of Labor and Industries," *Silent Worker* (September 1915): 12–13; "Address of Petra Howard," *Proceedings of the Thirteenth Biennial Convention of the Minnesota Association of the Deaf* (n.p., 1915), 40, 38–42 (hereafter *Thirteenth Convention of the Minnesota Association*).

45. "Division for the Deaf," *Fifteenth Biennial Report Minnesota Department of Labor and Industries* (n.p., 1919), 191–92.

46. "Division For The Deaf," *Sixteenth Biennial Report Minnesota Department of Labor* (n.p., 1921), 184–87. For a second report which points out minor inaccuracies in this report and indicates that deaf adults were observing the activities of the Division, see "The Labor Bureau," *Companion* (29 January 1919): 5.

47. "Division for the Deaf," *Sixteenth Biennial Report Minnesota Department of Labor*, 184–87.

48. Ibid.

49. For an overview, begin with Reverend James H. Cloud, "A Bureau for the Deaf in the U.S. Department of Labor," *Jewish Deaf* (July 1918); Dr. James H. Cloud, "The Labor Division for the Deaf," *Companion* (February 1919): 18–19. In addition, the proposed official would study the causes of deafness and work to eliminate the condition.

50. All bills were essentially the same.

51. Cloud, "A Bureau for the Deaf."

52. Representative Dudley Hughes, Chair House Committee on Education, to Secretary of Labor James B. Wilson, 30 April 1914; James B. Wilson to Dudley Hughes, 5 June 1914, RG 174, National Archives, Department of Labor, Chief Clerks File, box 15, folder: Bureau of Deaf and Dumb, folder 8/56.

53. *Twentieth CAID*, 195–96; "A Proposed Bureau of Labor," *Annals* (September 1914): 415–17. Committee members included Dr. Harris Taylor

of New York's Lexington School; Dr. Albert H. Walker of the Florida School; and James H. Cloud, the deaf representative. For background on Cloud, see Gallaher, *Representative Deaf Persons,* 126–27; Berg and Buzzard, *Thomas Gallaudet,* 75–76.

54. "NAD," *DMJ* (15 October 1914): 2; Correspondence, *DMJ* (31 December 1914): 1.

55. Anson Spear, 1 January 1915, to *DMJ* (7 January 1915): 2. For an example of one leader who followed Spear's requests, see the correspondence of Marcus L. Kenner, in *DMJ* (18 February 1915): 2.

56. "Report of the Civil Service Committee," *Proceedings of the Eleventh (Special) Convention of the National Association of the Deaf* (Kansas City, Mo.: Walkenhorst, 1916), 45–49, 52–53 (hereafter, *Eleventh NAD*). The report on the bill was prepared by B. R. Allabough of Ohio.

57. Francis W. Neuboer to Secretary of Labor W. B. Wilson, June 8, 1917, RG 174, Department of Labor, Chief Clerks File, box 15, folder, Bureau of Deaf and Dumb, National Archives.

58. "The Lady From Montana," *Jewish Deaf* (May 1917): 1; Editorial, *Jewish Deaf* (May 1918): 1–2. See also Editorial, *Jewish Deaf* (May 1920): 1–2. For biographical information on Rankin, see Hannah Josephson, *Jeannette Rankin, First Lady In Congress.* Rankin never sponsored the legislation.

59. "National Association of the Deaf," *DMJ* (7 February 1918): 2.

60. Cloud, "A Bureau for the Deaf."

61. For a rare expression of opposition to labor bureaus see Alexander Pach, "With the Silent Workers," *Silent Worker* (May 1919): 144. Proponents of labor bureaus, Pach argued, were demeaning and paternal. He claimed that bureau advocates assumed deaf adults were "a helpless lot of people, who stumble and fall by the wayside unless there is some charitable welfare organization that extends a fatherly hand." This critique was consistent with the general gender-based code of responsibility espoused by nearly every male deaf leader. Instead, Pach's argument varied only insofar as he directed his animus at bureau officials.

62. U.S. Congress, House, Committee on Education, *To Create a Bureau for the Deaf and Dumb in the Department of Labor and Prescribing the Duties Thereof,* H.R. 244, 65th Congress, 2d. Session, 13 February 1918, 7.

63. "Death of A. R. Spear," *Companion* (19 December 1917): 10.

64. Congress, House, Committee on Education, *To Create a Bureau for the Deaf and Dumb,* 10.

Chapter 5. *"For One's Daily Bread" Entering Industry*

1. Jonathan Eddy, "Independence in the Country," in *Fourteenth Convention of the Empire State Association of Deaf-Mutes, DMJ* (20 August 1891): 2.

2. Robert Taylor, "Farming as an Occupation for the Deaf," *Annals* 53 (November 1908): 482, 479–83.

3. As expected, the *DMJ*'s Hodgson publicly chided Rider's plan, see Editorial, *DMJ* (26 September 1912): 2. There is no evidence that the plan came to fruition. See also "Farm Colony of Deaf-Mutes To Be Formed," *DMJ* (3 August 1912): 2 (reprint, *Syracuse Post-Herald*, 1 August 1912).

4. "A Chance for the Deaf," *DMJ* (22 February 1912): 2 (reprint, William Cowles, *Minneapolis Journal*, 16 February 1912); "Correspondence," *Companion* (17 December 1913): 5–6.

5. Sarah Porter, "Back to the Soil," *Annals* 52 (March 1907): 117. See also Warren Robinson, "An Inquiry by the Chairman of the Industrial Section," *American Industrial Journal* (October 1908): 1–5. In an earlier meeting of the CAID, Superintendent Francis Clarke of Michigan offered some explanation for this inattention. Most parents preferred that their children be provided trades training at school; agricultural instruction could be learned at home. See Charles P. Fosdick, "Gardening for the Deaf" *Seventeenth CAID*, 97–99, 123.

6. Warren Robinson, "Tendencies to be Guarded Against in the Family Life of our Schools," *Thirteenth CAID*, 179. For biographical information, see "Warren Robinson, Litt. D.," in Braddock, *Notable Deaf Persons*, 186–89; Gallaher, *Representative Deaf Persons*, 219–22.

7. Edward Hodgson argued that schools were able to provide instruction in no more than a few areas. See Editorial, *DMJ* (19 December 1895): 2. For a comparable defense of manual training, see Philip Emery, "Manual Training vs. Machine Operation," *DMJ* (4 February 1904): 2. On the limitations of school programs, see "Syracuse, Convention of the Empire State Association," *DMJ* (9 August 1906): 1.

8. C. A. Boxley, "The Industrial Pursuits of the Deaf," in *Troy, The Twenty-third Convention of the Empire State Association of Deaf-Mutes, DMJ* (4 September 1902): 1, 4.

9. W. G. Shanks, "Manual Training of the Deaf," *Thirteenth Convention of the Empire State Association*, 19–24; Olof Hanson, "The Industrial Problem Among the American Deaf," *Seventh Convention of the NAD*, 141–45.

10. See, for example "Proceedings of the Eleventh Conference of Superintendents and Principals of American Schools for the Deaf," *Annals* 65 (May 1920): 226–29.

11. See, for example, L. K. Thompson, "Industrial Training for Girls," *Fourteenth CAID*, 175–81. See also Mrs. John Schwirtz, "Domestic Science," *Sixteenth CAID*, 269, 267–70.

12. May Martin, "Employments Open to Deaf Women," *Sixth NAD*, 76–81.

13. For a general statement on behalf of expanding instruction for women, see Charles Ely, "The Best 'Bread and Butter' Trades for the Schools in the East," *Twentieth CAID*, 37–38. See also R. Cory Montague, West Virginia, "What of Women?" *Proceedings of the Tenth Conference of Superintendents and Principals of American Schools for the Deaf* (Washington, D.C.: American Annals of the Deaf, 1913), 374 (hereafter, *Tenth Conference of Superintendents and Principals*).

14. On the shortcomings of residential schools, see E. J. Bending, "How Far Should Manual Training Be Carried Before Trades Teaching Is Begun?" *Sixteenth CAID*, 260–69. On changes in New York's schools, see C. A. Boxley, "The Industrial Pursuits of the Deaf," in "Troy, The Twenty-third Convention of the Empire State Association of Deaf-Mutes," *DMJ* (4 September 1902): 1, 4. On broadening Gallaudet College, see Amos G. Draper, "Education of the Deaf in America," *Seventh NAD*, 22–30.

15. D. S. Rogers, "A Plea for a Polytechnic Institute for Deaf-Mutes," *Annals* 28 (July 1883): 184–85.

16. Warren Robinson, "The Necessity of Technical Schools for the Deaf," *Proceedings of the World's Congress of the Deaf and the Report of the Fourth Convention of the National Association of the Deaf* (n.p., 1893), 231–35; Charles R. Ely, "Gallaudet College and Vocational Training," *Proceedings of the Twenty-first Meeting of the CAID Convention of the American Instructors of the Deaf* (Washington, D.C.: Government Printing Office, 1918), 90–93 (hereafter, *Twenty-first CAID*); Editorial, *DMJ* (21 June 1888): 2.; "Industrial," *Silent Worker* (29 January 1892): 4; Jack Gannon, *Deaf Heritage*, 79.

17. Francis D. Clarke, "A National Training School for the Deaf," *Proceedings of the Seventh National Conference of Superintendents and Principals of Institutions for the Deaf* (Colorado Springs: Colorado School, 1892), 80–81 (hereafter, *Seventh Conference of Superintendents*).

18. Maxine Boatner, "Vocational Education under the Gallaudets," *Annals* 102 (May 1957): 308–11.

19. Amos Draper, "The Higher Education of the Deaf," *Thirteenth CAID*, 45–51; Gannon, *Deaf Heritage*, 79.

20. On the origins of the journal, see *American Industrial Journal* (January 1906): 1. On its funding problems and demise, see *American Industrial Journal* (October-December 1910): 12–13.

21. *Twentieth CAID*, 63, 62–66; Louis Cohen, "The Society for the Welfare of the Jewish Deaf," *Silent Worker* (November 1914): 35–36.

22. "Sixth Annual Report-Year of 1917," *Jewish Deaf* (February 1918): 45–49; "Eighth Annual Report-Year of 1919," *Jewish Deaf* (February 1920): 50–73.

23. Harvey Doane, "The Labor World," *American Industrial Journal* (December 1906): 14.

24. Philip Morin, "Trade Unions," *DMJ* (30 August 1906): 1.

25. George Sawyer, "Some of the Difficulties which Beset the Deaf as Breadwinners," *DMJ* (13 September 1900): 1.

26. Sawyer's recommendation came ninety years too soon. The Americans with Disabilities Act signed by President George Bush in 1990 enacted the types of prohibitions envisioned by Sawyer.

27. "Chicago," *DMJ* (28 August 1902): 3. A later account maintains that over 250 deaf women and men were employed prior to the 1903 strike. See "Chicago Firm Employs 150 Deaf Mutes in Big Phone Factory," *Deaf Herald* (June 1906): 2.

28. "Deaf Mutes Go On Strike," *Chicago Tribune* (23 April 1903): 2; "Chicago," *DMJ* (7 May 1903): 3.

29. "Chicago Firm Employs 150 Deaf Mutes in Big Phone Factory," *Deaf Herald* (June 1906): 2.

30. J. Frederick Meagher, "The Spotlight," *The Frat* (February 1939): 2; "The Spotlight," *The Frat* (August 1938): 2.

31. Typically, workers were paid approximately $2.50 per day, the established rate in the industry. See Robert Lacey, *Ford, the Men*. See also Nevins and Hill, *Ford, Expansion and Challenge*, 525.

32. S. S. Marquis, "The Factory Doctor," speech to the American Association of Industrial Surgeons, Detroit, 12 June 1916, 3, Accession 293, Soci-

ology Department, Henry Ford Museum and Greenfield Village, Dearborn, Michigan (hereafter, Ford Museum).

33. Ibid., 117–20. This was a profit sharing plan that workers could qualify for after six months with the company. Management did not extend the offer to women workers.

34. Henry Ford with Samuel Crowther, "My Life and Work," *McLure's* (August 1922): 28–38.

35. Greenleaf, *From These Beginnings*, 3.

36. Ford, *My Life and Work*, 107.

37. Ford, *My Life*, 106–8; Henry Ford with Samuel Crowther, "My Life and Work," *McLure's* (August 1922): 30. Additional works have described the ways that management policies marginalized workers according to their sex and race. See, for example, Greenleaf, *From These Beginnings*, 3, 114–18; Meyer, *The Five Dollar Day*.

38. W. D. Brown, "The Disabled as Productive Workers," *Proceedings, National Conference on Employment of the Disabled* (National Rehabilitation Association, 1941), 91. Brown argued that the safety department was the most appropriate section to appraise these positions as its staff would not be unduly by concerns regarding cost or efficiency. The changes suggested by the Safety Department are suggestive of the mandates regarding reasonable accommodation established in the Americans with Disabilities Act.

39. J. E. Mead, M.D., "Training and Employment of Disabled Workmen in the Ford Plant," *Monthly Labor Review* (November 1923): 1164.

40. *DMJ* (16 September 1915): 2.

41. "Detroit," *The Frat* (January 1916): 6; "Detroit," *The Frat* (April 1916): 5; "Detroit, Michigan," *Ohio Chronicle* (29 January 1916): 2.

42. S. S. Marquis, "The Factory Doctor."

43. Ford with Crowther, "My Life and Work," 31. Henry Ford explained, "No particular consideration has to be given to deaf and dumb employees. They do their work one hundred percent." For additional background, see Ford, *My Life*, 110; Nevins and Hill, *Ford, Expansion and Challenge*, 513–14; David Lewis, *The Public Image of Henry Ford*.

44. On the movement of deaf workers into the Ford Company, see "Deaf Workers in the Industrial World," *Companion* (13 December 1916): 1 (reprint, *Silent Hoosier*).

45. On Akron at the turn of the century, see Grismer, *Akron and Summit County*, 380–82. On the rubber-based industries, see Lief, *The Firestone Story*, 43.

46. Benjamin S. Schowe, "The Akron That Endures," *The Frat* (March 1932): 2–4; Marcus Miller, "The Deaf and the Hard of Hearing in Akron Industry," (master's thesis, University of Akron, Akron, Ohio, 1943), 1–13. On the takeoff of the rubber industry, see Harold Roberts, *The Rubber Workers*, 5–10.

47. Burr, "Akron," *Ohio Chronicle* (8 January 1910): 1; J. O. Hammersly, "Akron," *The Frat* (July 1935): 8. One account identified a deaf woman, Etta Major, as one of the first deaf employees at the Goodrich Company, "Akron," *Ohio Chronicle* (19 March 1910): 2.

48. One account indicated that Ware joined R. A. Henderson. a deaf man already employed. See "Akron," *Ohio Chronicle* (8 October 1910): 2.

Benjamin M. Schowe to Marcus Miller, 16 July 1943, box 13, folder 5, Benjamin Schowe Papers, GUA. Schowe also argued that the Goodyear and Firestone corporations hired a small number of deaf employees during 1910. Deaf women may have been the state's first industrial workers. Female students from the state residential school were recruited as garment workers in a factory in Piqua, a small town in southeast Ohio. See "Piqua," *Ohio Chronicle* (21 May 1910): 2. For a representative story that describes the efforts of deaf workers to secure work, see "Akron," *Ohio Chronicle* (12 February 1912): 2.

49. "Akron," *Ohio Chronicle* (11 November 1911): 2. A later account identifies Park Meyers as the first worker at Goodyear. See "Park Meyers, First Deaf Worker," *Cavalier* (April 1945): 1. Alternate explanations for the hiring of deaf workers exist. The first emphasizes the initiative of management, "Ohio," *DMJ* (12 April 1928): 3; Paul W. Litchfield, "Hiring of Deaf-Mutes," *Some Wingfoot Clan Editorials* (Akron, Ohio: Superior, n.d.). A second theory emphasized the role of Ohio's Department of Labor, J. Schuyler Long, "What the Goodyear Tire and Rubber Company of Akron Ohio is Doing for the Deaf," *Silent Worker* (February 1919): 180 (reprint, *Iowa Hawkeye*). A final theorist argued that the Minnesota state labor bureau assisted in these changes, J. Frederick Meagher, "NadFratities," *Silent Worker* (October 1919): 25. These accounts do not stand up under scrutiny. On the initial recruitment of workers, see "Akron," *Ohio Chronicle* (17 May 1913): 2; "Akron," *Ohio Chronicle* (31 May 1913): 2; "Akron," *Ohio Chronicle* (28 March 1914): 2.

50. Roberts, *The Rubber Workers*, 5.

51. On the migration in Akron, "Several Hundred Men Given Work at Goodyear," *Akron Beacon Journal* (2 February 1914): 7; "Rubber Factories

Here Hiring Men," *Akron Beacon Journal* (13 February 1915): 1; "Goodyear Plans Eight Hour Day for all Workers," *Akron Beacon Journal* (17 March 1916): 1; "Big Demand For Labor in Akron," *Akron Beacon Journal* (2 August 1917): 7; Lief, *The Firestone Story*, 89–101.

52. Karl Grismer, *Akron and Summit County* (Akron: Summit County Historical Society, n.d.), 379, 381.

53. Ibid.

54. Editorial, *Akron Beacon Journal* (26 April 1917): 4.

55. On the decision to recruit deaf workers, see rough draft for "Deaf Workers on the Home Front," (n.d.), box 13, folder 4, Schowe, GUA. Schowe noted that Charles Sieberling at Goodyear and Harvey Firestone supported this initiative. For background, see Allen, *The House of Goodyear*; Lief, *Harvey Firestone*; Litchfield, *Industrial Voyage*; O'Reilly and Keating, eds. *The Goodyear Story*.

56. "Akron, Ohio," *DMJ* (18 January 1917): 3. This account lists some twenty incoming deaf workers, including Troy Hill from Texas and Warren Shafer, the boys' supervisor from the Ohio School. See also, *Companion* (29 November 1916): 10; "Deaf Workers in The Industrial World," *Companion* (9 January 1918): 3; "Deaf Workers in The Industrial World," *Companion* (3 December 1919): 4 (reprint, *Indiana Hoosier*).

57. J. Frederick Meagher, "Akron, O.," *DMJ* (8 August 1918) 3.

58. "Akron," *DMJ* (1 March 1917): 1; "Akron," *Ohio Chronicle* (14 April 1917): 2.

59. Benjamin M. Schowe, Sr., "Akron, City of Opportunity?" *Silent Worker* (January 1922, reprint, *Buff and Blue*).

60. J. Schuyler Long, "What the Goodyear Tire and Rubber Company is Doing for the Deaf," *Silent Worker* (February 1919): 181 (reprint, *Iowa Hawkeye*).

61. Schowe, "Akron, The City of Opportunity?"

62. Lief, *The Firestone Story*, 93; O'Reilly and Keating, ed., *The Goodyear Story*, 43. Including the entire labor force, five hundred women worked at Firestone and three thousand were employed at Goodyear. Definitive figures regarding the number of deaf women who labored during the war years is not available. See "Akron," *The Frat* (October 1918): 17; "Tire Workmen Rank Highest on Payroll," *Akron Beacon Journal* (25 August 1916): 1.

63. For a portrait of a deaf work group, see "Shop Operates Without Word Being Spoken," *Ohio Chronicle* (15 January 1916): 1 (reprint, *Akron Press*); "Akron, O., A City of Opportunity!" *DMJ* (27 January 1916): 1.

64. On the safe work record of deaf employees, see Long, "What the Goodyear Tire and Rubber Company is Doing."

65. *DMJ* (13 March 1919): 1; "Akron, O.," *DMJ* (26 June 1919): 1; "Akron," *DMJ* (16 November 1919): 3; Thomas J. Blake, "The Deaf At Akron," *Proceedings of the Thirteenth Convention of the NAD*, The NAD (December 1920), 57–60 (hereafter, *Thirteenth NAD*).

66. Blake, "The Deaf At Akron," 58–59; Grover C. Farquhar, "The Pick of Industry Goodyear's Flying Squadron," *Silent Worker* (January 1920): 101–2. In August 1918, the company established a Flying Squadron with sixty deaf men and a hearing foreman. At the same time, union proponents properly argued that management relied upon "Squadron" members as a bulwark against strikes.

67. "Akron, O.," *DMJ* (4 December 1919): 1; Grover C. Farquhar, "The Deaf in Industrial Rubber Chemistry," *Silent Worker* (March 1920): 151–52; Blake, "The Deaf At Akron," 57–60.

68. J. Frederick Meagher, "Last to Fight," *Silent Worker* (April 1919): 112.

69. On educational opportunities, see "Akron, Ohio," *DMJ* (18 January 1917): 3; "An Educational Opportunity," *Companion* (10 March 1920): 4; "Goodyear Company Has School for Deaf-Mute Employees," *Ohio Chronicle* (20 March 1920); "Goodyear Institute," *Annals* 65 (May 1920): 338.

70. G. C. Farquhar, "A Winter's Tale," *Silent Worker* (February 1920): 123.

71. Philip J. Dietrich, foreword, *The Silent Men* (Akron: Goodyear Tire and Rubber Company).

72. On various organizations, see *Ohio Chronicle* (12 May 1920); "What the Goodyear Tire and Rubber Company is Doing for the Deaf," *Silent Worker* (February 1919): 182 (reprint, *Iowa Hawkeye*); "Akron," *Ohio Chronicle* (9 May 1914): 2; "Akron, O," *DMJ* (11 March 1920).

73. For an overview of activities, see Ralph Busby, "A Woman Who Is Doing Wonderful Work," *Silent Worker* (June 1920): 277. On church services, see "Akron," *Ohio Chronicle* (17 October 1914): 2. On deaf elders, see *Ohio Chronicle* (28 September 1918). On the activities of the knitting club, *Ohio Chronicle* (12 October 1918) and (3 May 1919). Regarding literary clubs, see "Akron, Ohio," *DMJ* (11 January 1917): 2; "J. F. Meagher, Last to Fight," *Silent Worker* (October 1918): 45. Regarding lectures, see "Akron," *Ohio Chronicle* (10 October 1914): 2; "Akron, O.," *DMJ* (11 March 1920).

74. *DMJ* (30 October 1919): 4.

75. On the transfer of deaf workers, see "Akron," *The Frat* (January-February 1919): 16–17. On the cutoff of women employees, see ibid.

76. See "Firestone Tire and Rubber Company Wants Deaf Workers," *Ohio Chronicle* (8 June 1918): 2; "Firestone Sees the Light," *The Frat* (April 1919): 2 (reprint, *Kentucky Standard*); C. A. Reece, ed., "Those Who Hear Not-In Akron," *Firestone Non-Skid* (19 December 1919): 1–4; "Akron," *The Frat* (June 1918): 9.

77. On Goodyear's plan to establish a division for deaf workers, see "Akron," *The Frat* (November 1919): 10.

78. For background, see "How the Era of Great Prosperity Passed," *Ohio Chronicle* (25 December 1920): 4. For work conditions after the downturn, see *Ohio Chronicle* (15 January 1921), (21 December 1921), and (22 December 1921). For the downturn, see "Akron," *The Frat* (September 1920): 12; "Akron," *The Frat* (November-December 1920): 21; "Akron. O." *DMJ* (7 October 1920): 3.

79. "Akron, O." *DMJ* (29 July 1920): 3.

80. Goodyear sales in 1920 of $192 million, for example, led to profits of $51 million dollars. In 1921, sales dropped to one hundred and five million dollars. A net loss of five million dollars contributed to turnover in the top management. See O' Reilly, *The Goodyear Story*, 43.

81. "Akron, Ohio," *DMJ* (17 February 1921): 3.

82. "Akron, Ohio," *DMJ* (2 December 1920): 1; Harold Igo, "Youngstown's Colony of Deaf Mutes," *Ohio Chronicle* (15 January 1921): 1; "Akron, Ohio," *DMJ* (17 February 1921): 3; "Akron," *DMJ* (9 June 1921): 6.

83. "Goodyear Aircraft Head Relates Experience with Deaf," *Cavalier* (April 1945): 1, 7.

84. Thomas J. Blake, "The Deaf At Akron," *Thirteenth NAD*, 59.

85. Editorial, "Out of Work," *Ohio Chronicle* (12 October 1921): 2.

86. "Division Notes," *The Frat* (June 1917): 5.

87. On inroads into various industries, see "Akron," *Ohio Chronicle* (8 December 1917): 2. On inroads in the auto industry, B. R. Allabough, "Report of the Civil Service Committee," *Twelfth NAD*, 78. On inroads at Nash Motors, see "Employment Chances," *The Frat* (October 1918): 10.

88. "Hartford," *The Frat* (April 1916): 6. See also, Harry J. Goldberg, "Remember Pearl Harbor," *Empire State News* (January-February 1942): 3.

Goldberg worked in a munitions plant in Connecticut with fifty deaf compatriots.

89. "Goodrich Tries Employment of Disabled Men," *Akron Beacon Journal* (30 July 1918): 1; "Akron," *DMJ* (16 November 1919): 3; "Chicago," *DMJ* (7 January 1926): 2.

90. J. Frederick Meagher, "The Deaf Barred," *DMJ* (20 July 1916): 1.

91. Arthur Bailey, "Open Letter to NAD," *DMJ* (1 February 1917): 2.

92. Editorial, *DMJ* (1 February 1917): 2.

93. "The Goodyear Way," *The Frat* (June-July 1920): 7 (reprint, *Alabama Messenger*). For a similar argument, see "Oscar H. Regensburg, The Deaf Apprentice," *Sixth NAD*, 69–71.

94. "Wants Deaf Workers," *Silent Worker* (January 1921): 138 (reprint, *Iowa Hawkeye*).

Chapter 6. *"Conspiracy of Silence" Contesting Exclusion and Oral Hegemony*

1. The national deaf population was 57,804, as noted in the 1930 census. Of this group, 15,881 individuals were between the ages of five (an early age for admission to most schools) and nineteen. I derived the estimate of 40,000 adults by subtracting the number of student-age individuals from the overall group. See *The Blind and Deaf-Mutes in the United States, 1930* (Washington, D.C.: Government Printing Office, 1931), 16 (Table 6).

2. For representative discussions, see "Training for Girls in This Machine Age," *Vocational Teachers* (September 1930): 1; Odie Underhill, "Here and There," *The Frat* (November 1933): 4; Norman G. Scarvie, "Practical Training For Underprivileged Pupils," *Twenty-ninth CAID*, 136–37.

3. Regarding the percentage of deaf teachers in 1935, see Leonard Elstad, "Normal Training of Deaf Teachers," *Report of the Proceedings of the Convention of American Instructors of the Deaf* (Washington, D.C.: Government Printing Office, 1935), 194–97. Regarding the status of deaf teachers, see Norman G. Scarvie, "Practical Training For Underprivileged Pupils," *Twenty-ninth CAID*, 136–37; "This Vocational Business," *Vocational Teachers* (June 1931): 17 (reprint, *Pennsylvania Society News*).

4. J. Schuyler Long, "How Can We Further Advance the Education of the Deaf by Consultation with Our Graduates?" in "Proceedings of the Fifteenth Conference of Superintendents and Principals of American Schools for the Deaf," *Annals* 76 (January 1931): 136.

5. On the Connecticut school, J. Pierre Rakow, "Typewriters Mechanics," *American Era* March 1938): 61–62, 72; "Deaf Workers Make Good," *American Era* (May-June, 39): 90–91; "Mr. Boatner's Address," *American Era* (November 1939): 14–15; Edmund Boatner, "Placement-An Increasingly Important Function of the School," *American Era* (March 1940): 61–62; Editorial, "Placement Record," *American Era* (May-June 1940): 90; Edmund Boatner, "Address," *American Era* (October 1940): 1.

6. At the 1930 NAD convention, Troy Hill argued that a college open to all students, whatever their skills in written English, would substantially advance the position of deaf workers. See Troy E. Hill, "The NAD and the Future of the Deaf in America," *Proceedings of the Sixteenth Triennial Convention of the NAD and Fourth World Congress of the Deaf* (New York: Fanwood Press, 1930), 52. Applicants to Gallaudet College had to pass a demanding written examination.

7. For proposals from Roy Conkling, the editor and publisher of the independent *American Deaf Citizen,* and from Harvey Barnes, a vocational instructor at Illinois's residential school, see "Advanced Vocational Training at Gallaudet," *American Deaf Citizen* (7 May 1932): 2; Barnes, *Proposal to Establish an Opportunity School.*

8. Editorial, "What the Deaf Need, A Moses," *Companion* (26 November 1936): 6–7; Editorial, "What Shall the Solution Be?" *Companion* (29 April 1937): 6–7.

9. William J. Marra, "The Federal Adult Education Project For The Deaf," *Annals* 82 (November 1937): 406–10; "Kansas City, MO.," *DMJ* (22 July 1937): 5. For background on Marra, see Georgetta Graybill, "A Man of Many and Varied Talents; Pioneer in Adult Education for the Deaf," *Deaf American* (September 1971): 3–6. In addition, programs were also held in Chicago, Oklahoma, and New Jersey. See Alan B. Crammatte, "Vocational Guidance in Schools for the Deaf," *Annals* 84 (March 1939): 404.

10. On Tom Anderson, likely the most influential advocate for improved vocational instruction, see Tom L. Anderson, "The Handwriting on the Wall," *Proceedings of the Thirtieth Convention of American Instructors of the Deaf* (Washington, D.C.: Government Printing Office, 1938), 211, 211–15 (hereafter, *Thirtieth CAID*). Deaf writers lashed out at these policies in the pages of *Vocational Teachers,* an independent national periodical edited by Anderson. See "Salt Risin,'" *Vocational Teachers* (June 1931): 21.

11. Margaret McKellar, "Suggested Vocational Training Courses for Girls," *Vocational Teachers* (March 1931): 6–9.

12. As one frustrated respondent explained, "There are lots of things deaf girls can do. They only need a chance, which they never get." Bertha Peterson and Clara Brown, "Home Economics in Schools for the Deaf and the Marital and Occupational Status of the Alumni," *Annals* 78 (March 1933): 197.

13. For a frank discussion, see the views of the superintendent of Louisiana's residential school, L. R. Divine, "Trades Open to Deaf Girls in the South," *Thirtieth CAID*, 68–70.

14. On Indiana, see Robert Baughman, "Trades Open to Deaf Girls in Indianapolis," *Thirtieth CAID*, 70–72. For broadly comparable reports, see Leila Gerry, "Vocational Placements of Deaf Girls in the East," *Thirtieth CAID*, 72–75; "Present Occupations of Former Pupils," *Fanwood Journal* (1 February 1933): 11.

15. On instruction to deaf African Americans in Louisiana, see "Who Will Give This Little Boy a Chance?" *Volta Review* (October 1937): 548; "New State School for Negro Deaf in Louisiana Started," *Ohio Chronicle* (24 December 1938): 1 (reprint, *Annals*). On the position of deaf women in Georgia, see Georgia State Department of Public Welfare, *Georgia's Deaf* (Atlanta, Georgia: Report on the United States Work Projects Administration of Georgia Official Project, 665-34-3-90), 18–23.

16. Warren M. Smaltz, "The Deaf in Modern Industry," *Eighteenth Triennial Convention of the National Association of the Deaf* (n.p., 1937), 67, 63 (hereafter, *Eighteenth NAD*). On Smaltz, see Berg, *A Missionary Chronicle*, 166–67. For an illustration of Superintendent Elbert Gruver's views, see Elbert Gruver, "A New Emphasis in the Education of Deaf Children," *Vocational Teachers* (October 1932): 1.

17. Norman G. Scarvie, "Practical Training For Underprivileged Pupils," *Twenty-ninth CAID*, 136. For a comparable opinion, see Arthur G. Norris, "A Review and a Prophecy," *Twenty-seventh CAID*, 36–41.

18. Roy Conkling ended publication of the paper in December 1942. On Conkling and the paper, see *Ohio Chronicle* (5 December 1942): 1, 2.

19. "Keep Them within Bonds," *American Deaf Citizen* (24 March 1933): 4. See also, "It's Our 'Language,'" *American Deaf Citizen* (12 April 1929): 2.

20. On Idaho, see *NAD Bulletin* (December 1934): 2; "NAD Activities," *NAD Bulletin* (January 1935): 1; J. F. M., "Combined System Wins Out in Idaho," *NAD Bulletin* (May 1935): 2. On Virginia, see "Ouster Proceedings Start," *American Deaf Citizen* (6 April 1934): 1; William Schaub, "President's

Address," *Proceedings of the Seventeenth Triennial Convention of the National Association of the Deaf* (n.p., 1934), 7–11 (hereafter, *Seventeenth NAD*); "Executive Board Report" *Eighteenth NAD*, 21–24; "No Deaf Graduate From Virginia School," *American Deaf Citizen* (10 June 1938): 1 (reprint, *Staunton Evening Leader*); "Alumni Vindicated," *Modern Silents* (May 1939): 9 (reprint, *Staunton News Leader*). On Montana, see Marcus L. Kenner, "President's Address," *Eighteenth NAD*, 11–12.

21. Minimized, if mentioned at all, in school records and only intermittently cited in mainstream newspapers, most accounts of these contests were recorded in the publications of deaf organizations whose members led these challenges.

22. "Experimentation is Condemned by Deaf," *Modern Silents* (January 1938): 14 (reprint, *Dallas News*, (12 December 1937). Deaf activists had long opposed Scott. See "Investigation of Deaf Association's Charges Made on May 5 to 7," *Modern Silents* (September 1938): 4–7.

23. "Protests and Charges by Association before the House Eleemosynary Institutions Investigating Committee Corroborated by Sworn Testimony and Evidence," *Modern Silents* (June 1938): 3–4.

24. "PROTESTS AND CHARGES as Presented by the Texas Association of the Deaf," *Modern Silents* (December 1938): 4–5.

25. On the investigation, see "Protests and Charges by Association," 3–4; "Investigation of Deaf Association's Charges Made on May 5 to 7," 4–7; "Additional Information on Investigation," *Modern Silents* (October–November 1938): 8.

26. On Scott's claim regarding the lipreading abilities of students, see "Additional Information On Investigation," 8. Scott's assertions exceeded the estimates of even the most optimistic oralist professionals.

27. "Investigation of Deaf Association's Charges Made on May 5 to 7," *Modern Silents* (September 1938): 4–7.

28. "Proceedings of the Special Called Convention," *Modern Silents* (August 1938): 9–10.

29. "Investigation of the Texas School for the Deaf," *Modern Silents* (October–November 1938): 2.

30. Governor-elect Lee O'Daniel publicly questioned Scott's competence and endorsed the investigation. "Deaf Fight for Justice and a Fair Deal," *Modern Silents* (December 1938): 6; "Children Sent Home for Recounting Incidents of Cruel Treatment at Investigation," *Modern Silents*

(January 1939): 3; "Representative Ross Harding Decries Cruelty to Deaf Children," *Modern Silents* (February 1939): 4.

31. "Legislative Committee Approves Resolution Recommending Ouster, Deaf Association Victorious," *Modern Silents* (March–April 1939): 9; "Oust Scott March By Pupils Averted," *Modern Silents* (March–April 1939): 12 (reprint, *Austin Statesman*, 24 February 1938).

32. "Superintendent-Elect E. R. Wright," *Modern Silents* (September 1939): 2; "An Open Message," *Modern Silents* (September 1939): 3.

33. On the NAD, begin with Gannon, *Deaf Heritage*, 264–65; Editorial, *DMJ* (24 July 1930): 2; George Veditz, "The Genesis of the National Association of the Deaf," *DMJ* (1 June 1933): 1; Altor Sedlow to *DMJ* (28 March 1934): 6; Frank Andrewjeski, "The Ailing NAD," *American Deaf Citizen* (8 June 1934): 1. Marcus Kenner, elected President of the NAD in August 1934, was aware of these criticisms. See Marcus L. Kenner, "The Missing Link," *Seventeenth NAD*, 36.

34. "Financiers to Raise $150,000 Each Week to Give Jobs to Idle," *New York Times* (16 October 1930): 1; "Businessmen Will Map Jobless Aid Today," *New York Times* (22 October 1930): 20; "Relief Work Unified to Widen Aid to Idle," *New York Times* (31 October 1930) 1; Editorial, "A Job Well Done," *New York Times* (18 December 1930): 24; "Job Fund $8,269,000 as Campaign Closes," *New York Times* (18 December 1930): 1, 18.

35. Editorial, "A Special Handicap," *New York Times* (29 January 1931): 22. During this period, the Empire State Association of the Deaf was in a period of severe decline and ill-positioned to negotiate for local men. New York's residents revived the state association but not until the latter years of the Depression.

36. On the NFSD see "Lean Years and Lush," *The Frat* (December 1944): 5.

37. On community efforts, see "Akron," *American Deaf Citizen* (16 October 1931): 2; "Houston Deaf Organize for Relief," *American Deaf Citizen* (30 October 1931): 1; Miles Sweeney, "New Jersey News," *American Deaf Citizen* (9 December 1932): 1; J. W. Ferg, "Louisville," *The Frat* (January 1932): 11; "Organize for Relief of Needy," *American Deaf Citizen* (1 April 1932): 1.

38. For representative reports, see "Present Occupations of Former Pupils," *Fanwood Journal* (1 February 1933): 11; Louise Odencrantz, "The Vocational Adjustment of the Deaf, A Study of the Work Histories of 749 Deaf Men And Women," *Proceedings of the Conference of American Instructors of*

the Deaf (Washington, D.C.: Government Printing Office, 1935), 80–94; Leila Gerry, "A Study of Two Hundred and Ninety-Two Deaf Persons Listed with the Employment Center for the Handicapped in New York City," *Annals* 75 (May 1930): 177–91.

39. See *Twenty-seventh Biennial Report, Maryland State School for the Deaf* (Frederick, Md.: Maryland State School for the Deaf, 1932), 87.

40. Frank Thompson to General Hugh Johnson, 16 September 1933, National Recovery Administration, folder 567, Handicapped-Deaf, RG 69, National Archives, Washington, D.C. (hereafter, NRA). See also Marcus Kenner to General Hugh Johnson, 27 November 1933, NRA; Gerald Tussing to General Hugh Johnson, 24 November 1933, NRA; Nathan Fritz to General Hugh Johnson, 23 August 1933, NRA.

41. In his reply to Kenner, an assistant to General Johnson simply noted that the NRA was neither empowered to assist deaf workers directly nor authorized to compel private employers to hire deaf workers. A. R. Forbush, Assistant to General Hugh Johnson, to Marcus Kenner, 27 November 1933, NRA.

42. On the CCC, see Salmond, *The CCC 1933–1942*; Saalberg, "Roosevelt, Fechner and the CCC"; James Woods, "The Legend and the Legacy of F.D.R. and the CCC."

43. U.S. Department of Labor, *Handbook for Agencies Selecting Men for Emergency Conservation Work,* Bulletin No. 3, 1 May 1933 (Washington, D.C.: Government Printing Office, 1933), quote 4, 3–6. See also *A Chance to Work in the Forests, Emergency Conservation Work*, Bulletin No. 1, 17 April 1933 (Washington, D.C.: Government Printing Office, 1933), 1, 3.

44. For background figures, see Salmond, *The CCC 1933–1942*, preface.

45. For a representative letter from a deaf applicant, see Sterling Summers to Robert Fechner, 27 July 1933, Civilian Conservation Corps, General Correspondence, 1933–42, series 100, box 132, folder, Sterling Summers, RG 35, National Archives, Washington, D.C. (hereafter, CCC).

46. William Allen to Robert Fechner, 15 April 1935, and Robert Fechner to William Allen, 1 May 1935, CCC, General Correspondence, 1933–42, series 100, box 4, folder, William Allen; Louis Alphonse, "Says Deaf Ought to Get Equal Chance in CCC Or a Similar Group," *Jersey Journal* (29 March 1937) in CCC, General Correspondence, 1933–42, series 100, box 889, folder, Enrollment Deaf Mutes.

47. On Bjorlee, see "Ignatius Bjorlee, An Autobiography," *DMJ* (4 April 1929): 2.

48. *Twenty-ninth Biennial Report: Sixty-seventh and Sixty-eighth Annual Report Maryland State School for the Deaf* (Frederick, Md.: Maryland School for the Deaf, 1936), 24, 25.

49. Robert Fechner to William Allen, 1 May 1935; Robert Fechner to Honorable Abe Murdock, 10 May 1935, CCC, General Correspondence, 1933–42, series 100, box 889, folder, Enrollment of Deaf Mutes.

50. Salmond, *The CCC 1933–42;* 55, 63.

51. On a proposal from Minnesota, see Blanche La Du to Robert Fechner, 6 February 1934; and Robert Fechner to Blanche La Du, 13 February 1934, CCC, General Correspondence, 1933–42, series 100, box 671, folder 500, Minnesota Department of Public Institutions. On a proposal from J. H. Stone, the Superintendent of the Mississippi School, see Mississippi School for the Deaf, 5 September 1935; CCC to Buford Yeager, Emergency Relief Coordinator, Jackson Mississippi, 21 September 1935, CCC, General Correspondence, 1933–42, series 100, box 889, folder, Enrollment of Deaf Mutes. Although neither Stone's nor La Du's proposals were scrutinized, deaf leaders typically opposed segregated camps, arguing that deaf adults had a right to be included in the main body of the CCC; detached camps implied a subordinate status and were unacceptable. Regarding camp proposals, see J. E. Dunn to Robert Fechner, 15 July 1935, CCC, series 100, box 889, folder, Enrollment of Deaf Mutes; "FERA Aid for the Deaf of the North-West," *NAD Bulletin* (January 1935): 1; "Worth Considering," *NAD Bulletin* (January 1935): 2; "O.A.D. Convention," *Oregon Outlook* (September 1935): 3; "The Dunn-McNary Bill," *NAD Bulletin* (October 1935): 2; "More About the Dunn-McNary Plan," *NAD Bulletin* (January 1936): 1; J. E. Dunn to *Oregon Outlook* (February 1936): 4–5; Editorial, *The Frat* (February 1936): 4; "The Dunn-McNary Plan," *DMJ* (16 April 1936): 6; "Experience," *NAD Bulletin* (April 1936): 3; J. Frederick Meagher, "The Spotlight," *The Frat* (March 1937): 2.

52. Charles Taylor to Millard Tyding, 3 December 1940, CCC, General Correspondence, 1933–42, series 100, box 889, folder, Enrollment of Deaf Mutes.

53. Robert Fechner to Edward Blake, 8 April 1935, CCC, General Correspondence, 1933–42, series 100, box 889, folder, Enrollment of Deaf Mutes.

54. On Native Americans, see Parman, "The Indian Civilian Conservation Corps." On African Americans in the CCC, see Kifer, "The Negro Under the New Deal, 1933–1941"; Olen Cole, Jr., "Black Youth in the Civilian Conservation Corps."

55. For background on these efforts, see "School and Industrial Legislation," *DMJ* (28 May 1936): 1.

56. Deaf workers—as well as other workers with physical differences—were admitted into the WPA under an Executive Order that prohibited the exclusion of "physically handicapped persons, otherwise employable, where such persons may be safely assigned to work which they can ably perform." Some deaf people objected to their classification as "handicapped" but interpreted this order as proof they had a right to undertake any job they could safely perform. *Executive Orders Numbers 6915–7089* (Washington, D.C.: Government Printing Office, 1934), 4 (No. 7046).

57. "Notice to the Deaf of America," *Companion* (24 December 1936): 8; "W.P.A., Social Security and Civil Service," *NAD Bulletin* (January 1937): 1; Marcus L. Kenner, "President's Address," *Eighteenth NAD*, 12.

58. Howard, *The WPA*, 368, 378, 379, 452.

59. "Akron W.P.A. Consents to Hire Deaf Workers on Some of Its Projects," *Ohio Chronicle* (19 March 1938): 1 (reprint, *Akron Division Journal*); B. M. Schowe, "A Worm's Eye View of W.P.A." *St. Ann's Quarterly Review* (July 1938): 3–7.

60. See Anderson, "Report of the Industrial Committee of the NAD," 45.

61. The Fanwood School joined with the Lexington School and St. Joseph's to place Hemle at the Employment Center of the Deaf. Hemle had prior experience at a private employment agency, the YMCA and as an administrative assistant at the New York State Employment Center. See *DMJ* (16 November 1933): 2.

62. For Hemle's views on deaf applicants, see Margarette Hemle, "The Deaf Worker," *Maryland Bulletin* (December 1935): 45 (reprint, *Fanwood Journal*); "The Vocational Attitude of the Deaf," *Companion* (23 May 1935): 1–2 (reprint, New York State Employment Services, Placements).

63. For an early criticism of Hemle and state services for deaf adults, see Altor Sedlow to *DMJ* (25 October 1934): 7. See also "Dunny" to *DMJ* (8 November 1934): 2; C. Allan Dunham to *DMJ* (21 February 1935): 6.

64. Generally, workers with disabilities were not to be paid less than 75 percent of the minimum wage or constitute more than 5 percent of the work force, unless a variance was granted by the Department of Labor. See Enforcement of Code Provisions Limiting Employment of Handicapped Workers, in "Unemployment Conditions and Unemployment Relief," *Monthly Labor Review* 38 (May 1934): 1058–59.

65. One survey of adults placed by Hemle in 1939 noted that some workers earned as little as $5.50 per week—scarcely more than half the

weekly base pay of the minimum wage. See "Special Employment Services For the Deaf," *New York Journal of the Deaf* (9 February 1939): 4. Also see "Report of Placement Officer," *DMJ* (26 July 1934): 7; "Report of Placement of the Deaf," *DMJ* (4 October 1934): 4.

66. Editorial, "False Impressions," *Empire State News* (March-April 1942): 3. Moreover, critics were aware of the advances secured by Edmund Boatner in finding well-paid industrial positions for deaf applicants in Connecticut.

67. On Hemle's placements during the Depression, see "Vocational Guidance," *Annals* 85 (May 1940): 280–81. For a defense of Hemle's work, see Editorial, *DMJ* (4 November 1937): 4; Editorial, *DMJ* (2 December 1937): 4. Superintendent Victor Skyberg, Hemle's supporter, rather than Thomas Fox, the recently appointed editor, probably wrote these commentaries. In 1938, Fox, a deaf teacher at the Fanwood School, opposed the hiring of deaf workers at the sub-minimum wage. See Editorial, *DMJ* (22 September 1938): 4.

68. The provision of pensions was not uniformly supported. Some worried that these benefits would lock blind adults into dependency without lowering the obstacles in the work force that impeded their access and advance. See Robert C. Irwin and Evelyn McKay, "The Social Security Act and the Blind," *Law and Contemporary Problems* (April 1936): 271–78; Committee on Economic Security, *Social Security in America, The Factual Background of the Social Security Act as Summarized from Staff Reports* (Washington, D.C.: Government Printing Office, 1937).

69. "The Deaf and National Legislation," *NAD Bulletin* (October 1935): 1. "The Blind Get $400,000.00," *DMJ* (17 December 1936): 6. For comments ascribed to Tom Anderson, see J. Frederick Meagher, "The Spotlight," *The Frat* (September 1936): 2.

70. In 1936, Fox argued that dollars dispersed to blind pensioners brought no return to the state, whereas funds spent on the education of deaf students were reimbursed as students become wage earners. See "The Blind get $400,000.00," *DMJ* (17 December 1936): 6.

71. On Wood's petitions to the president in 1934 and to Eleanor Roosevelt in 1937, see "Mrs. Anna Eleanor Roosevelt Praises This Magazine," *Digest of the Deaf* (June 1939): 1. Disgruntled at the administration's activities regarding deaf adults, Wood urged the NAD to sue the government, charging that the administration neglected deaf workers in comparison to blind adults, African Americans, and foreign countries. See William H. Wood, "Impossible?" *Silent Broadcaster* (April 1941): 1.

72. See Kenner, "President's Address," *Eighteenth NAD*, 13. For background on Kenner, see Sol Garson, "Marcus Kenner for NAD President," *American Deaf Citizen* (11 July 1930): 2; Bernard Teitelbaum, "A Graduate of the School of Hard Knocks, Marcus L. Kenner," *Silent Worker* (December 1957): 3–5.

73. *Jersey Booster* (January 1938): 7.

74. Regarding discriminatory private employers, see Altor Sedlow, "Empire State Association of the Deaf," *DMJ* (26 December 1935): 3; Altor Sedlow to *DMJ* (16 January 1936): 6; Altor Sedlow, "The Deaf in Industry," *DMJ* (4 June 1936): 6; Arthur G. Leisman, "Some Observations in the Deaf World," *Nineteenth Triennial Convention of the National Association of the Deaf* (n.p., 1940), 74–77 (hereafter, *Nineteenth NAD*); "Educating the Employers as to the Capabilities of the Deaf," *Ohio Chronicle* (21 May 1938): 1; James Smith, "What About a Labor Bureau For the Deaf of Arkansas?" *The Ark* (1–4 July 1938): 2.

75. Max Hesel Lewis, "Wisconsin," *DMJ* (8 July 1937): 2.

76. "Convention of Indiana Association," *DMJ* (2 July 1936): 6. The newspaper did not indicate how many firms were contacted.

77. For the study, see Elise H. Martens, *The Deaf and the Hard of Hearing*. Half of the respondents identified themselves as hard-of-hearing. On the unemployment of deaf workers, see pp. 23 and 28. See also Elise Martens, "Guidance for Deaf and Hard of Hearing," *Companion* (15 April 1937): 1–3 (reprint, *School Life*). For a critique, see "The Right Focus," *The Frat* (March 1934): 4.

78. Martens, *The Deaf and the Hard of Hearing*, 82.

79. For arguments in favor of state and national labor bureaus, see Leisman, "Some Observations in the Deaf World," 74–77; "Report of the NAD Civil Service Committee," *Nineteenth NAD*, 24.

80. On failed efforts in Iowa, West Virginia and Texas, see "NAD Activities," *NAD Bulletin* (March 1935): 4; "Items of Interest," *NAD Bulletin* (April 1935): 3. On failed efforts in Kentucky, West Virginia, and Washington, see "NAD Activities," *NAD Bulletin* (February 1935): 1; Editorial, *Washington Deaf Record* (October 1938): 4; "Bureau of Labor or Placement Office," *Silent Cavalier* (1 April 1941): 2. On Ohio's pursuit, see "The Need For a Labor Bureau for the Deaf of Ohio," *Ohio Chronicle* (4 June 1938): 2.

Wisconsin's deaf citizens established a state-funded Service Bureau in 1940. See Max Hesel Lewis, "Wisconsin," *DMJ* (8 July 1937): 2; Jobs Are

Found For Wisconsin Deaf," *Ohio Chronicle* (9 October 1937): 1; *DMJ* (11 February 1937): 2.

81. The labor bureau drive was proposed by the newly established Metropolitan Civic Association of the Deaf (MCAD) in 1937. See *DMJ* (4 November 1937): 1; Jack Ebin, "Why A Labor Bureau For the Deaf?" *Empire State News* (January 1940): 3. On Ebin, see Deaf Biographical Files and Deaf Subject Files, Empire State Association for the Deaf, GUA.

82. For an overview, see New York State Commission, *Third Report of the Temporary State Commission,* 31–33. On ESAD's perspectives, see Albert Davis, "Report of Our Legal Advisor," *Empire State News* (January 1939): 2. On the expiration of legislation, see "Assembly Bill for Labor Division Killed by Ways & Means Com.," *Empire State News* (April 1940): 1; Paul Blanshard, "Labor Bill Again Defeated But Hope Exists For Other Remedies" *Empire State News* (May 1940): 1.

83. New York State Commission, *Second Report of the Temporary State Commission to Examine, Report Upon and Recommend Measures to Improve Facilities for Care of Hard of Hearing and Deaf Children and Children Liable to Become Deaf* (Albany: J. B. Lyon, 1939), 31–33.

84. On the bureau, see "Mich. Deaf to Create Commission of Labor," *Ohio Chronicle* (10 April 1937): 1 (reprint, *American Deaf Citizen*); Jay Cooke Howard to *DMJ* (15 July 1937): 2; "Michigan Labor Bureau," *Companion* (3 March 1938): 5 (reprint, *Detroit Daily News*).

85. Henry P. Crutcher, "The Division of the Deaf and Deafened of the Michigan State Department of Labor," *Silent Worker* (June 1949): 13–14.

86. On the role of state politicians and labor organizations, see Jay Cooke Howard, "Work of Michigan Division for the Deaf and Deafened," *American Deaf Citizen* (1 July 1938): 1; "Michigan Comes Through," *DMJ* (1 July 1937): 5. On Jay Cooke Howard's role, see Henry P. Crutcher, "The Division of the Deaf and Deafened of the Michigan State Department of Labor," *Silent Worker* (June 1949): 13–14. On the bureau, see Leon D. Case, comp., *Public and Local Acts of the Legislature of the State of Michigan* (Lansing, Michigan: Franklin De Kleine, 1937), 97–98.

87. Regarding unemployment see "Report of Labor Relations Committee," *Pennsylvania Society News* (December 1935): 11; "Report of Labor Relations Committee," *Pennsylvania Society News* (December 1935): 14; "P.S.A.D. Convention," *DMJ* (19 September 1935): 7; "Rehabilitation of the Deaf in Pennsylvania is Well Established," *Ohio Chronicle* (1 March 1941): 1 (reprint, *Pennsylvania Society News*). On the bureau, see "President Clark's

Address," *DMJ* (3 October 1929): 1; "P.S.A.D. Convention," *DMJ* (19 September 1935): 7; W.M.S. "Pennsylvania Deaf Organize," *Ohio Chronicle* (8 February 1936): 1 (reprint, *Silent Missionary*); "The Deaf Win," *The Frat* (August 1937): 4.

88. On the use of state assistance before 1937, see "Report of Labor Relations Committee," *Pennsylvania Society Bulletin* (December 1935): 3–16; Editorial, "Rehabilitation Prevents and Protects," *Monthly News* 19 (August 1932): 2. See also *Pennsylvania Labor and Industry Review* (March 1940): 64–65; Warren F. Smaltz, "The Case for Rehabilitation," *Annals* 84 (November 1939): 387–91.

89. "Twelve Points," *The Frat* (February 1938): 4.

90. "Pennsylvania Comes Through," *DMJ* (24 June 1937): 6. One account claims that 20,000 letters and telegrams were sent to the state legislature. This figure appears extravagant. See "Pittsburgh, Pa.," *DMJ* (10 June 1937): 7.

91. "Pittsburgh, Pa.," *DMJ* (10 June 1937): 7.

92. Warren F. Smaltz to *DMJ* (17 February 1938): 3; "From Dependence to Independence," *Department of Labor and Industry Biennium Report, 1937–1938, Special Bulletin no. 47* (Harrisburg, Pa.: Department of Labor and Industry, 1939), 111–21.

93. On the endorsement of vocational services, see "Report of the Industrial Committee," *Nineteenth NAD,* 22–23; James Vestal, "Employment Adjustments of the Deaf," *Eighteenth NAD,* 68–72; Warren F. Smaltz, "The Case for Rehabilitation," *Annals* 84 (November 1939): 387–91.

94. Regarding limits in Michigan, see "Division for the Deaf," *Twenty-fourth Biennial Report Department of Labor and Industry* (n.p., 1935), 62–69. For an overview, see Jay Cooke Howard, "The Deaf and the Deafened in Industry," *Volta Review* (December 1940): 845–46, 874.

Chapter 7. *"To Stand on Their Own" Looking to the Future*

1. Estimates regarding the number of deaf citizens in the war era ranged between 60,000 and 120,000. See Mark Walter, "The Disabled Employee in National Defense," *Proceedings, National Conference on Employment of the Disabled* (National Rehabilitation Association, 1941), 83.

2. U.S. Congress, House Committee on Labor. *To Investigate Aid to the Physically Handicapped*, Hearings before the Committee on Labor Subcommittee, 78th Cong., 2d sess., 12 September 1944, 252. Testimony of Alan B. Crammatte.

3. "Into Their Own," *The Frat* (December 1942): 4.

4. For suggestions concerning a national publicity campaign, see Tovio Lindholm, "A Publicity Program," *The Frat* (May 1941): 10. For a proposal that apparently preceded Strachan's efforts to establish a national week to encourage the hiring of disabled workers, see "Deaf Might Contribute by National Deaf Week," *Ohio Chronicle* (24 January 1942): 1 (reprint, *California News*).

5. Benjamin M. Schowe, "Building for Tomorrow," *New York Journal of the Deaf* (26 September 1940): 4, 5.

6. Jay Cooke Howard to Benjamin Schowe, 20 May 1941, Schowe, box 3, folder 21, GUA.

7. On ESAD's entreaties, see "National Defense," *Empire State News* (September 1940): 4; Charles Joselow to President Franklin Roosevelt, 5 August 1940, Franklin Roosevelt Library, personal papers, Hyde, New York (hereafter, FDR), file 592, Deaf. See also Editorial, *New York Journal of the Deaf* (18 December 1941): 2.

8. "Why Not?" *The Frat* (June 1941): 4.

9. Richard E. Fraser, Denver, 24 November 1941, to Thomas L. Anderson, Thomas L. Anderson Papers, GUA, Gallaudet University, Washington, D.C. (hereafter, TLA).

10. H. Jay McMahon to Thomas Anderson, 6 December 1941, TLA. McMahon also sent correspondence to the *New York Times*. See H. Jay McMahon, "Rehabilitation Urged," *New York Times* (28 December 1941): 6 (e). ESAD's leaders supported McMahon's initiative. See Charles Joselow, "For Your Record," *Empire State News* (January-February 1942): 3.

11. Success, Barnes concluded, would come when "each group and each individual accepts the implication of the truth that our own good, our own security, is bound up with the welfare and security of all others." See Harvey Barnes to Anderson, n.d., TLA.

12. Anderson to Richard E. Fraser, 30 November 1941, TLA.

13. On Strachan's background, see John White, "Did You Happen To See . . . Paul Strachan." Papers of the President's Council on Employment of the Handicapped, series 1, box 17, Archives, Marquette University, Milwaukee, Wisconsin (hereafter PCEH). (Reprint, *Washington D.C. Times Herald*, 3 January 1948.)

14. Paul A. Strachan to Thomas L. Anderson, 11 September 1941, TLA.

15. Anderson to Marcus L. Kenner, 13 September 1941, TLA.

16. "President's Address," *Nineteenth NAD* (n.p., 1940): 7–8. Benjamin M. Schowe, "Labor Laws and Deaf Employment" *Annals* 86 (March 1941): 117–30.

17. Carl Curtis to Anderson, 7 April 1941, Attachment, C. V. McLaughlin, acting secretary Department of Labor, to Mary Norton, chair of the Committee on Labor, n.d., TLA.

18. Strachan to Anderson, 18 September 1941, TLA.

19. Strachan to Anderson and Kenner, 22 September 1941, TLA.

20. Participants included Marcus Kenner, Ignatius Bjorlee and Percival Hall, President of Gallaudet College. Anderson to Strachan, 28 September 1941, TLA.

21. "Report and Recommendations of Paul A. Strachan to the President and Executive Board, National Association of the Deaf" (part 2), n.d., TLA.

22. Ignatius Bjorlee to Anderson, 22 October 1941, TLA.

23. Kenner to Anderson, 21 October 1941; Kenner to Anderson, 4 November 1941, TLA.

24. Paul Strachan, "Points to Be Considered by the Committee on Legislation for the NAD" n.d., TLA.

25. "Statement of P. A. Strachan on Interpretations of Section (2)e of the amended Bill, to establish a Bureau of Welfare of the Deaf, etc.," 20 October 1941, 2, TLA.

26. Anderson to Strachan, 9 November 1941, TLA.

27. Strachan to Anderson, 18 November 1941, 8, TLA.

28. Anderson to Strachan, 16 November 1941, TLA; Anderson to Strachan, 20 November 1941, TLA.

29. Anderson to Kenner, 20 November 1941, TLA.

30. On the NAD in the early 1940s, see Gannon, *Deaf Heritage,* 222–23.

31. Anderson to Strachan, 16 November 1941, TLA.

32. Anderson to Benjamin Schowe, 7 February 1942, TLA.

33. Anderson to Kenner, 20 November 1941, TLA.

34. Ignatius Bjorlee, "The Deaf In Industry and their Greatest Handicap," in *Proceedings, National Conference on Employment of the Disabled* (National Rehabilitation Association. n.d.), 38–42.

35. U.S. Department of Labor, Bureau of Labor Statistics, *Impact of the War on Employment,* 2.

36. "Akron," *American Deaf Citizen* (29 November 1940): 4; J. F. M. "The Spotlight," *The Frat* (March 1941): 2; "Akron," *American Deaf Citizen* (11 April 1941): 4; J. F. Meagher "The Spotlight," *The Frat* (August 1941): 2; "Ohio," *New York Journal Of The Deaf* (10 December 1941): 3.

37. On the recruitment of deaf workers and the expansion of Akron's deaf community, see "AKN," *New York Journal Of The Deaf* (12 February 1942): 4; J. Frederick Meagher, "The Spotlight," *The Frat* (March 1942): 2; "Goodyear Gets Rubber Recruits," *Ohio Chronicle* (4 April 1942): 1; "New York City," *New York Journal Of The Deaf* (1 October 1942): 1; *New York Journal Of The Deaf* (5 November 1942): 6; "New York City," *New York Journal Of The Deaf* (19 November 1942): 1; Art Kruger, "Metropolitan Civic Association of the Deaf," *Empire State News* (January 1943): 2; *Silent Cavalier*, January 1943): 2; J. Frederick Meagher, "The Spotlight," *The Frat* (March 1943): 2; T. W. Osborne, "Akron," *The Frat* (March 1943): 7.

38. On Akron's industries, see Grismer, *Akron and Summit County*, 495, 507–9. On the deaf community, see "Ohio," *New York Journal Of The Deaf* (4 March 1943): 2; J. Frederick Meagher, "The Spotlight," *The Frat* (March 1943): 2; T. W. Osborne, "Akron," *The Frat* (March 1943): 7.

39. "Actions Speak Louder Than Words," n.d., Deaf Biographical Files and Deaf Subject Files, Employment, GUA; "Akron," *American Deaf Citizen* (17 July 1942): 4. Benjamin M. Schowe to Wallace Green, 26 May 1943, Schowe, box 13, folder 5.

40. Benjamin M. Schowe to D. W. Carnahan, 13 May 1943, Schowe, box 13, folder 14.

41. At Firestone, deaf men worked at twenty-eight positions and women at eight including office work. See following note.

42. On deaf supervisors, see Jerome D. Schein, *A Rose for Tomorrow*, 7, 8; J. F. Meagher, "The Spotlight," *The Frat* (June 1943): 2; "Akron," *American Deaf Citizen* (27 November 1942): 3; Frederick George Fancher, Supervisor Goodyear Aircraft Corporation, *Aid to the Physically Handicapped*, 340–43.

43. Report, "Duplicates," Deaf Workers (n.d.), Schowe, box 13, folder 3, GUA; Benjamin M. Schowe, "The Development of Postwar Employment," *American Era* (May–June 1944): 80–83. See also Miller, "The Deaf and the Hard of Hearing in Akron Industry," 1–13; "How Handicapped Workers Fill Manpower Needs," *Factory Management and Maintenance* (March 1943): 108–11, 204–7.

44. J. O. Hammersley, "Akron NAD Stronghold," *Silent Worker* (December 1948): 9; Lily Andrewjeski, "A Brief History of the Akron Club of the Deaf," *Deaf American* (January 1967): 27–28; "Akron Club," *Silent Cavalier* (June 1944): 1; J. Frederick Meagher, "The Spotlight," *The Frat* (May 1945): 2.

45. "Akron, Ohio," *New York Journal of the Deaf* (25 March 1943): 6.

46. Art Kruger, "American Athletic Association of the Deaf," in Van Cleve, ed., *Gallaudet Encyclopedia*, vol 1, 17–19.

47. J. Frederick Meagher, "The Spotlight," *The Frat* (September 1942): 2.

48. "Training Program," *The Frat* (January 1941): 5 (reprint, *The Michigan Mirror*); "Fanwood," *New York Journal of the Deaf* (6 March 1941): 1; "Deaf in National Defense," *Empire State News* (February-March 1941): 1.

49. Arthur L. Sedlow, "Alabama," *The Frat* (January 1942): 9.

50. "Curtiss-Wright Willing to Hire Deaf Workers," *Ohio Chronicle* (14 March 1942): 1.

51. "Commando Mary," *New York Journal of The Deaf* (18 March 1943): 1.

52. Loy E. Golladay, "Organizing Our Thinking for Post-War Problems," *Ohio Chronicle* (October 1943): 1.

53. The business was managed by George Barr and Mitchell Echovitz and had been in operation since 1935. See "They Also Serve," *The Frat* (July 1943): 10 (reprint, *Chicago Daily News*).

54. On the movement of workers through Jay Cooke Howard's office, see Jay Cooke Howard, "Our In-Migrants," *Sign Post* (October 1945): 1. Although deaf workers flocked to Detroit, they never migrated en masse to the Ford Motor Company. By 1944, only two hundred adults were estimated to work at Ford's various plants in greater Detroit although the Congress of Industrial Organizations (CIO) local welcomed deaf workers. See " 'List of Deaf Mutes' As of 12–14–42," Record Group, War Manpower Commission, box 63, Historical Analysis, folder, 5-3D Physically Handicapped, National Archives, Washington, D.C. (hereafter, WMC).

55. "Reynolds Research Pleased With Deaf Workers," *Silent Cavalier* (April 1943): 1.

56. On deaf workers at United Aircraft, see "Connecticut," *New York Journal Of The Deaf* (10 December 1942): 1; "Connecticut," *New York Jour-*

nal Of The Deaf (23 September 1943): 3; J. Frederick Meagher, "The Spotlight," *The Frat* (November 1943).

57. Inez Robb, "Kaiser Sees War Need for Handicapped," *Washington Post* (18 October 1942) in PCEH, series 1, box 7.

58. George Billey, "Deaf Workers In Defense Industries," *Washington Deaf Record* (January 1943): 3–4.

59. "Deaf Woman on Air Job, Bomber Plant Seeks More," *New York Times* (13 February 1943): 15.

60. R. N. Trowbridge, "Red Caps for Deaf Workmen," *Safety Engineering* (August 1944): 29.

61. "The Deaf and Defense Work," *Washington Deaf Record* (January 1943): 3.

62. Winfield Runde, "Bordering S. F.," *New York Journal Of The Deaf* (24 December 1942): 2; "Into Their Own," *The Frat* (January 1942): 9; "Use of Handicapped Workers in War Industry," *Monthly Labor Review* 57 (September 1943): 435–43, quote, 443.

63. This readiness to integrate deaf workers was part of the broader—but still limited—willingness of some employers to consider workers with a range of physical disabilities. See Walter, "The Disabled Employee," 86–89.

64. Forrest Finney, "Placement Officer Writes on Status of Deaf in War Work," *Ohio Chronicle* (28 November 1942): 1; Benjamin Schowe to Walter Carl, 9 November 1942, TLA; "Ohio," *New York Journal Of The Deaf* (9 April 1942): 2.

65. Evidence from Minnesota's Labor Bureau was fragmentary. On trends in North Carolina and Michigan, see *Biennial Report of the Department of Labor 1 July 1942 to 30 June 1944* (Raleigh: North Carolina Department of Labor, 1944), 71–75; Howard, "Our In-Migrants," 1.

66. Arthur G. Leisman, "Goodbye Old Man," *Wisconsin Pilot* (December 1942): 5.

67. On the growth of the AFPH, see White, "Did You Happen to See?" PCEH, series 1, box 17.

68. Strachan restated the AFPH program in written testimony he submitted to later hearings before Congress regarding vocational rehabilitation services. See U. S. Congress, Senate Committee On Education and Labor, *To Provide for Vocational Rehabilitation*, 77th Cong. 2d. sess., 13 November 1942 (Washington, D.C.: Government Printing Office), 78–80.

69. Strachan argued that there were 23 million citizens with disabilities in the United States, a claim based on the results of a national health survey undertaken during the Depression.

70. "War Work to Use the Handicapped," *New York Times* (1 August 1942): 9.

71. "Nine Cripples, Seeking Jobs, Besiege McNutt," *Washington Post* (12 May 1941); "End 'Sit-Down' at Capital," *New York Times* (12 May 1941): 19.

72. On McNutt and the War Manpower Commission, see Parrish, ed., *Encyclopedia of World War II*, 667.

73. "War Work to Use the Handicapped," 9; "Rationing Dr.'s Hinted by McNutt," *New York Times* (11 November 1942): 20. For background, see McNutt's testimony, U.S. Congress, Senate, Committee on Education and Labor, *To Provide for Vocational Rehabilitation*, 11–16.

74. "Progress report" received from Placement, March 1943, WMC, box 63, Historical Analysis, folder 5-3D, Physically Handicapped.

75. Ibid.; "Summary of 'The Physically Handicapped in the Labor Reserve,'" Confidential, 26 February 1943, WMC, box 27, War Manpower Historical Analysis, folder 1-B4, Manpower Allocation in Physically Handicapped.

76. *Silent Cavalier* (September 1942): 1.

77. Regarding early conflicts between AFPH proponents and detractors, see "National Association of the Deaf," *New York Journal Of The Deaf* (8 October 1943): 3; "Empire State Ass'n of the Deaf," *New York Journal Of The Deaf* (12 November 1942): 4; "A.F.P.H. Introduces Nothing New in Bill," *Empire State News* (January 1945): 1.

78. "In Demand," *The Frat* (February 1943): 4–5.

79. "American Federation for the Physically Handicapped," *Companion* (15 January 1943): 6–7.

80. "300,000 Cripples Hired in 44," *New York Times* (23 February 1945): 19.

81. U.S. Congress, Senate, Committee on Education and Labor, *To Provide for Vocational Rehabilitation*, 11–12.

82. Ronald W. Conley, *The Economics of Vocational Rehabilitation* (Baltimore: John Hopkins Press, 1965), 136–38. For overview of legislative history, see U.S. Congress, Senate, Committee on Education and Labor, *Report No. 53 to Accompany S. 180, Vocational Rehabilitation of Disabled Persons*, 78th Cong., 1st sess., 15 February 1943.

83. U.S. Senate, *To Provide for Vocational Rehabilitation* (9 October 1942), 13.

84. Apparently, discussion of affiliation had been underway between Anderson and the NRA as early as September 1943. See "Official Communication of the Executive Board, no.12," 22 January 1944, TLA.

85. U.S. Senate, Committee on Education and Labor, *To Provide for Vocational Rehabilitation of Individuals* (9 October 1942), 78–80.

86. Golladay, "Organizing Our Thinking," 1.

87. "Deafness a Handicap—Deafness an Inspiration," *Companion* (15 January 1944): 6.

88. Roy Conkling, "Writer Says the Deaf Do Not Need A.F.P.H," *Ohio Chronicle* (15 January 1944), Deaf Biographical Files and Deaf Subject Files, AFPH, GUA.

89. Anderson to Winfield S. Runde, 11 January 1944, TLA. See also, Anderson to Alice Terry, 11 January 1942, TLA.

90. Anderson to Arthur Roberts, 3 February 1944, TLA. See also, Anderson to Roberts, 5 February 1944, TLA.

91. On Kelley, see *Memorial Services Held in the House of Representatives and Senate of the United States, Together with Remarks Presented in Eulogy of Augustine B. Kelley, Late Representative from Pennsylvania* (Washington, D.C.: Government Printing Office, 1958).

92. *New York Journal of the Deaf* (12 October 1944): 2.

93. Tom L. Anderson, U.S. Congress, House Committee on Labor, *Aid to the Physically Handicapped* (Sept. 12–14): 1944, Appendix, 345. See also Schowe to Anderson, 10 October 1944, TLA. Jay Cooke Howard ridiculed Anderson's postcard drive. See "He Sent A Card," *New York Journal of the Deaf* (7 December 1944): 3.

94. U.S. Congress, House Committee on Labor, *Aid to the Physically Handicapped*, Oct. 2–4, 1944, 603–5, Sept. 12–14, 1994, 275–82. See also "NAD," *New York Journal of the Deaf* (28 September 1944): 2.

95. *New York Journal of the Deaf* (12 October 1944): 2.

96. U.S. Congress, House Committee on Labor, *Aid to the Physically Handicapped*, 275–82.

97. Ibid., 603–5.

98. Ibid., 243–54.

99. Deaf Biographical Files and Deaf Subject Files, Alan B. Crammatte, GUA.

100. *Aid to the Physically Handicapped* (12–14 September 1944): 244.

101. He proposed a three-point program including establishment of a Presidential Commission to appraise existing schools; creation of a Division for the Deaf in the Office of Education; and the accreditation of Gallaudet College. Ibid., 243–54.

102. "NAD," *New York Journal of the Deaf* (28 September 1944): 2; *New York Journal of the Deaf* (12 October 1944): 2.

103. Thomas L. Anderson, "President's Address," *Proceedings of the Twentieth Triennial Convention of the NAD* (n.p., 1946): 18–19 (hereafter, *Twentieth NAD*).

104. U.S. Congress, Committee on Labor, *Aid to the Physically Handicapped*, 1. In the twenty-one page summary of the full report, members also recommended that Gallaudet College admit African Americans to the campus.

105. For TLA's attack on Kelley, see Anderson to Schowe, 2 November 1944, TLA. See also Anderson to Schowe, 18 September 1944, TLA.

106. "Placement of Handicapped Workers in 1944," *Monthly Labor Review* 60 (May 1945): 1008–9; "300,000 Cripples Hired in 44," *New York Times* (23 February 1945): 19.

107. "Rehabilitation Plans for Disabled Returned 44,000 Men and Women to Jobs," *New York Times* (12 March 1945): 21.

108. Overall, the legislation was comparable to the British Disabled Persons Act. See Michigan Legislature, *House Bill No. 428.* Michigan 63d Legislature, Session of 1945.

109. Jay Cooke Howard, "War for Survival," *Sign Post* (July 1945): 1.

110. Jay Cooke Howard, "House Bill No. 428," *Sign Post* (June 1945): 1; "Michigan Considers Bill to Require Hiring Handicapped," *Cavalier* (July 1945): 1 (reprint, *Signpost*).

111. Jay Cooke Howard, "War for Survival," 1; "The Observer," *Sign Post* (August 1945): 1.

112. Lewis Swellenbach, Secretary of Labor, "Hire the Handicapped," *Progress* (February 1948): n.p., PCEH, series 1, box 17.

113. *Digest of Public General Bills* (Washington, D.C.: Government Printing Office, 1946), 47–48. The proposal sought to establish a national

register of disabled applicants to serve as a pool for employers. Recalcitrant employers could be fined up to $1,000. In turn, the commission would help businesses to accommodate workers. The proposal also supported efforts to cure deafness, polio, and epilepsy. For hearings on the proposed legislation, see U.S. Congress, House Committee on Labor, *To Investigate Aid to the Physically Handicapped,* Part 23, *H.R. 5206.*

114. Paul Strachan, *H.R. 5206,* 2319, 2320.

115. Warren M. Smaltz, "Anent House Resolution 5206," *Cavalier* (April 1946): 4. See also Warren Smaltz to *Sign Post* (June–July 1946): 2. For a comparable argument, see Isadore Zisman, "First NEGA Meet Since 1940 Held," *Cavalier* (October 1946): 1. Opponents held that businesses would use the legislation as a lever to exploit workers. As the legislation established nominal monthly allocations to workers deemed unemployable, detractors claimed that businesses would lure workers by offering paid compensation slightly over this nominal amount.

116. For opposition to the bill, see *H.R. 5206,* 2302, 2307–13, 2485–90, 2500–2503.

117. Ibid., 2333–40, 2454; Howard A. Rusk, M.D., "Rehabilitation," *New York Times* (19 May 1946): 31.

118. *H.R. 5206,* 2345–48, 2516–22.

119. National Federation of the Blind, *H.R. 5206,* 2421–25. For background, see Scotch, *From Goodwill to Civil Rights,* chapter 2.

120. Ibid., 2295–97, 2355–61.

121. Fred Zusy, "Physically Handicapped Have Real Friend in Paul Strachan Who Founded NEPH Week," in PCEH, series 1, box 17 (reprint, *Sarasota Herald-Tribune,* 5 February 1948).

122. George Lavos and Earl W. Jones, "The Deaf Worker in Industry," *Annals* 91 (January 1946): 154–76. For the second study, see United States Department of Labor, Bureau of Labor Statistics, *of Physically Impaired Workers in Manufacturing Industries,* Bulletin no. 923, by Henry S. Hammond (Washington, D.C.: Government Printing Office, 1948). On the cases involving deaf and workers with hearing losses, see *The Performance,* 74–83. See also Verne K. Harvey and E. Parker Luongo, "Physical Impairment and Job Performance," *Journal of American Medical Association* 127 (7 April 1945): 902–7, 961–70. This study included a small number of deaf workers in its sample population.

123. *Biennial Report of the Department of Labor*, 115–22; Clyde Walker, "Crutcher Succeeds Howard," *Detroit Sign Post* (April 1946): 1; Henry P. Crutcher, "The Division of the Deaf and Deafened of the Michigan State Department of Labor," *Silent Worker* (August 1949): 7–8; Petra Howard, "Bureau for the Deaf," *Companion* (15 October 1946): 1–2; Benjamin Schowe, "The Deaf at Work," *Annals* 103 (March 1958): 285–87.

124. "President's Address," *Twentieth NAD*, 12–25.

125. Boyce Williams, "The Deaf and Vocational Rehabilitation," *Twentieth NAD*, 41–46.

126. Tom L. Anderson, *Twentieth NAD*, 18–19.

127. Speech before the NFSD local in Akron, Ohio, 16 July 1959, Schowe, box 9, folders 4, 9.

Epilogue

1. For an overview, begin with John B. Christiansen and Sharon Barnartt, "The Socioeconomic Status of Deaf People," in *Understanding Deafness*, ed. Higgins and Nash, 171–96; and John B. Christiansen and Sharon Barnartt, "The Socioeconomic Status of Deaf Workers, A Minority Group Perspective," *Social Science Journal* 22 (1985): 19–32. For a sketch of problems and prospects of industrial workers, see Benjamin Schowe, "The Deaf at Work," *Annals* 103 (March 1958): 283–92. On the responses of employers, see Pino, *Employer Ratings*, 103–105; and Schroedel, *Attainment of Occupational Status*, 1–4.

2. For an overview of these developments begin with R. Stuckless, et. al., *A Report on the National Task Force*, 1–14.

3. See Gannon, *The Week the World Heard Gallaudet*; Sacks, *Seeing Voices*.

4. See, for example, Robert Buchanan, "The *Silent Worker* Newspaper and the Building of a Deaf Community, 1890–1925," in Van Cleve's *Deaf History Unveiled*, 172–97.

5. Holcomb and Wood, *Deaf Women*, 142–43; "Reflections of Five Deaf Women," *Gallaudet Today* 14 (Summer, 1984): 1–4; Gertrude Galloway, "We the Outsiders . . ." *Gallaudet Today* 14 (Summer, 1984): 6–7; Roslyn Rosen, "We Were There Too!" *Deaf American* 36 (1984): 4–9.

6. For a provocative and well argued recent study that places these efforts in an international, historical framework, see Charlton, *Nothing About*

Us Without Us; Shapiro, *No Pity*; Stone, *Awakening to Disability*; Jankowski, *Deaf Empowerment*.

7. For a general overview of strategies to increase employment during the 1970s, see Gliedman and Roth, *The Unexpected Minority*, 274–300.

8. See The National Center for Law and Deafness, *Legal Rights*; Fersh and Thomas, *Complying with the Americans with Disabilities Act*.

Bibliography

Primary Sources

Collections

Akron City Library, Akron, Ohio: Goodyear and Firestone Collections.

Henry Ford Museum and Greenfield Village. Dearborn, Mich.: Industrial Relations: Medical Department at Highland Park. Oral History: William C. Klann; Samuel Marquis Papers. Sociological Department: Samuel Marquis.

Gallaudet University Archives, Washington, D.C.: Tom L. Anderson Papers. Henry L. Buzzard Collection. Thomas Gallaudet Papers. Olof Hanson Papers. National Association of the Deaf Papers. Pennsylvania School for the Deaf Papers. Percival Hall Presidential Papers. Benjamin M. Schowe Papers.

Marie Katzenbach School for the Deaf, Trenton, New Jersey: Assorted Papers.

Marquette University Archives, Milwaukee: Presidents Council on Employment of the Handicapped.

Minnesota Historical Society, Minneapolis: Minnesota Association of the Deaf, Proceedings.

National Archives, Washington, D.C.: Civilian Conservation Corps. Civil Service. Civilian Works Administration. Department of Labor. Federal Employment Relief Agency. War Manpower Commission. Works Progress Administration.

National Association of the Deaf Library, Silver Spring, Md.: Convention Proceedings and Assorted Papers.

National Fraternal Society of the Deaf Library, Mount Prospect, Ill.: Assorted Papers.

Diocese of New York of the Episcopal Church Archives, New York: St. Ann's Church for the Deaf Papers.

New York School for the Deaf, White Plains, N.Y.: Assorted Papers.

New York Society for the Deaf, New York: Oral Interview Tanya Nash and Assorted Papers.

Franklin Roosevelt Library, Hyde Park, N.Y.: Personal Papers, Franklin and Eleanor Roosevelt.

Wayne State University, Archives of Labor History and Urban Affairs, Detroit: United Auto Workers, Local 600.

State Historical Society of Wisconsin, Madison: Wisconsin School for the Deaf Papers. William Taft Presidential Papers (microfilm). Theodore Roosevelt Presidential Papers (microfilm).

State Documents and Publications

California. *Statutes of California, 1927.* San Francisco: Bancroft and Whitney, 1927.

Case, Leon, comp. *Public and Local Acts of the Legislature of the State of Michigan.* Lansing: Franklin De Kleine, 1937.

Georgia State Department of Public Welfare. *Georgia's Deaf.* Atlanta: Works Project Administration of Georgia (official project no. 665–34–3-90), 1942.

Michigan Legislature. *House Bill No. 428.* Michigan 63d Legislature, sess. of 1945. Minnesota Legislature. *General Laws of the State of Minnesota Passed by the Thirty-eighth Session of the State Legislature.* St. Paul: Pioneer Printing, 1913.

———. *Legislative Manual of the State of Minnesota.* Minneapolis: Harrison and Smith, 1916.

———. *Session Laws of the State of Minnesota,* Minneapolis: Syndicate Printing, 1919.

New Jersey Board of Education. *Annual Report of the State Board of Education and of the Commissioner of Education of New Jersey, 1919–1945.* Trenton, 1950.

New Jersey Legislature. *New Jersey State Report.* Trenton, 1928.

New York State Legislature. *Report of the Temporary State Commission to Examine, Report Upon, and Recommend Measures to Improve Facilities for Care of Hard of Hearing and Deaf Children and Children Liable to Become Deaf.* Albany: J. B. Lyon, 1938.

———. *Second Report of the Temporary State Commission to Examine, Report Upon, and Recommend Measures to Improve Facilities for Care of Hard of Hearing and Deaf Children and Children Liable to Become Deaf.* Albany: J. B. Lyon, 1939.

————. *Third Report of the Temporary State Commission to Examine, Report Upon, and Recommend Measures to Improve Facilities for Care of Hard of Hearing and Deaf Children and Children Liable to Become Deaf.* Albany: J. B. Lyon, 1940.

North Carolina. *State of North Carolina Public Laws and Resolutions Passed by the General Assembly at Its Session of 1923.* Raleigh: Commercial Printing, 1923.

Parker, Warren Downs. *First Annual Report of the Inspector of Schools for the Deaf.* Madison: Democrat Printing, 1902.

Winnie, A. J. comp., *History and Handbook of Day Schools for the Deaf and Blind.* Madison: Democrat Printing, 1912.

Wisconsin Phonological Institute. *The Wisconsin System of Public Day Schools for the Deaf with Limited State Aid.* Milwaukee: Wisconsin Phonological Institute, 1896.

Federal Government Documents and Publications

Martens, Elise. *The Deaf and the Hard of Hearing in the Occupational World,* U.S. Department of the Interior, Office of Education. Washington, D.C.: Government Printing Office, 1936.

United States Civil Service Commission. *First Annual Report of the United States Civil Service Commission,* 2d edition. Washington, D.C.: Government Printing Office, 1884.

————. *Ninth Report of the United States Civil Service Commission.* Washington, D.C.: Government Printing Office, 1893.

————. *Nineteenth Annual Report of the United States Civil Service Commission.* Washington, D.C.: Government Printing Office, 1902.

———— *Twenty-first Report of the United States Civil Service Commission.* Washington, D.C.: Government Printing Office, 1905.

————. *Twenty-second Annual Report of the United States Civil Service Commission.* Washington, D.C.: Government Printing Office, 1905.

————. *Twenty-fourth Annual Report of the United States Civil Service Commission.* Washington, D.C.: Government Printing Office, 1908.

————. *Twenty-fifth Annual Report of the United States Civil Service.* Washington, D.C.: Government Printing Office, 1909.

————. *Twenty-sixth Annual Report of the United States Civil Service Commission.* Washington, D.C.: Government Printing Office, 1910.

————. Office of Public Affairs. *Biography of an Ideal: A History of the Federal Civil Service.* Washington, D.C.: Government Printing Office, 1974.

U.S. Congress. *Social Security in America: The Factual Background of the Social Security Act as Summarized from Staff Reports to the Committee on Economic Security.* Washington, D.C.: Government Printing Office, 1937.

U.S. Congress. *Digest of Public General Bills.* Washington, D.C.: Government Printing Office, 1946.

U.S. Congress. House of Representatives. Committee on Education. *To Create a Bureau for the Deaf and Dumb in the Department of Labor and Prescribing the Duties Thereof. Hearing before the Committee on Education,* 65th Cong., 2d sess., 13 February 1918. Washington, D.C.: Government Printing Office, 1918.

————. Committee on Labor Subcommittee. *To Investigate Aid to the Physically Handicapped. Hearings before the Committee on Labor Subcommittee,* Part 3: Aid to the Deaf and Hard of Hearing. 78th Cong., 2d sess., 12–14 September 1944. Washington, D.C.: Government Printing Office, 1944.

————. *To Investigate Aid to the Physically Handicapped. Hearings before the Committee on Labor Subcommittee,* Part 4. 78th Cong., 2d sess., 2–4 October 1944. Washington, D.C.: Government Printing Office, 1944.

————. *To Investigate Aid to the Physically Handicapped. Hearings before the Committee on Labor Subcommittee,* Part 7: Federal Aid to the Physically Handicapped. 78th Cong., 2d sess., 27, 29, 30 November 1944. Washington, D.C.: Government Printing Office, 1944.

————. *To Investigate Aid to the Physically Handicapped. Hearings Before the Committee on Labor Subcommittee,* Part 23: H.R. 5206. 79th Cong., 2d sess., 30 April, 1, 2, 3, 6, 7, 8, 9, 15, and 16 May 1946. Washington, D.C.: Government Printing Office, 1946.

————. *Aid to the Physically Handicapped Report of the Committee on Labor Subcommittee, to H. Res 45.* 79th Cong., 2d sess., 10 October 1946. Washington, D.C.: Government Printing Office, 1946.

————. Senate Committee on Education and Labor. *To Provide for Vocational Rehabilitation of Individuals Suffering from War Connected or Other Disabilities: Hearings before a Subcommittee of the Committee,* 77th Cong., 2d. sess., 9–10 October, and 13 November 1942. Washington, D.C.: Government Printing Office, 1942.

————. *Report No. 53 to Accompany S. 180, Vocational Rehabilitation of Disabled Persons,* 78th Cong., 1st sess., 15 February 1943. Washington, D.C.: Government Printing Office, 1943.

U.S. Bureau of the Census. *Tenth Census of the United States: 1880.* Washington, D.C.: Government Printing Office, 1883.

————. *Eleventh Census of the United States: 1890.* Washington, D.C.: Government Printing Office, 1895.

————. *Special Reports: The Blind and the Deaf, 1900.* Washington, D.C.: Government Printing Office, 1906.

———— *Summary of State Laws Relating to the Dependent Classes, 1913.* Washington, D.C.: Government Printing Office, 1914.

————. *Deaf-Mutes in the United States: Analysis of the Census of 1910 with Summary of State Laws Relative to the Deaf as of January 1, 1918.* Washington, D.C.: Government Printing Office, 1918.

————. *The Deaf-Mute Population of the United States, 1920: A Statistical Analysis of the Data Obtained at the Fourteenth Decennial Census.* Washington, D.C.: Government Printing Office, 1928.

————. *Fifteenth Census of the United States: 1930, The Blind and Deaf-Mutes in the United States, 1930.* Washington, D.C., Government Printing Office, 1931.

U.S. Department of Labor. *A Chance to Work in the Forests, Emergency Conservation Work Bulletin No. 1, 17 April 1933.* Washington, D.C.: Government Printing Office, 1933.

————. *Handbook for Agencies Selecting Men for Emergency Conservation Work Bulletin No. 3, 1 May, 1933.* Washington, D.C.: Government Printing Office, 1933.

————. Bureau of Labor Statistics. *Impact of the War on Employment in 181 Centers of War Activity, Bulletin No. 826.* Washington, D.C.: Government Printing Office, 1945.

————. *The Performance of Physically Impaired Workers in Manufacturing Industries, Bulletin No. 923.* Washington, D.C.: Government Printing Office, 1948.

————. Manpower Commission, Bureau of Training. *The Training Within Industry Report 1940–1945.* Washington, D.C.: Training Within Industry Service, 1945.

Newspapers, Periodicals, and Journals

Akron Beacon Journal (Akron, Ohio)

American Annals of the Deaf (CAID and CEASD, Washington, D.C.)

American Deaf Citizen (Versailles, Ohio)

American Era (American School for the Deaf, West Hartford, Conn.)

American Federation of Physically Handicapped Tribune (AFPH, Washington, D.C.)

American Industrial Journal (Wisconsin School for the Deaf, Delavan, Wisc.)

The Ark (n.p., available on microfilm at Gallaudet University, Washington, D.C.)

Buff and Blue (Gallaudet University, Washington, D.C.)

California News (California School for the Deaf)

Cavalier (previously *Silent Cavalier*) (Virginia Association of the Deaf)

Companion (Minnesota School for the Deaf)

Deaf American (Omaha, Nebraska)

Deaf American (contemporary) (National Association of the Deaf)

Deaf Carolinian (North Carolina School for the Deaf, Raleigh)

Deaf Herald (New York, N.Y.)

Deaf Mute's Journal (*DMJ*) (New York School for the Deaf)

Deaf Spectrum (Beaverton, Ore.)

Dee Cee Eyes (Washington, D.C.)

Detroit Signpost (earlier *Signpost*) (Detroit)

Digest of the Deaf (Springfield, Mass.)

Empire State News (New York Association of the Deaf)

Fanwood Journal (New York School for the Deaf)

Firestone Non-Skid (Firestone Corporation, Akron, Ohio)

The Frat (National Fraternal Society of the Deaf, Mount Prospect, Ill.)

Gallaudet Alumni Newsletter (Gallaudet University, Washington, D. C.)

Gallaudet Today (Gallaudet University, Washington, D.C.)

Jersey Booster (Newark, N.J.)

Jewish Deaf (New York, N.Y.)

Lone Star (Texas School for the Deaf)

Maryland Bulletin (Maryland School for the Deaf)

Modern Silents (Texas Association of the Deaf)

Monthly Labor Review (U.S. Bureau of Labor Statistics, Washington, D.C.)

Mount Airy World (Pennsylvania School for the Deaf)

The NAD Broadcaster (National Association for the Deaf)

NAD Bulletin (National Association for the Deaf)

Nadic (National Association for the Deaf)

Nebraska Journal (Nebraska School for the Deaf)

New Jersey School News (New Jersey School for the Deaf, Trenton, N.J.)

New York Journal of the Deaf (New York School for the Deaf)

New York Times (New York, N.Y.)

Ohio Chronicle (Ohio School for the Deaf)

Oregon Outlook (n.p., available on microfilm at Gallaudet University, Washington, D.C.)

Pennsylvania Society News (Pennsylvania Association of the Deaf, Philadelphia)

Signpost (later *Detroit Signpost*) (Detroit, Mich.)

Silent Courier (Chicago)

Silent Worker 1892–1929 and *1948–1960* (New Jersey School for the Deaf and National Association of the Deaf)

St. Ann's Bulletin (St. Ann's Church for the Deaf, New York, N.Y.)

TBC News (The Bicultural Center, Riverdale, Md.)

Tri-State News (Hickory, N.C.)

Vocational Teacher (Council Bluffs, Iowa)

Volta Review (Alexander Graham Bell Association for the Deaf)

Washington Deaf Record (Vancouver, Wash.)

Washington Post (Washington, D.C.)

Secondary Sources
Books, Studies, and Reports

Allen, Robert L. *Reluctant Reformers: Racism and Social Reform Movements in the United States.* Washington, D.C.: Howard University Press, 1974.

Allport, Gordon W. *The Nature of Prejudice.* Boston: Beacon, 1954.

Alsberg, Henry G. *On the CWA Front: A Photographic Record of the Civil Works Administration.* New York: Coward-McCann, 1934.

Atwood, Albert. *Gallaudet College: Its First One Hundred Years.* Lancaster, Penn.: Intelligencer, 1964.

Axinn, June, and Herman Levin. *Social Welfare: A History of the American Response to Need.* New York: Harper and Row, 1982.

Babson, Steve. *Working Detroit: The Making of a Union Town.* New York: Adama Books, 1984.

Barnard, Henry, ed. *Tribute to Gallaudet: A Discourse in Commemoration of the Life, Character, and Services of the Reverend Thomas Hopkins Gallaudet, L.L.D., Delivered before the Citizens of Hartford, January 7, 1852.* Hartford: Brockett and Hutchinson, 1852.

Baynton, Douglas C. *Forbidden Signs: American Culture and the Campaign Against Sign Language* Chicago: University of Chicago Press, 1996.

Bell, Alexander Graham. *Memoir upon the Formation of a Deaf Variety of the Human Race.* Washington, D.C.: Government Printing Office, 1884; reissued by the Alexander Graham Bell Association for the Deaf, 1969.

Benderly, Beryl Lieff. *Dancing without Music: Deafness in America.* Washington, D.C.: Gallaudet University Press, 1990.

Berg, Otto. *A Missionary Chronicle: Being a History of the Ministry to the Deaf in the Episcopal Church.* Hollywood, Md.: St. Mary's, 1984.

Berg, Otto Benjamin, and Henry L. Buzzard. *Thomas Gallaudet: Apostle to the Deaf.* New York: St. Ann's Church for the Deaf, 1989.

Berkowitz, Edward D. *America's Welfare State: From Roosevelt to Reagan.* Baltimore: Johns Hopkins University Press, 1991.

Berkowitz, Edward D. *Disabled Policy: America's Programs for the Handicapped.* Cambridge: Cambridge University Press, 1987.

Berkowitz, Edward D., and Kim McQuaid. *Creating the Welfare State.* Lawrence: University Press of Kansas, 1988.

Berkowitz, Monroe, William G. Johnson, and Edward Murphy. *Public Policy Towards Disability.* New York: Praeger, 1976.

Bernstein, Irving. *The Lean Years.* Boston: Houghton Mifflin, 1960.

Best, Harry. *Deafness and the Deaf in the United States: Considered Primarily in Relation to Those Sometimes More or Less Erroneously Known as Deaf-Mutes.* New York: Macmillan, 1943.

———. *The Deaf: Their Position in Society and the Provision for Their Education in the United States.* New York: Thomas Y. Crowell, 1914.

Boatner, Maxine Tull. *Voice of the Deaf: A Biography of Edward Miner Gallaudet.* Washington, D.C.: Public Affairs, 1959.

Bodnar, John. *Worker's World: Kinship, Community, and Protest in an Industrial Society, 1900–1940.* Baltimore: Johns Hopkins University Press, 1982.

Bowe, Frank. *Changing the Rules.* Silver Spring, Md.: T. J. Publishers. 1986.

————. *Handicapping America*. New York: Harper and Row, 1978.

————. *Rehabilitating America*. New York: Harper and Row, 1978.

Bowler, Peter J. *Evolution: The History of an Idea*. Berkeley: University of California Press, 1989.

Boyer, Paul S. *Urban Masses and Moral Order in America, 1820–1920*. Cambridge: Harvard University Press, 1978.

Braddock, Guilbert C. *Notable Deaf Persons*. Washington, D.C.: Gallaudet College Alumni Association, 1975.

Brown, Roy M. *Public Poor: Relief in North Carolina*. Chapel Hill: University of North Carolina Press, 1928.

Bruce, Robert V. *Alexander Graham Bell and the Conquest of Solitude*. Boston: Little Brown, 1973.

Bullard Douglas. *Islay*. Silver Spring, Md.: T.J. Publishers. 1986.

Burkhauser, Robert V., and Robert Haveman. *Disability and Work: The Economics of American Policy*. Baltimore: Johns Hopkins University Press, 1982.

Burnet, John R. *Tales of the Deaf and Dumb with Miscellaneous Poems*. Newark, N.J.: Benjamin Olds, 1835.

Calkins, Earnest Elmo. *Louder Please! The Autobiography of a Deaf Man*. Boston: Atlantic Monthly, 1924.

Charlton, James I. *Nothing about Us without Us: Disability, Oppression, and Empowerment*. Berkeley: University of California Press, 1998.

Clarke, Bonaventure, comp. *An Account of St. Ann's Church for Deaf-Mutes and Articles of Prose and Poetry by Deaf Mutes*. New York: John A. Gray and Green, 1865.

Clawson, Mary Ann. *Constructing Brotherhood: Class, Gender, and Fraternalism*. Princeton: Princeton University Press, 1989.

Cloward, Richard A., and Frances Fox Piven. *Regulating the Poor: The Functions of Public Welfare*. New York: Random House, 1971.

Cohen, Leah. *TRAIN GO SORRY*. Boston: Houghton Mifflin, 1994.

Cole, Charles Burt. *Social Technology, Social Policy, and the Severely Disabled: Issues Posed by the Blind, the Deaf, and Those Unable to Walk*. Berkeley: University of California Press, 1979.

Conley, Ronald W. *The Economics of Vocational Rehabilitation*. Baltimore: Johns Hopkins University Press, 1965.

Crammatte, Allan B. *Deaf Persons in Professional Employment*. Springfield, Ill.: Charles C. Thomas, 1968.

Currier, E. Henry. *The Deaf: By Their Fruits Ye Shall Know Them.* New York: New York Institution for the Deaf and Dumb, 1912.

Darwin, Charles. *The Origin of Species.* New York: Oxford University Press, 1996.

Day, Herbert, Irving Fusfeld, and Rudolf Pinter. *A Survey of American Schools for the Deaf, 1924–1925.* Washington, D.C.: National Research Council, 1928.

De Mott, Benjamin. *The Imperial Middle: Why Americans Can't Think Straight about Class.* New York: William Morrow, 1990.

Dietrich, Philip J. *The Silent Men.* Akron: Goodyear Tire and Rubber, n.d.

Edelman, Murray. *The Symbolic Uses of Politics.* Urbana: University of Illinois Press, 1967.

Eller, Ronald. *Miners, Millhands, and Mountaineers: Industries of the Appalachian South, 1880–1930.* Knoxville: University of Tennessee Press, 1982.

Erting, Carol, Robert Johnson, Dorothy Smith, and Bruce Snider, eds. *Deaf Way: Perspectives from the International Conference on Deaf Culture.* Washington, D.C.: Gallaudet University Press, 1994.

Fay, Edward Allen, ed. *Histories of American Schools for the Deaf 1817–1893,* 3 vols. Washington, D.C.: Volta Bureau, 1893.

Fersh, Don, and Peter Thomas. *Complying with the Americans with Disabilities Act.* Westport, Conn., Quorum Books, 1993.

Fischer, Renate, and Harlan Lane, eds. *Looking Back: A Reader on the History of Deaf Communities and Their Sign Languages.* Hamburg: Signum-Verlag, 1993.

Fishman, Joshua. *Language Loyalty in the United States.* The Hague: Mouton, 1966.

Ford, Henry, with Samuel Crowther. *My Life and Work.* Garden City, N.Y.: Doubleday, Page, 1923.

Gallaher, James E. *Representative Deaf Persons of the United States.* Chicago: James E. Gallaher, 1898.

Gallaudet, Edward Miner. *Life of Thomas Hopkins Gallaudet: Founder of Deaf-Mute Instruction in America.* New York: Henry Holt, 1888.

Galper, Jeffrey H. *The Politics of Social Services.* Englewood Cliffs, N.J.: Prentice Hall, 1975.

Gannon, Jack. *Deaf Heritage: A Narrative History of Deaf America.* Silver Spring, Md.: National Association of the Deaf, 1981.

————. *The Week the World Heard Gallaudet*. Washington, D.C.: Gallaudet University Press, 1989.

Garfinkel, Herbert. *When Negroes March*. Glencoe, Ill.: Free Press, 1959.

Gliedman, John, and William Roth. *The Unexpected Minority: Handicapped Children in America*. New York: Harcourt Brace Jovanovich, 1980.

Gordon, Linda. *Heroes of Their Own Lives: The Politics and History of Family Violence: Boston, 1880–1960*. New York: Viking Penguin, 1988.

————. *Pitied but Not Entitled: Single Mothers and the History of Welfare, 1890–1935*. New York: Free Press, 1994.

Green, James R. *The World of the Worker: Labor in Twentieth-Century America*. New York: Hill and Wang, 1980.

Greenleaf, William. *From These Beginnings: The Early Philanthropies of Henry and Edsel Ford, 1911–1936*. Detroit: Wayne State University Press, 1964.

Grismer, Karl H. *Akron and Summit County*. Akron: Summit County Historical Society, [1952].

Groce, Nora. *Everyone Here Spoke Sign Language: Hereditary Deafness on Martha's Vineyard*. Cambridge: Harvard University Press, 1985.

Hairston, Ernest, and Linwood Smith. *Black and Deaf in America: Are We That Different*. Silver Spring, Md.: T. J. Publishers. 1983.

Higgins, Paul. *Outsiders in a Hearing World: A Sociology of Deafness*. Beverly Hills, Calif.: Sage, 1980.

Higgins, Paul, and Jeffrey Nash, eds. *Understanding Deafness Socially*. Springfield, Ill.: Charles C. Thomas, 1987.

Higham, John. *Strangers in the Land: Patterns of American Nativism, 1860–1925*. New York: Athenaeum, 1974.

Hofstadter, Richard. *The Age of Reform: From Bryan to F.D.R.* New York: Knopf, 1955.

————. *Social Darwinism in American Thought*. Boston: Beacon Press, 1955.

Holcomb, Mabs, and Sharon Wood. *Deaf Women: A Parade Through the Decades*. Berkeley: Dawn Sign Press, 1989.

The Holy Bible. Philadelphia: John C. Winston and Company, 1915.

Holycross, Edwin Isaac, comp. *The Abbé de l'Épée: Founder of the Manual Instruction of the Deaf and Other Early Teachers of the Deaf*. Columbus, Ohio: Nitsche, 1913.

Howard, Donald. *The WPA and Federal Relief Policy*. New York: Russell Sage: 1943; Reprint. New York: Da Capo, 1973.

Humphrey, Heman. *The Life and Letters of the Reverend T. H. Gallaudet.* New York: Robert Carter and Brothers, 1857.

Jacobs, Leo M. *A Deaf Adult Speaks Out.* Washington, D.C.: Gallaudet College Press, 1974.

Jones, Jacqueline. *The Dispossessed: America's Underclasses from the Civil War to the Present.* New York: Basic Books, 1992.

Josephson, Hannah. *Jeanette Rankin, First Lady in Congress: A Biography.* Indianapolis: Bobbs-Merrill, 1974.

Kaestle, Carl. *Pillars of the Republic: Common Schools and American Society, 1780–1860.* New York: Hill and Wang, 1983.

Katz, Michael B. *In the Shadow of the Poorhouse: A Social History of Welfare in America.* New York: Basic Books, 1986.

Keating, James T., ed. *The Goodyear Story.* Elmsford, N.Y.: Benjamin, 1972.

Kesselman, Louis. *The Social Politics of FEPC: A Study in Reform Pressure Movements.* Chapel Hill: University of North Carolina Press, 1947.

Kevles, Daniel J. *In the Name of Genetics: Genetics and the Uses of Human Heredity.* New York: Alfred A. Knopf, 1985.

Kisor, Henry. *What's That Pig Outdoors? A Memoir of Deafness.* New York: Hill and Wang, 1990.

Klima, Edward, and Ursula Bellugi. *The Signs of Language.* Cambridge: Harvard University Press, 1979.

Koestler, Frances A. *The Unseen Minority: A Social History of Blindness in the United States.* New York: David McKay, 1976.

Kovarsky, Irving. *Discrimination in Employment.* Iowa City: University of Iowa Press, 1976.

Lacey, Robert. *Ford, the Men and the Machine.* Toronto: McClelland and Stewart, 1986.

Lane, Harlan. *When the Mind Hears: A History of the Deaf.* New York: Vintage Books, 1989.

———. *The Mask of Benevolence: Disabling the Deaf Community.* New York: Random House, 1993.

Lefler, Hugh Talmadge, and Albert Ray Newsome. *North Carolina: The History of a Southern State,* 3d. ed. Chapel Hill: University of North Carolina Press, 1973.

Levine, Edna S. *The Psychology of Deafness.* New York: Columbia University Press, 1960.

Lewis, David. *The Public Image of Henry Ford: An American Folk Hero and His Company*. Detroit: Wayne State University Press, 1976.

Lief, Alfred. *The Firestone Story: A History of the Firestone Tire and Rubber Company*. New York: McGraw Hill, 1951.

————. *Harvey Firestone: Free Man of Enterprise*. New York: McGraw Hill, 1951.

Litchfield, Paul. *Industrial Voyage: My Life as an Industrial Lieutenant*. Garden City, N.Y.: Doubleday, 1954.

Long, J. Schuyler. *Out of the Silence: A Book of Verse*. Council Bluffs, Iowa: J. Schuyler Long, 1909.

————. *The Sign Language: A Manual of Signs*. Iowa City: Athens, 1918.

Lunde, Anders, and Stanley K. Bigman. *Occupational Conditions among the Deaf*. Washington D.C.: Gallaudet College, 1959.

Martens, Elise H. *The Deaf and the Hard of Hearing in the Occupational World*, bulletin no. 13. Washington, D.C.: U.S. Office of Education, 1936.

McLaughlin, Doris B. *Michigan Labor: A Brief History from 1818 to the Present*. Ann Arbor: University of Michigan Press, 1970.

Meyer, Stephen, III. *The Five Dollar Day: Labor, Management, and Social Control in the Ford Motor Company, 1908–1921*. Albany, N.Y.: State University of New York Press, 1981.

Mindel, Eugene D., and McCay Vernon. *They Grow in Silence: The Deaf Child and His Family*. Silver Spring, Md.: National Association of the Deaf, 1974.

Montgomery, David. *The Fall of the House of Labor: The Workplace, the State, and American Labor Activism, 1865–1925*. Cambridge: Cambridge University Press, 1989.

National Center for Law and Deafness. *Legal Rights: The Guide for Deaf and Hard of Hearing People*. Washington D.C.: Gallaudet University Press, 1992.

Neisser, Arden. *The Other Side of Silence: Sign Language and the Deaf Community in America*. New York: Alfred A. Knopf, 1983.

Nelson, Daniel. *American Rubber Workers and Organized Labor, 1900–1941*. New Jersey: Princeton University Press, 1988.

Nevins, Alan, and Frank Ernest Hill. *Ford, Expansion and Challenge, 1915–1933*. New York: Charles Scribner and Sons, 1957.

Newby, Ida A. *Jim Crow's Defense: Anti-Negro Thought in America, 1900–1930*. Baton Rouge: Louisiana State University Press, 1965.

Nichols, Kenneth. *Yesterday's Akron: The First One Hundred and Fifty Years.* Miami: E.A. Seaman, 1976.

O'Connor, James. *The Fiscal Crisis of the State.* New York: St. Martin's, 1973.

O'Reilly, Maurice, and James T. Keating, eds. *The Goodyear Story.* Elmsford, N.Y.: Benjamin, 1912.

Padden, Carol, and Tom Humphries. *Deaf in America: Voices from a Culture.* Cambridge: Harvard University Press, 1988.

Parrish, Thomas, ed. *Simon and Schuster Encyclopedia of World War II.* New York: Simon and Schuster, 1978.

Patten, J. Alexander. *Lives of the Clergy of New York and Brooklyn: Embracing Two Hundred Biographies of Eminent Living Men in All Denominations.* New York: Atlantic, 1874.

Patterson, James T. *America's Struggle against Poverty: 1900–1980.* Cambridge: Harvard University Press, 1981.

Reed, Merle E. *Seedtime for the Modern Civil Rights Movement: The President's Committee on Fair Employment Practice, 1941–1946.* Baton Rouge: Louisiana State University Press, 1991.

Roberts, Harold. *The Rubber Workers: Labor Organization and Collective Bargaining in the Rubber Industry.* New York: Harper and Brothers, 1944.

Rusk, Howard A., and Eugene Taylor. *New Hope for the Handicapped: The Rehabilitation of the Disabled From Bed to Job.* 4th ed. New York: Harper and Brothers, 1949.

Sacks, Oliver. *Seeing Voices: A Journey into the World of the Deaf.* Berkeley: University of California Press, 1988.

Salmond, John A. *The CCC 1933–1942: A New Deal Case Study.* Durham, N.C.: Duke University Press, 1967.

Schein, Jerome D. *At Home Among Strangers: Exploring the Deaf Community in the United States.* Washington, D.C.: Gallaudet University Press, 1989.

———. *The Deaf Community: Studies in the Social Psychology of Deafness.* Washington, D.C.: Gallaudet College Press, 1968.

———. *A Rose for Tomorrow: A Biography of Frederick C. Schreiber.* Silver Spring, Md.: National Association of the Deaf, 1981.

Schein, Jerome D., and Marcus T. Delk, Jr. *The Deaf Population of the United States.* Silver Spring, Md.: National Association of the Deaf, 1974.

Schowe, Benjamin M. *Identity Crisis in Deafness: A Humanistic Perspective.* Tempe, Ariz.: Scholars, 1979.

Schultz, Stanley K. *The Culture Factory: Boston Public Schools, 1789–1860.* New York: Oxford University Press, 1973.

Scotch, Richard K. *From Goodwill to Civil Rights: Transforming Federal Disability Policy.* Philadelphia: Temple University Press, 1984.

Scott, Robert. *The Making of Blind Men: A Study of Adult Socialization.* New York: Russell Sage Foundation, 1969.

Shapiro, Joseph. *No Pity: People with Disabilities Forging a New Civil Rights Movement.* New York: Random House, 1993.

Sondik, Cindy. *The Ladies and Gentlemen of the Civil Service.* New York: Oxford University Press, 1987.

Stam, James. *Inquiries into the Origin of Language: The Fate of a Question.* New York: Harper and Row, 1976.

Stone, Karen G. *Awakening to Disability: Nothing About Us Without Us.* Volcano Press, 1997.

Van Cleve, John V., ed. *Gallaudet Encyclopedia of Deaf People and Deafness.* New York: McGraw Hill, 1987.

———. *Deaf History Unveiled: Interpretations from the New Scholarship.* Washington, D.C.: Gallaudet University Press, 1993.

Van Cleve, John V., and Barry Crouch. *A Place of Their Own: Creating the Deaf Community in America.* Washington, D.C.: Gallaudet University Press, 1989.

Vash, Carolyn L. *The Psychology of Disability.* New York: Springer, 1981.

Walker, Forrest A. *The Civil Works Administration: An Experiment in Federal Work Relief, 1933–1934.* New York: Garland, 1979.

Weinstein, James. *The Corporate Ideal in the Liberal State, 1900–1918.* Boston: Beacon Press, 1968.

Williams, Job. *A Brief History of the American Asylum at Hartford for the Education and Instruction of the Deaf and Dumb.* Hartford, Conn.: Case, Lockwood and Brainard, 1893.

Winefield, Richard M. *Never the Twain Shall Meet: Bell, Gallaudet, and the Communications Debate.* Washington, D.C.: Gallaudet University Press, 1987.

Wineman, Steven. *The Politics of Human Services: Radical Alternatives to the Welfare State.* Boston: South End Press, 1984.

Woodward, James. *How You Gonna Get to Heaven if You Can't Talk with Jesus: On Depathologizing Deafness.* Silver Spring, Md.: T. J. Publishers. 1982.

Wright, David. *Deafness: A Personal Account.* London: Allen Lane, 1969.

Wright, Mary Herring. *Sounds Like Home: Growing Up Black and Deaf in the South.* Washington, D.C.: Gallaudet University Press, 1999.

Articles, Pamphlets, and Proceedings Not Cited in the Notes

Barnes, Harvey P. *A Proposal to Establish an Opportunity School to Meet the Need for Better Technical, Agricultural, and Vocational Training for the Deaf of the Nation.* Jacksonville: Illinois School for the Deaf, [1939].

Baynton, Douglas. " 'A Silent Exile on This Earth': The Metaphorical Construction of Deafness in the Twentieth Century." *American Quarterly* 44 (June 1992): 216–43.

Berkowitz, Edward. "Professionals as Providers: Some Thoughts on Disability and Ideology." *Rehabilitation Psychology* 29 (1984): 211–16.

Boatner, Edward B., E. R. Stuckless, and Donald F. Moores. *Occupational Status of the Young Deaf Adult of New England and Demand for a Regional Technical-Vocational Training Center.* West Hartford, Conn.: American School for the Deaf, 1964.

Christiansen, John B., and Sharon Barnartt. "The Socioeconomic Status of Deaf Workers: A Minority Group Perspective." *Social Science Journal* 22 (1985): 19–32.

Copp, Tracy. "The Physically Disabled and the War Effort." *Social Science Review* 17 (September 1943): 320–27.

Coudroglou, Aliki. "Professional Ideology: A Response to a Critique." *Rehabilitation Psychology* 29 (1984): 205–10.

De Jong, Gerben. "Independent Living: From Social Movement to Analytic Paradigm." *Archives of Physical Medicine and Rehabilitation* 60 (October 1979): 435–46.

Edelman, Murray. "The Political Language of the Helping Professions." *Politics and Society* 4 (1974): 295–310.

Fenderson, Douglas A. "Rehabilitation Services as Ideology: A Response to Stubbins, Coudroglou, and Berkowitz." *Rehabilitation Psychology* 29 (1984): 217–19.

Gallaudet, Edward Miner. "The Intermarriage of the Deaf and their Education." *Science* 16 (8 November 1890): 295–99.

Gillett, Philip. "The Inter-Marriage of the Deaf and Their Education." *Science* 16 (26 December 1890): 353–57.

Goodwin, E. McK. *Brief Sketch of the North Carolina School for the Deaf.* Press of the North Carolina School for the Deaf, 1932.

Groce, Nora. "Everyone Here Spoke Sign Language." *Natural History* 89 (June 1980): 10–16.

Harvey Verne K., and E. Parker Luongo. "Physical Impairment and Job Performance." *Journal of American Medical Association* 127 (7 April 1945): 902–7, 961–70.

Ianacone, Barbara. "Historical Overview: 'From Charity to Rights.' " *Temple Law Quarterly* 50 (1977): 955–56.

Irwin, Robert C., and Evelyn McKay. "The Social Security Act and the Blind." *Law and Contemporary Problems* (April 1936): 271–78.

Muraskin, William A. "The Social-Control Theory in American History: A Critique." *Journal of Social History* 9 (Summer 1976): 559–69.

Proceedings: National Conference on Employment of the Disabled. National Rehabilitation Association, 1941.

Seiberling, Charles, and L. V. Hannah. *Deaf Men and Women at Work: Excerpts from Addresses.* Akron: National Association of the Deaf, 1940.

Stokoe, William C., *Sign Language Structure: An Outline of the Visual Communication Systems of the American Deaf. Studies in Linguistics, Occasional Papers,* 8 Buffalo: University of Buffalo Department of Anthropology and Linguistics, 1960.

Stubbins, Joseph. "Rehabilitation Services as Ideology." *Rehabilitation Psychology* 29 (1984): 197–203.

Stuckless, E. Ross, Donnell H. Ashmore, John G. Schroedel, and J. Richard Simon. "Introduction: A Report on the National Task Force on Quality of Services in the Postsecondary Education of Deaf and Hard of Hearing Students." Rochester, NY: Northeast Technical Assistance Center, Rochester Institute of Technology, 1997.

Van Cleve, John V. "Nebraska's Oral Law of 1911 and the Deaf Community." *Nebraska History* 65 (Summer 1984): 195–220.

Dissertations and Theses

Carmel, Simon J. "A Study of Deaf Culture in an American Urban Deaf Community." Ph.D. diss., American University, 1987.

Cole, Owen, Jr. "Black Youth in the Program of the Civilian Conservation Corps for California, 1933–1942." Ph.D. diss., University of North Carolina, 1986.

Erting, Carol. "Deafness, Communication, and Social Identity: An Anthropological Analysis of Interaction among Parents, Teachers, and Deaf Children in a Preschool." Ph.D. diss., American University, 1982.

Gough, John Albert. "The Status of the School Paper in American Schools for the Deaf." Master's thesis, Indiana University, 1934.

Johnston, George William Jr. "History of the New Jersey School for the Deaf." Master's thesis, Catholic University, 1962.

Jones, Earl W. "A Survey to Determine the On-The-Job Efficiency of the Deaf in Industry." Master's thesis, University of Michigan, 1945.

Jones, Nancy C. "Don't Take Any Aprons to College! A Study of the Beginning of Co-Education at Gallaudet College." Master's thesis, University of Maryland, 1983.

Kannapell, Barbara. "Language Choice Reflects Identity Choice: A Sociolinguistic Study of Deaf College Students." Ph.D. diss., Georgetown University, 1985.

Kifer, Alan. "The Negro under the New Deal, 1933–1941." Ph.D. diss., University of Wisconsin, 1961.

Meadow, Kathryn. "The Effect of Early Manual Communication and Family Climate on the Deaf Child's Development." Ph.D. diss., University of California, Berkeley, 1987.

Miller, Marcus S. "The Deaf and the Hard of Hearing in Akron Industry." Master's thesis, University of Akron, 1943.

Nomeland, Ronald E. "Beginnings of Vocational Education in Schools for the Deaf." Master's thesis, University of Maryland, 1967.

Parman, Donald L. "The Indian Civilian Conservation Corps." Ph.D. diss., University of Oklahoma, 1967.

Pino, Jacobo Felix, "Employer Ratings of the Suitability of Certain Occupations for Deaf Persons and the Vocational Status of Deaf Employees in Certain Industries." Ed.D. diss., University of Illinois, 1970.

Saalberg, John Jacob. "Roosevelt, Fechner, and the CCC, a Study in Executive Leadership." Ph.D. diss., Cornell University, 1962.

Schroedel, John G. "Variables Related to the Attainment of Occupational Status among Deaf Adults." Ph.D. diss., New York University, 1976.

Turechek, Armin. "A Comparative Investigation of the Vocational Aspirations of Deaf High School Boys." Ed.D. diss., University of Arizona, 1987.

Winefield, Richard M. "Bell, Gallaudet, and the Sign Language Debate: A Historical Analysis of the Communications Controversy in the Education of the Deaf." Ed.D. diss., Harvard University, 1981.

Woods, James Russell. "The Legend and the Legacy of F.D.R. and the CCC." Ph.D. diss., Syracuse University, 1964.

Index

Page references in italics indicate photographs.

79